AFRIC
Series Editors Ale

C000155474

Congo-
Paris Transnational
Traders on the
Margins of the Law

JANET MACGAFFEY & REMY BAZENGUISSA-GANGA

Africa
Works Disorder
as Political
Instrument

PATRICK CHABAL & JEAN-PASCAL DALOZ

The Criminalization
of the State
in Africa

JEAN-FRANÇOIS BAYART, STEPHEN ELLIS
& BEATRICE HIBOU

Famine
Crimes Politics & the
Disaster Relief Industry
in Africa

ALEX DE WAAL

Above titles
Published in the United States & Canada
by Indiana University Press

Peace
without How the IMF
Profit Blocks Rebuilding
in Mozambique

JOSEPH HANLON

The Lie
of the Challenging
Land Received Wisdom on the
African Environment

Edited by
MELISSA LEACH & ROBIN MEARNS

Fighting
for the War, Youth
Rain Forest & Resources in
Sierra Leone

PAUL RICHARDS

Above titles
Published in the United States & Canada
by Heinemann (N.H.)

DEDICATION

This book is dedicated
to my parents, Norman and Marjorie Richards,
to my partner Esther Yei Mokuwa,
to Esther's parents, James Mokuwa and Kumba Bona,
and to our two daughters – Mayiatta Lahai and Gladys Mokuwa –
in the hope that a peaceful millennium
might yet dawn.

AFRICAN ISSUES

Fighting for the Rain Forest

War, Youth & Resources in Sierra Leone

PAUL RICHARDS
Professor of Anthropology
University College London

The International
African Institute

in association with
JAMES CURREY
Oxford

HEINEMANN
Portsmouth (N.H.)

The International
African Institute
in association with

James Currey
73 Botley Road
Oxford OX2 0BS

Heinemann
A division of Reed Elsevier Inc
361 Hanover Street
Portsmouth
New Hampshire
03801-3912

British Library Cataloguing in Publication Data

Richards, Paul, 1945 May 14 –
Fighting for the rain forest: war, youth and
resources in Sierra Leone. – (African issues)
1. Rain forests – Sierra Leone – Management
2. Youth – Sierra Leone
3. Sierra Leone – History
4. Sierra Leone – Social conditions – 1961 –
I. Title
966.4'04

ISBN 0-85255-398-6   (James Currey Cloth)
ISBN 0-85255-397-8   (James Currey Paper)

Library of Congress Cataloging-in-Publication Data applied for
ISBN 0-435-07405-9 (Heinemann Cloth)
ISBN 0-435-07406-7 (Heinemann Paper)

Typeset in
9/11 Melior with Optima display by
Exe Valley Dataset
Exeter, Devon

Printed & bound in Great Britain
by Woolnough, Irthlingborough

CONTENTS

LIST OF PHOTOGRAPHS
MAPS & GRAPHS

ABBREVIATIONS

APC	All People's Congress
ECOMOG	Economic Community of West African States Monitoring Group
INPFL	Independent National Patriotic Front of Liberia
NPFL	National Patriotic Front of Liberia
NPRC	National Provisional Ruling Council
NTFPs	Non-timber forest products
PANAFU	Pan-Africa Union of Sierra Leone
RSLMF	Republic of Sierra Leone Military Force
RUF	Revolutionary United Front
SLPP	Sierra Leone People's Party
ULIMO	United Liberian Movement for Democracy

FOREWORD

Small wars are very much on the minds of policy makers and thinkers as they seek to anticipate trends in global peace and security. Sierra Leone has long been a measure of the sincerity with which the richer countries of the Atlantic basin regarded their global commitments. It is no accident that a small war in Sierra Leone has focused some of the current debates about violence as a global social trend; the country was shaped by a similar debate surrounding the ending of the slave trade. The present book is intended as a warning to those modelling global futures not to disregard complexity of historical and sociological detail when thinking about post-Cold War conflict. Small wars need fine-grained explanation.

Writing the book has been a harrowing experience, first and most obviously because so many people close to me have been caught up in and damaged by the events I describe. I, too, have felt traumatized by what I have seen and learnt. But I have also had to struggle to overcome scholarly reserve in writing close to events still unfolding. It was Alex de Waal who persuaded me, by his published example and through his editorial help, including the recruitment of two highly critical but supportive anonymous referees, that being wise after the event was no great intellectual accomplishment; social scientists ought to re-focus their skills on complex political emergencies *as they happen*, and perhaps try to anticipate the trend of events. But having accepted this challenge I failed to spot its practical consequences – the Expanding Forth Bridge Phenomenon. I knew that the painters of the Forth Bridge, in legend at least, begin their work again every time they reach the other side. What I had not realized was that the structure expands as they do so. My publisher is now about to lock my word processor and throw away the key. My family will be relieved.

A number of other debts must be acknowledged. The work could not have been carried out without the energy and interest of my long-standing research assistant Samuel Mokuwa and his team of schoolteacher interviewers. Colleagues in Wageningen and London backed me up, and allowed me to make repeated passes through the material at considerable inconvenience to their own work plans. I must mention, in particular, Guido Ruivenkamp and Dineke Wemmenhove in Wageningen, and four collaborators in the Department of Anthropology at UCL, Phil Burnham, Murray Last, Mike Rowlands, and Barrie Sharpe, thanking them for support and inspiration. The data in the present book derive from research supported by the Global Environmental Change programme of the Economic and Social Research Council, and ESRC funding is gratefully acknowledged. Professor Bobor Kandeh and colleagues at Njala University College have provided long-term support and intellectual stimulus for my research in Sierra Leone and it is especially sad to have to report that the war has now wrecked and closed their institution. The bravery of our African colleagues in keeping the intellectual project alive in such circumstances deserves the widest support and acknowledgement. In UK, Steve Riley and Max Sesay (Staffordshire University), Tunde Zack-Williams (Central Lancashire University), Melissa Leach (IDS, Sussex), James Fairhead (SOAS) and Kate Longley, Ron Fennell and Caspar Fithen (UCL) have helped with timely advice and information. Long-term conversations with Jane Guyer and Keith Hart are reflected throughout the book. Finally, I want to acknowledge three sources of inspiration of fundamental significance in shaping my understanding of the events I describe. Robert Bates, of Harvard, suggested to me that anarchic violence is often highly rational, and provided timely support on the draft even in its pre-rational incarnation. The late M. G. Smith, in a brilliant seminar shortly before he died, reminded us that the civilized have long denied the functional connection between their sophisticated standing in the world and mayhem on the periphery, and social science needs to re-establish the connection. Perhaps most important of all, Mary Douglas provided me with the insight that the makers of mayhem are often irresponsible 'excluded intellectuals'. 'In the stagnation of empire when the educated found themselves unesteemed, they denied political realities, espoused contradictory and impossible projects and cherished ultramontane loyalties.' (Douglas 1986). This I take as a warning to myself as well as to those about whom I have chosen to write. Over-theorization may break the connections between social science ideas and their community context. Instead we should seek 'group-wise intelligent effort to heal the widening divisions' (Douglas 1986: 83). Mary's comment that my material 'sounded like Jerusalem 500 BC' opened a door through which enlightenment rushed in.

Zetten, 1996.

War in Sierra Leone | New Barbarism in Africa?

Small wars in a post-Cold War world

As the Cold War nightmare fades more attention is paid to small wars, fought with conventional weapons and for complex local reasons. Africa is scarred by a rash of small wars. Factors internal to the continent are now being offered as explanations for this troublesome rise in modern low-level insurgency. Episodes of apparently bizarre violence in Liberia, Somalia, Rwanda seem to fit a pattern. Surely this is evidence that Africa is, inherently, a wild and dangerous place? Here is violence driven by environmental and cultural imperatives which the West has had no hand in shaping, and now has no responsibility to try and contain. These violent urges are politically meaningless and beyond the scope of conventional diplomacy or conciliation. They are best understood as natural forces – the cultural consequences of a biological tendency by Africans to populate their countries to the point of environmental collapse.

Arguments linking environmental determinism and cultural essentialism are hardly new. They have been regularly refuted by Africanists. Just as quickly they spring up again. The fear of the revenge of the enslaved and dispossessed is hard to quell. Recent versions of the argument offer a new twist by adding modern weapons and the spread of drug culture. Most journalistic reportage and not a little academic writing reflects this view, which is becoming more, not less, influential, obliging their dissenters to return to the fray.

Are these proponents of Malthus-with-guns saying anything new about war and Africa? It is time to submit the environmentalist argument to re-examination, but taking the cheap AK-47s and crack cocaine fully into account. To distinguish this post-Cold War argument from earlier Malthusian visions of African dystopia[1] I propose the label 'New Barbarism'. The book is a critique of the New Barbarism thesis.

[1] A word signifying the opposite of Utopia.

Malthus-with-guns: the New Barbarism thesis

Three central ideas underpin the New Barbarism thesis[2] in Africa and more widely.

First, cultural identity is an essential and durable, rather than context-dependent, feature of social systems. Different cultures and civilizations are thereby prone to clash (Huntington 1993).

Second, war in the post-Cold War world has changed. States have lost the monopoly of military violence once underwritten by nuclear balance of terror. The equipment is cheap, and widely available to religious, cultural and criminal organizations prepared to pursue armed conflict independently of sovereign states and without reference to international opinion (van Creveld 1992).

Third, culture clash, resource competition and environmental breakdown provoke a rash of small, localized and essentially uncontrollable armed conflicts. Many are anarchic disputes – i.e. apolitical events indistinguishable from banditry and crime. Insulation rather than intervention is the rational response of the major powers.

This potent mix of ideas was brought together in a book on the Balkan conflict by American journalist Robert Kaplan (Kaplan 1993).[3] When the Yugoslavian state broke up suppressed ethnic and religious animosity broke out like a disease. Kaplan then extended the argument to Africa in an influential essay ('The coming anarchy', *Atlantic Monthly*, February 1994).[4] Violence in Liberia, Rwanda, Somalia is not war in any ordinary political sense of the term (a continuation of diplomacy by other means, as Clausewitz viewed it[5]). Far from fully

---

[2]Duffield (1995) relates New Barbarism to so-called 'new racism' (cf. Barker 1982). The old racism was hegemonic. It sought to legislate between slaves and free. The 'new racism' is non-hierarchical – proposing a level playing field for the accommodation of groups whose differences are as essential as they are irreconcilable. Others, however, consider the New Barbarism a global phenomenon, as likely in London or Moscow as in Africa (Bradshaw 1996).

[3]Kaplan's writing on the Balkans comes under critical anthropological scrutiny in Schwartz (1996).

[4]Tim Wirth, Under-Secretary at the US Department of Global Affairs, faxed Kaplan's article to every US embassy around the world (Bradshaw 1996). According to the same source the article 'so rattled top officials at the United Nations that they called a confidential meeting to discuss its implications'.

[5]Carl von Clausewitz, *Vom Kriege* (1832), (trans. as *On War*, by J. J. Graham, 1908, and republished in an abridged edition with an introduction by Anatol Rapoport, Pelican Classics, Penguin Books, Harmondsworth, 1968). Clausewitz is interested not in the causes or consequences of war, but in what war is. This ontological question tends to be answered in two ways – either war is a fundamental expression of a biological competitiveness (a viewpoint often espoused by neo-Malthusians) or in the Clausewitzian way ('War belongs to the province of social life . . . It would be better . . . to liken it to business competition . . . and it is still more like State policy . . .' [von Clausewitz, 1832/1968, pp. 202–3]). Rapoport (1968) suggests that Cold War strategy was basically neo-Clausewitzian. Neo-Barbarism is a reversion to the biologically-based point of view. In this book I attempt to illustrate a third, cultural, ontology of war – the concept of war as a drama of social exclusion.

understood even by the participants themselves, these conflicts, in Kaplan's eyes, were clear evidence of Africa's gathering environmental crisis. Maintaining peace in such conditions is beyond the scope of regular diplomacy or peace-keeping intervention.[6]

New Barbarism in Sierra Leone?

Kaplan's thesis has proved extraordinarily influential in the U.S. His article was faxed to every American embassy in Africa, and has undoubtedly influenced U.S. policy. This is less because of the cogency of thought and quality of evidence, than because of the way Kaplan tapped into broader currents of thinking.

Kaplan's essay begins and ends in the small West African country of Sierra Leone. Arguably the oldest modern state in West Africa (with a constitutional history dating back to 1787) Sierra Leone first experienced war in 1991 when a small rebellion took shape on the eastern border with Liberia, launched from territory controlled by one of the factions fighting the Liberian civil war. Lacking any Cold War roots, or evident religious or ethnic dimensions, but possessing a high quotient of apparently bizarre and random acts of violence, many perpetrated by children, this conflict is cited by Kaplan as a prime instance of the New Barbarism.

By the time Kaplan visited Sierra Leone (in late 1993) government troops maintained only tenuous control of large parts of forested eastern and southern Sierra Leone. What had caused anarchy to spread so quickly through these West African forests? According to Kaplan, the war was a product of social breakdown caused by population pressure and environmental collapse.

Throughout West Africa, drought and land hunger (he argues) had driven young people to the teeming and only superficially modernized shanty-town suburbs of the coastal cities. Spun off from a failing traditional society, these criminally-inclined young migrants were 'loose molecules in a very unstable social fluid' (Kaplan 1994). The perpetrators of the violence in eastern and southern Sierra Leone lacked any clear political purpose. They were better pictured as criminals and

---

[6]Some ex-Cold War security analysts, seeking a new role, have taken up this hypothesized link between violence and environmental pressure with enthusiasm. New Barbarism asks whether it makes sense for international diplomats to broker peace, e.g. between Somali warlords, when global climatic change might make nonsense of their carefully-phrased appeals to human reason. The thesis has quickly bitten deep. Greenhouse (1995) reports that 'American policy makers are [now] looking more than ever before at natural phenomena in their search for the *deeper* roots of war and threats to global security' (my emphasis). Consider 'the threats . . . are not communism or aggression but rather overpopulation, migration, environmental degradation, ethnic conflict, and economic instability, all phenomena that traditional security forces find hard to address' (Chase, Hill and Kennedy 1996, p. 36, cf. Garrett 1996).

bandits. Reverting to old, superstition-riddled, forms of violence, these gangs of youngsters, roaming the Sierra Leone countryside, armed with AK-47s and killing for scraps, are likened by Kaplan to the hungry mercenary hordes ravaging seventeenth-century Germany prior to the ending of the Thirty Years War.

Testing New Barbarism

The present book is a critical examination of the New Barbarism thesis. The scrutiny is based on ethnographic analysis of the insurgency in Sierra Leone. New Barbarism's essential propositions are found wanting in several major respects.

Although the local history of resource acquisition is relevant to understanding the war there is no run-away environmental crisis in Sierra Leone. Young people caught up in the dispute specifically point to political failures as a cause of the war, and deny the relevance of Malthusian factors. The data on population trends and land resources confirm the essential soundness of this point of view.

Whereas it is true that the war in Sierra Leone is a terror war, and involves horrifying acts of brutality against defenceless civilians, this sad fact cannot in any way be taken to prove a reversion to some kind of essential African savagery. Terror is *supposed* to unsettle its victims. The confused accounts of terrorized victims of violence do not constitute evidence of the irrationality of violence. Rather they show the opposite – that the tactics have been fully effective in disorientating, traumatizing and demoralizing victims of violence. In short, they are devilishly well-calculated.[7]

Lacking heavy weapons, both rebels and government forces have made extensive use of cultural resources in their campaigns. In particular, the rebels deploy forest knowledge in both practical and symbolic ways to make converts to their cause and demoralize opponents. By these cultural ploys they manifest a distinctly 'post-modern' awareness of modern media and the propaganda opportunities they provide. The skills on view are those of the hybrid and globalized world of Atlantic commerce rather than the 'traditional' subsistence worlds of the African bush.

New Barbarism pays scant regard to the insurgents' own claims concerning the purpose of their movement (that they took up arms to fight for multi-party democracy and against state corruption). Kaplan

---

[7]The extent to which insurgent movements can gain strategic advantage from the systematic terrorization of relief workers and diplomats is an intriguing aspect of contemporary research on African war. I was informed by one relief worker in Freetown on April 30th 1991 that 'the rebels were everywhere, they had captured Bo', and she was leaving for home the next day because the country was finished. The fact that I had just travelled down from Bo without incident cut no ice, since she had been informed of the capitulation of Bo by a European ambassador.

(1994) prefers instead to endorse a view widespread among capital city elites and in diplomatic circles at the time of his visit, but now known to be incorrect, that the rebel movement had been destroyed and the violence was exclusively the work of bandits and military splinter groups.[8] In fact the war has a clear political context, and the belligerents have perfectly rational political aims, however difficult it may be to justify the levels of violence they employ in pursuit of these aims. The rebel leadership has a clear political vision of a reformed and accountable state. Failure to communicate that vision owes more to the poverty, incompetence, and sectarian isolation of the movement than to any inherent trend towards anarchy in today's devastated West African forests.

As in any war opportunist individuals and groups muddy the waters with atrocities and looting. But these opportunist acts by themselves are insufficient to explain the continuation of the conflict. The war in Sierra Leone drags on essentially because there are social factors feeding the conflict, and because the main rebel group feels it has not yet had a chance to get its political point of view across, and that it needs to do so to honour activists who died in its cause.

Contra New Barbarism the violence of the Sierra Leone conflict is shown to be moored, culturally, in the hybrid Atlantic world of international commerce in which, over many years, Europeans and Americans have played a prominent and often violent part. Although a small and highly localized conflict, the war has a global range of symbolic and dramaturgical reference. It deserves to be regarded as one of the world's first truly post-Cold War conflicts, since it owes little if anything to Super Power rivalry, and everything to the media flows and cultural hybridizations that make up globalized modernity (cf. Waters 1995). The challenge is to understand that 'we' and 'they' have made this bungled world of Atlantic-edge rain-forest-cloaked violence together. In a world of globalization disengagement from Africa's violence is no longer an option.

Fighting for the Rain Forest: a crisis of the patrimonial state

If we reject New Barbarism what better explanations of the war in Sierra Leone might be offered?

---

[8]Cf. '[The RUF] seem[s] to have no ideology or politics. Most of the violence is almost certainly carnage for the sake of it. Bandits, teenage hoodlums, Kaplan's "juju warriors", have joined together in a rag-tag army intent on destruction.' (Bradshaw 1996) and 'The chaos that now engulfs [Sierra Leone] cannot be described as a civil war, inasmuch as the contending forces – notably including the "government" – represent nobody but themselves; nor can it be described as a guerrilla war, for no side seriously pretends to be fighting for a cause . . .' (Luttwak 1995). My own essay on the early part of the war (Richards 1995a) drafted in January 1993, is guilty of adding some fuel to this anarchist fire.

Long-term patterns of 'primitive accumulation' of forest and mineral resources in Sierra Leone have fed a modern politics dominated by patrimonial redistribution (Reno 1995, Kpundeh 1995). The political elite builds support through distributing resources on a personal basis to followers. Relatively few resources are distributed according to principles of bureaucratic rationality or accountability. In the 1980s, through a combination of circumstances, the resources available for patrimonial redistribution in Sierra Leone went into sharp decline, a decline exacerbated by the ending of the Cold War and a general reduction and tightening up of overseas aid budgets. This crisis has tested the loyalty of the younger generation in particular. Meanwhile, as a result of political machinations and resource shortages the state's capacity to control some of its peripheral regions was weakened. The Liberian border region was a particular casualty of this aspect of state recession, allowing dissidents to enter the country from Liberia and deploy methods of violent social destabilization invented in the course of the Liberian civil war (1989-96). The Sierra Leone war, it will be argued, is a product of this protracted, post-colonial, crisis of patrimonialism.

The book advocates no heavy-footed international military intervention as an alternative to the disengagement proposed by New Barbarism. As in Somalia, intervention by peace-keeping forces might serve little useful purpose, and even lead to escalation of conflict. Even large-scale top-down style relief initiatives are problematic, since they inject resources into the local economy that often end up, through raiding and other forms of 'leakage', supporting the belligerent parties.

Instead, it is suggested that the 'creolized' cultural understandings drawn upon by the belligerents in making war are also the resources through which civil communities in this part of the African rain forest might make peace. To explore the pacific potential of this highly complex cultural heritage local groups need both encouragement and opportunity. To the extent that there is a role at all for outside intervention it should concentrate on what is termed, in a concluding essay, 'smart relief'. This is shorthand for any low-key assistance that supports culturally informed analysis of the war, and effective local mobilization to meet its challenges. New Barbarism should be resisted since it undermines respect for those hybrid aspects of the West African cultural heritage that might be of greatest potential value in making peace.

A war more barbaric than most?

The Sierra Leone insurgency began on 23 March 1991 (Musa and Musa 1993). Seeking to overthrow the patrimonial rule of President Joseph Saidu Momoh and the All People's Congress (APC) a small and lightly armed rebel force fought for a year in the forested districts of eastern and southern Sierra Leone before Momoh and the APC were ousted in a coup by junior officers disenchanted by government lack of support for their efforts in confronting the rebels.

Rebel violence in the first phase of the war fell mainly upon unarmed villagers, and civilian support for the young officers' regime, the National Provisional Ruling Council (NPRC), was based on a promise to the victims of the violence to bring the war to a brisk conclusion.

After the NPRC coup fighting between government troops and rebels resumed. The rebels suffered major losses but vowed to fight on. Dissension within the army gave them the chance to counter-attack. Having initially taken up arms to oust the APC, the rebels justified further extension of the long-drawn-out bush war with the claim that the NPRC regime, after a bright start, had reverted to the patrimonial politics of the APC. By January 1995 the insurgents were within sight of the capital Freetown. Suffering subsequent reverses they declared an interest in peace negotiations. The first tentative contacts concerning a peace process took place during the latter half of 1995, but without any obvious reduction in the intensity of the fighting.

The rebel group appears to be remarkably small. It is run by a War Council of 21 people, and has several thousand young members. It has little if any territorial base, and few settlements of any size under its firm control, apart from its forest camps. It obtains resources by mining diamonds in the forest and capturing food and weapons, mainly from NPRC sources. It builds membership by conscription of young people it judges amenable to its political message.

Most of these youngsters, in fact, have little option about whether or not they join. Terrorized in the process of capture they are later treated generously by the rebels and the secrets of the movement are revealed. This process amounts to a type of initiation, for several centuries a near-universal feature of forest society in the western half of West Africa. Initiation separates young people from their immediate family and builds adult loyalties to a wider society.[9]

In a country of c. 4 million, an estimated 15,000 civilians have been killed and more than 40 per cent of the total population displaced during five years of war. Local communities are still ruled by widely-respected Paramount Chiefs. It is some measure of the dislocation caused by the conflict that half the country's Paramount Chiefs are displaced, living in Freetown or one of the three main provincial towns (Bo, Kenema and Makeni). Manifestly not an ethnic conflict, and therefore failing to fit the main international media 'slot' reserved for the reporting of African war, the Sierra Leone insurgency has had little coverage apart from incidents involving the capture of foreign hostages by the rebels.

[9]Capture by the rebels, by contrast, seems to induce the apparently paradoxical loyalties between hostage and captor known in Western psychiatric models as the Stockholm Syndrome.

Superficially, some of the facts of the war seem to fit the theory of New Barbarism. Fighting takes place mainly by means of hit-and-run raids and ambushes in thickly forested country. With little hardware, the rebels have to rely upon bushcraft, misinformation and terror tactics to control villagers and demoralize the better-armed government troops. This leads them into actions (beheading chiefs, cutting the hands and fingers off villagers) that cause outsiders to assume a wanton and mindless violence. Further reflection shows it to be nothing of the sort.

Take, for instance, a spate of incidents in villages between Bo and Moyamba in September-October 1995 in which rebels cut off the hands of village women. What clearer instance could there be of a reversion to primitive barbarity? Images flood into the mind of hands cut off for the manufacture of magic potions.

But behind this savage series of incidents lay, in fact, a set of simple strategic calculations. The insurgent movement spreads by capturing young people. Short of food in the pre-harvest period, some captives, irrespective of the risks, sought to defy the movement and return to their villages where the early harvest was about to commence. How could the rebels prevent such defections? By stopping the harvest. When the news of rebel amputations spread in central Sierra Leone (the rice granary of the war-affected region) few women were prepared to venture out into the fields. The harvest ceased.[10]

Conflict in Sierra Leone is no exception to the generalization that modern warfare targets civilians as well as enlisted troops. Whether the rebels in Sierra Leone were in any way justified in their decision to take up violence is highly debatable. The consequences have been tragic. But their actions are not the actions of madmen or mindless savages. Once a decision to resort to violence had been taken, hand cutting, throat slitting and other acts of terror become rational ways of achieving intended strategic outcomes. There is little if any analytical value, it seems to me, in distinguishing between cheap war based on killing with knives and cutlasses, and expensive wars in which civilians are maimed or destroyed with sophisticated laser-guided weapons. All war is terrible. It makes no sense to call one kind of war 'barbaric' when all that is meant is that it is cheap.

Some theoretical considerations

The present study is primarily ethnographic in orientation. By that I mean that it is mainly an attempt to contextualize some of the data relating to the conflict in Sierra Leone via description and analysis of

---

[10]Having decided not to take part in the February 1996 elections the rebels then started to use the same tactic to scare away would-be voters – cutting off the hands that might otherwise cast a vote.

concrete situations, events and discourses. But no ethnographic account is ever 'pure fact'. It may help readers to point out some of the main theoretical assumptions and influences that have shaped my own understanding of the materials at my disposal. Four related bodies of ideas in particular should be acknowledged: practice, performance, discourse and culture theory.

War as practice
Practice theory takes the standpoint that knowledge (in this case knowledge of how to promote war in forests beyond the edge of the state) is a product of context and action as well as of cognition and training (Bourdieu 1979; Giddens 1989). This implies that some domains of knowledge work kinetically, rather than through formal calculus. That is to say they work through routines (often improvisatory routines) rather than through abstract analytical devices, but without being any the less rich or powerful for that (Guyer and Richards 1996, Hardin 1992, Richards 1993). By applying formalistic rather than kinetic standards to 'war knowledge' the proponents of New Barbarism blunder into a misunderstanding of their own devising. Unable to perceive the practical rationality of war caught on the wing, New Barbarism assumes that the conflict makes no sense according to outsiders' rules and must be a throwback to some African 'Dark Age'.

Let me briefly indicate how practice theory seeks to avoid confusion (or conflation) of formalistic and kinetic knowledge.

In a cross-cultural study of practical computation Lave (1986) shows that people in supermarkets correctly carry out calculations in their heads that they cannot carry out on paper in a classroom. A shopper, initially at a loss for words to describe to the researcher the decision she was about to make, then went ahead, integrated the variables, and made a correctly calculated choice once arriving at the right section of shelving and meeting the items in a familiar layout. Lave's point is that in practical (as opposed to schoolroom) arithmetic, environment and action – in this case the goods, the shelves, and the act of scanning them – are important parts of the computational process. Shoppers do not just compute – they compute through the actions of shopping. Ignore (or remove) the context and the computational operations are *indescribable*, and/or fall apart.

The mental maps and histories we accumulate moving through environments serve as a kind of abacus for our practical arithmetical operations. Without a good description of the environmental 'abacus' our computational procedures may seem to make little or no sense.

Insurgency in Sierra Leone fails to 'add up' if described from the standpoint of a formal logic of violence – from the perspective of, say, mathematical Game Theory, or the theories of warfare and diplomacy that dominate the fields of Conflict Studies and International Relations. What the following chapters seek to do, however, is to show that understanding can be transformed by taking note of the environment as a practical computational prop to belligerence.[11]

To do this we have to enter that environment, and understand it in some detail. This is why one chapter in particular (Chapter 3) is devoted to establishing various kinds of local 'forest' and 'Atlantic' cultural knowledge against which strategies of violence begin to assume coherence. The insurgency in Sierra Leone has been fought within rain forest, or in once-forested terrain, despoiled by mineral extraction operations. Specifically, I explore the idea that insurgents in Sierra Leone treat the forest, the history of resource struggles taking place within forests, and the character of forest social institutions, as a 'spur' to a series of practical judgements about the risks and benefits of political action based on violence. Remove the forest from the picture (or ignore it) and the rationality disappears – the violence makes no more sense than would the computations of market shoppers deprived of their shelves. It will become clear that I might just as appropriately have entitled this book 'Fighting *with* the Rain Forest' (in the sense of *using* it as a weapon, symbol, or dramatic backdrop).

War as performance
War, and coping with war, are matters of performance. The apparently pointless bitterness of a 'rebellion without cause' (Bradbury 1995) makes considerable sense as a drama of state recession, renewal and revenge. Performance theory concerns itself with the stage management of events. Applied to war, performance theory tries to understand how people make power through managing violence and terror as expressive resources.

A dramaturgical emphasis in analysis makes it possible, for example, to consider the Sierra Leone insurgents in terms of a rationalistic framework proposed by Lipsedge and Littlewood (1996) for the study of domestic sieges – violent events also commonly seen as crazy or incomprehensible.

Sieges typically involve an estranged father, distraught at being separated from children he loves, seizing them and threatening to kill them. This apparent contradiction generally leads to the conclusion that hostage takers are 'mad'. Lipsedge and Littlewood propose, however, that the rationality of the domestic siege lies in its coherence as drama. Sieges are events 'staged' in such a way as to attract wider media interest. Once media exposure is gained, the event then demands of onlookers that they ponder the question 'what external events have driven me, a reasonable person, to such despair, that I am prepared to behave like a lunatic, and threaten to kill my own children?'.

---

[11] It seems worth quoting Jean Lave's neat, if abstract, formulation: 'A politics of knowledge is thus embodied in mundane transformations of knowledge and value through activity constituted in relation with its daily settings.' (Lave 1986)

The Sierra Leone rebels indulged in a spate of (international) hostage taking in 1994-5. Possession of the hostages got the rebel movement TV exposure internationally. Releasing the hostages, rebel leader Foday Sankoh, a professional photographer as well as ex-soldier, and skilled, therefore, in *representation*, as well as trained in the practicalities of violence, explained that they had been seized 'for their own protection', since Sierra Leone was now such a dangerous place. This sounds like poor logic, since the rebels were the ones making the country so dangerous, but makes dramaturgical sense. Sankoh was, it seems, 'posing' his struggle in siege-like terms, to bring out the extent to which 'reasonable people' had turned to desperate measures, faced with the social dereliction caused by the extensive engagement, over many years, of patrimonial politicians and business elites in international commerce in gold, slaves, diamonds and tropical forest products.

Insurgents in Sierra Leone also draw upon more local dramaturgical resources, especially those associated with initiation. In Sierra Leone, the masked 'devil' is an expression of the secret energy of societies gathered together in this way. The young initiates captured by the rebels return to the countryside which they lay waste as 'bush devils'. Their terror campaign is more than *representation* of a crisis, therefore. It is an attempt *to mobilize power* through the expression of 'war as masquerade'. Theories of performance provide clues to the essential dramaturgical coherence, and powerfulness, of what it is the insurgents are trying to achieve.

War as discourse
Globalization Theory argues that the modern world is constructed as much from symbolic exchanges as from material transactions (Waters 1995). The worlds beyond the periphery of a patrimonial state in crisis are cut off, to greater or lesser extent, from regular material transactions the rest of us take for granted. In practical terms 'state collapse' means collapse of roads and other communications leading into these marginal regions. For regions 'beyond the pale' symbolic transactions assume a larger than normal significance in the attempt to re-establish contact with the wider world.

When insurgents entered Sierra Leone in 1991 they demanded an international press conference to talk to an international audience. They lacked sponsors and equipment, and the world ignored them. Once they had seized their first international hostages, outsiders were forced to try and locate the rebels and find out what they wanted. When negotiations opened, one demand of the insurgents (though not met) was for an international satellite phone link, to make up for lost time in promoting their cause. Subsequently (as noted) the rebels received TV coverage as part of a deal to recover the hostages.

This focusing upon violence (or the threat of violence) as discourse is common to several of the wars currently being fought within Africa (and elsewhere, e.g. the comparable Zapatista rebellion in Chiapas, in Mexico).[12] For this reason, discourse analysis is at least as important as the more usual, materially-oriented, analytical models (such as World Systems Theory, cf. Wallerstein, 1980) through which resource transactions on the global periphery are analysed.

Discourse analysis seeks to locate textual statements in their wider conversational background. Essentially, discourse analysis argues that texts are joint products – of readers as well as writers, listeners as well as speakers. It also suggests that 'innovative' texts are seldom if ever 'original', in any uncomplicated way. Discourse is, as it were, the conversational hubbub from which individual voices (texts) sometimes rise, occasionally with startling clarity. To understand the discourses of violence we need to identify, clearly, the social groups sustaining the conversation, as well as examining specific texts. My immediate concern in this book is to explore the state of conversations about violence and politics beyond the damaged edge of the Sierra Leone state. Who are the participants in these conversations and what do they discuss?

Kaplan does not appear to have visited the war zone, and reports few conversations with the 'loose molecules' about whom he writes. I attempt to remedy that deficiency by reporting how young people in Sierra Leone talk about politics, war, resources and the future. There is a particular focus on areas beyond the reach of the state. My aim is to enquire what the violence means to belligerents, and victims, themselves.

War itself is a type of text – a violent attempt to 'tell a story' or to 'cut in on the conversation' of others from whose company the belligerents feel excluded. Understanding war as text and discourse is not an intellectual affectation, but a vital necessity, because only when 'war talk' is fully comprehended is it possible for conciliators to outline other more pacific options in softer tones.

Culture theory
Mary Douglas (1986, 1987) and colleagues (e.g. Douglas and Wildavsky 1982; Rayner 1982) argue strongly against cultural essentialism. Instead, they believe that ideas, beliefs, classifications, perceptions of risk, etc. are tied to, and shaped by, systematic features of community organization (specifically, the degree to which people are bound into institutions reflecting hierarchical, egalitarian or individualistic orientations).

To take but one example, cannibalism may be quite unthinkable in one kind of community but in others it is àn all too readily imagined danger (irrespective of whether the danger is real or not). Douglas (1989) has speculated that only societies with a strong orientation towards individualism would be able to conjure up a mental procedure through which a victim might be selected. Richards (1995c) has hypothesized that *fear* of cannibalism is a feature of West African communities with a

[12] The Zapatistas apparently announced the launch of their rebellion over the Internet.

strong egalitarian background threatened by an excess of *uncontrolled* individualism.

Douglas (1986) has written with great insight into the mind-set of groups she describes as 'excluded intellectuals', caught between mass egalitarianism and the top-down power of hierarchs. The excluded intellectuals form a tiny, self-referencing, sectarian elite, prone to ambitiously irresponsible 'deconstruction' of the world.

In other contexts she and Aaron Wildavsky have pointed out that sectarians and hierarchs assess risks, including environmental risks, according to entirely different schemes (Douglas & Wildavsky 1982). An implication of this kind of argument is that sectarian thinkers may have more in common, across countries, than they have with the hierarchs in their own governments.

Far from isolating countries like Liberia and Sierra Leone from the wider world, as the New Barbarism literature attempts, we should be actively exploring, in the spirit of Mary Douglas, in what ways such national tragedies can be understood from a comparative sociological perspective. Here, it may pay to ponder possible similarities of cultural response to social exclusion evident in the thinking of forest rebels in Sierra Leone and anti-Federal forest survivalists in the United States. Structural position as 'excluded intellectuals' may be the common thread in the hostile response of both groups to perceived corruption at the federal or patrimonial (i.e. hierarchical) metropolitan core.

'Radical scepticism', Douglas writes, 'may flourish (and prove highly destructive) where an elite, educated and privileged, is faced with unacceptable arbitrary power, and is helpless to challenge it.' (Douglas 1986, p. 80). Excluded intellectuals are irresponsibly destructive. Where hierarchs look to their ancestors, sectarians need martyrs. Sometimes, as in Sierra Leone or Oklahoma City, these mutually reinforcing processes lead to real violence and tragic consequences.

Formal exploration of this argument is set aside for a later occasion. But it will become clear in the following account that I consider it plausible, and useful, to think of the rebel movement in Sierra Leone as a sectarian intellectual response to the perceived corruption of a metropolitan patrimonial elite. Far from random, the violence is an expression of the social exclusion of a group of educated exiles determined to force patrons 'in town' to imagine what life is like for the young minds stranded 'in the bush'. The antidote to this violence is not to be found in further intellectual analysis of the war, but in community action. As Douglas (1986) notes 'community is not separable from logic...the foundations of rational discourse are found in community commitment to stability and coherence'. It is on this insight that I later base my conclusion that, eschewing military intervention and top-down humanitarian assistance, peace-making initiatives in this small African war should be based on community indigenous knowledge supported by 'smart relief'.

Chapter synopsis

The book is organized in eight chapters and a concluding essay.

Chapter One is an account of five years of conflict started by the Revolutionary United Front (RUF), a small group of Sierra Leonean dissidents encouraged by Libyan leader Col. Muammar Gaddafi, and armed by the Liberian faction leader Charles Taylor. The chapter summarizes the main events and reviews the range of factors that seem relevant to explaining this low-level but highly disruptive conflict in the forests of eastern and southern Sierra Leone.

Chapter Two analyses the political economy of state recession in Sierra Leone, and its impact on youth. The diamond-rich forested border region where the insurgent movement first 'dug in' is introduced. The APC government opened the door to the rebels by weakening communications in this region along the Liberian border. The war is but one aspect of an extended crisis of the patrimonial state.

Chapter Three turns to the role of the forest in the rebellion. After failing in their initial attempt to reach the capital, the rebels were forced back into the forests of the Liberian border where they concentrated on building a revolutionary movement of captured young people in the bush. Fuller understanding of how and why this bush war works, and how it might end, requires some understanding of social and technical knowledge forged over 500 years of forest conversion – a process in which outside interests have long played a prominent part.

Chapter Four presents and discusses three local 'texts' linking forest resources and violence. The first account, of the actual fighting in the forest, is provided by a Sierra Leonean boy combatant. The second is *njɛpɛ wova* (a Mende oral historical story) from the Gola Forest, collected prior to the onset of hostilities, commenting on the violent exploitation of forest resources in the last days of the slave trade (in mid-nineteenth century). The third account describes the life of two young miners who make their living in the diamond camps of the border region peddling war films on a portable video rig.

The extent to which young people sucked into the conflict have been 'globalized' by media exposure is examined on a more general level in *Chapter Five*. More than 400 young people, sampled by gender and educational background in rural and urban environments, in war-torn and war-free zones, were interviewed about their exposure to international radio, TV and video sources. Even the most rural and least educated groups in the sample have exposure to war films and news footage of insurgencies across the globe. The way these media sources are interpreted by these young people is germane to understanding their ideas about where they stand in the total picture of global social change today. The rebels have sought, systematically, to exploit these ideas.

Chapter Six confronts the environmental determinism of the New Barbarism thesis directly. The suggestion that war in Liberia and Sierra

Leone is driven by population pressure and environmental crisis is refuted. Deforestation has a long history in Sierra Leone, and there is little evidence that the social and technical inventiveness displayed over several centuries by local populations engaged in forest conversion is at an end. Insurgency in Sierra Leone and Liberia is a response to political failures not environmental collapse.

Chapter Seven looks for the 'loose molecules' of the patrimonial state, living in the recession-damaged forested periphery. The chapter introduces a diamond village on the Liberian border on the eve of the war. Preoccupied by the problems of bringing up young families in a trackless wilderness, these 'loose molecules' are far from being the criminal anarchs envisaged by the New Barbarism thesis. Asked about the future, their ambitions were to establish a primary school and seek road connections to the rest of the country. IMF-imposed stringency, and international concern to keep the area 'remote' for conservation purposes, rendered these hopes futile. The rebels stepped into the breach. RUF bush schools, with only scraps and torn pages for readers, may not seem much, but they are more than could be found in this village on the border before the war began. Meanwhile, the chief agents of the patrimonial state sent their own children to expensive private schools in Britain.

Chapter Eight considers the environmental and political awareness of young people more generally across the nation, paying especial attention to those most directly affected by the war. Interviewees were quizzed about deforestation, responsibility for environmental resource management in Sierra Leone, and their future plans. Knowledgeable and highly realistic about environmental change, informants were keen to see forest resources managed sustainably, while rejecting talk of an environmental crisis. Only those most directly terrorized by the war would remove forest to flush out the rebels. Others firmly rejected the idea that the war had environmental roots, pointing instead to its political causes. Young Sierra Leoneans displayed a straightforward commitment to political modernity. They desired transparent and accountable institutions of state and civil society, not only to help remove the causes of war, but also to assist future effective environmental management. Judged by their own words, young people in Sierra Leone are poles apart from the superstition-addled young savages conjured up by the New Barbarism thesis.

War–peace transitions

The book concludes with a short essay on war-peace transitions in Sierra Leone. If there is a successful formal peace negotiation process, efforts will focus on making the state less vulnerable to the destabilizing factors documented in this study. Prospects are not encouraging, unless external donors can be found to support extensive institution-building activities. A senior official of the United Nations is reported (BBC World Service News, 27 October 1995) to have described donor responses to the crises in Liberia and Sierra Leone as 'pathetic'.

Another possibility is that with or without a token cease-fire the conflict might drag on for some time. Civilians in the war zone will then have to find ways of accommodating the risks of low-level insurgency as a normal condition of life. As Thomas Hobbes[13] pointed out, peace is an exceptional attainment and has to be worked for with all the ingenuity at human disposal.

Belligerent groups are likely to tolerate civil re-colonization of at least parts of the war-shattered zone to ensure better supply of basic commodities. Already, women from Bo in central Sierra Leone trade palm oil from the rebel-held palm plantation areas near the coast, passing through disputed territory. In the Biafran War such trading ventures were known, collectively, as the 'attack trade'. The 'attack trade', and other civilian innovations in a war zone, might contribute actively to the building of *peace from within*.

External donors are willing to try and support civilian enclave areas in Liberia and Sierra Leone, but overt support (e.g. massive feeding programmes) may be counter-productive (cf. Keen 1994). From early days, a pattern of RUF violence in Sierra Leone has been to concentrate attacks on arms dumps, hospital pharmacies and food stores. Faced with no alternative, rebels venture into farming areas to force villagers to harvest, thresh and transport rice back to their camps, but this is time-consuming and dangerous work. Attacking convoys or feeding centres is less risky. Given better appreciation of the unintended symbiosis between relief and war, it is possible to envisage sociologically 'smart', knowledge-intensive, ways to channel resources to the civil agrarian zones 'beyond the state' without exciting the attention of raiders or road-block troops.

One way might be to shift the focus in food security away from bulk food supply towards seed systems, genetic information and farmer invention. Another would be to help foster creative local responses to war-peace transition through broadcasting (e.g. via radio 'soap-opera'). A third, and perhaps key area, is to support *in situ* analysis of why the war has happened and what local groups might do to prevent its resurgence. In a climate of international neglect some interesting local developments have taken place. Some communities have organized effective civil defence through mobilizing local institutions such as the

---

[13]Thomas Hobbes, *Leviathan* 1651, published Pelican Books (1968) in an edition by C. B. Macpherson ('Hereby it is manifest, that during the time men live without a common Power to keep them all in awe, they are in that condition which is called Warre; and such a warre, as is of every man, against every man. For Warre, consisteth not in Battell onely, or the act of fighting; but in a tract of time, wherein the Will to contend by Battell is sufficiently known . . .' [pp. 185–6]).

Poro Society. A Women's Movement for Peace has begun to tap the potential of women's grass-roots organizations. Some groups have openly debated the extent to which the war reflects not only a lack of accountability in patrimonial politics but also the price society pays when the rising generation is neglected. More resources are needed to support this kind of local reflection and mobilization. More confidence should be placed in local capacity to arrive at sensible and durable solutions to the challenges of conciliation. This war is a terror war fought with local cultural resources. Those self-same cultural resources, I suggest, will be essential to the task of rendering the terror understandable (cf. Nordstrom 1992). Only if the community issues behind the terror are understood can the terror be deflated. Sustained intellectual support is now needed for Mary Douglas's 'group-wise' effort to heal widening divisions. This book has no aim other than the traditional anthropological aim of creating a climate of respect and support, among outsiders, for 'group-wise' community conciliation resources that might otherwise seem strange and inexplicably barbaric.

1

Insurgency in Sierra Leone

Context, Events & Interpretations

Introduction

The Revolutionary United Front (RUF) is a small but quite coherent movement, difficult to deal with in forested terrain with very poor communications. An inexperienced and divided army (RSLMF[1]) has proved ineffective against it in the field. Run by a group of about 20–30 quite highly educated dissidents, convinced that Sierra Leone has been robbed of its minerals and forest resources, the RUF sees itself as a people's movement for national recovery. It expands by capturing young people from the villages and towns that it attacks. The movement has gained only grudging tolerance in the rural areas in which it has fought. It has refused invitations to join the democratic process, uncertain of a fair hearing, or that it would gain much voluntary support. By-and-large the world view of the RUF leadership remains an exile standpoint. Convinced that it still has a chance to instruct the people, it fights doggedly on, wreaking havoc on the livelihoods of the rural poor it purports to champion. With schoolmasterly zeal insurgents preach to villagers, the only target group within their reach, and then scourge them for being slow to learn, burning their settlements and killing and maiming those who object to the revolutionary path. From the outset levels of atrocity have been high. The movement was never fully in control of mercenary elements, blooded in the civil war in Liberia, fighting on its behalf. A not dissimilar element has attached itself to the government side of the dispute. Some irregulars recruited at the war front have thrown in their lot with free-lance bandit factions who disguise their misdeeds as 'rebel action'. The RUF has failed to raise its political programme clear of this expatriated Liberian hubbub.[2] The

[1] Republic of Sierra Leone Military Force.
[2] A formal statement of the RUF political programme was published as this book went to press (RUF/SL 1995). I have managed to take account of this enlightening little document in footnotes. It provides firmer evidence for a number of my surmises about the character of the movement.

1

movement survives on the energy, wits and desperation of the young Sierra Leoneans it has captured and initiated. The best way to challenge the rebel leadership to enter a peace process, it is concluded, is unswervingly to follow a policy of offering amnesty and rehabilitation to young 'rebels' while continuing to press forward with negotiations.

Part One: Context

The Liberian civil war

The immediate origins of the insurgency in Sierra Leone are to be found in events associated with the civil war in neighbouring Liberia (Richards 1995a). The Liberian war began in 1989, nearly a decade after the rise to power, in a brutal coup, of an ill-educated army sergeant, Samuel Kanyon Doe.

Doe made many enemies, including Libyan leader Colonel Muammar Gaddafi.[3] Gaddafi supported a number of political dissidents from Liberia and Sierra Leone. Some Liberians and Sierra Leoneans received insurgency training in Benghazi.

Thomas Quiwonkpa, the corporal (later general) who, with Doe, had overthrown the True Whig Party regime of President Tolbert in Liberia in 1980 was implicated in a coup plot against Doe in 1985. Quiwonkpa was killed, and Doe had his head paraded round Monrovia on a pole. Doe loyalists in the army exacted random revenge on people from Quiwonkpa's home region, Nimba County. Soldiers and supporters of Quiwonkpa fled to neighbouring countries. Some ex-soldiers settled in Burkina Faso (Ellis 1995) and formed the nucleus of the National Patriotic Front of Liberia (NPFL).

Charles Taylor, an Americo-Liberian economist and 'one of those who had helped to down the Tolbert government' (Wonkeryor 1985), escaped jail in the United States, while being held pending extradition to account for his activities as director of the General Services

---

[3] Gaddafi had a direct interest in the overthrow of the Liberian military dictator. Doe came to power in a brutal military coup in 1980. Liberia under Doe is said to have been a base for US covert operations against Libya. Israeli interests in Liberia may have been a further factor. Liberia retained diplomatic ties with Israel after the 1973 Middle East war. The Israelis had business and strategic interests in diamonds from eastern Sierra Leone, many of which were smuggled across the border and exported through the Liberian capital Monrovia. Some of this diamond wealth went to support factions in the Lebanon civil war. Doe was assisted by Israeli security. Gaddafi may also have harboured a personal grudge against Sierra Leone's former president Siaka Stevens. Allegedly, the Libyan leader helped Stevens with some of the costs of the conference of the Organization of African Unity held in Freetown in 1980, an event that nearly bankrupted the Sierra Leonean treasury, in return for a promise (in the event unfulfilled) that Stevens would work to secure Gaddafi's nomination as his successor as chairman of the OAU.

Agency.[4] Taylor reached Ghana and allied himself with the broad-based democratic opposition movement to Doe. Later he secured an introduction to Gaddafi through future Burkinabe president Blaise Compaore (Tarr 1993). Taylor now saw himself as the man to over-throw Doe. Married to a woman from Nimba County (Ellis 1995), Taylor viewed the Libyan-backed nascent NPFL as the vehicle to advance his own longer-term presidential ambitions. A charismatic media figure, Taylor became the spokesman for the NPFL, and its *de facto* political leader.

A second key figure in the NPFL was dissident Liberian ex-soldier, Prince Yormeh Johnson. After training in Benghazi, Johnson became the NPFL's main combat strategist and guerrilla trainer (Ellis 1995).

The NPFL began an incursion into Nimba County, North East Liberia, from Côte d'Ivoire, on Christmas Eve, 1989. Doe assumed a general insurrection of Nimba County people had broken out. The NPFL seems to have been quite widely welcomed by Nimba County civilian populations. Further brutality by Doe's forces, sent to put down the rebellion, reinforced NPFL appeal. Villages burnt and parents and patrons massacred, Nimba youth, including girls and under-age orphans, rallied to the NPFL in considerable numbers.

Johnson's guerrilla know-how formed these youthful recruits into an effective insurgent force. Drugged on crack cocaine, recruits deployed terroristic methods apparently reflecting a knowledge of Renamo tactics in Mozambique (cf. Young 1990; Wilson 1992). Some of the terror may have been improvised on the spot by child soldiers (Brehun 1991; Ruiz 1992). The bizarre battle dress of these uninhibited young fighters, owing more to Kung Fu and Rambo than ideas of regular military uniform (Moran 1994; Furley 1995), featured regularly in photographs in the international press, even when journalists were at a loss for words.

Taylor was the movement's charismatic spokesman, but not a soldier. Johnson, as the military 'brains' behind NPFL mobilization, came increasingly into conflict with Taylor. Friction may have centred on Taylor's media effectiveness. The NPFL early acquired a satellite radio-telephone allowing Taylor regular direct access to international radio programmes, such as the BBC World Service's influential *Focus on Africa* evening news magazine. Broadcasters say they use Taylor's stuff because (however partial) it is cleverly expressed in clear and dramatic English. His rivals struggle, linguistically and dramaturgically, in his wake.

Accustomed to discipline his fighters with summary brutality, Johnson executed one of his followers in front of journalists. An

[4]Writing in 1985, a Quiwonkpa supporter, E. L. Wonkeryor described Taylor (well before the outbreak of hostilities) as a Doe loyalist. According to Wonkeryor '$3.5 million goods [were] bought but not delivered to Government' by the General Services Agency under Taylor's directorship, and 'had Taylor not been Doe's loyalist he would have been severely disgraced . . .' (p. 166).

alarmed Taylor broke with Johnson, but at the price of an apparent reduction in the movement's military effectiveness. Taylor paused outside Monrovia while international mediators tried to persuade Doe, holed up in the Monrovia Executive Mansion, to quit the country. In charge of a break-away Independent National Patriotic Front of Liberia (INPFL) Johnson picked this moment to snatch Doe from under the noses of the regional peace-keeping force.[5] Doe was dragged off to the Johnson camp outside Monrovia where the INPFL leader organized a startling media event to hit at Taylor. Johnson caused a video to be made of Doe's torture and death (Davidson 1992). This video circulated widely in West Africa, undermining Taylor's chances of claiming the presidency as the man who rid the country of the tyrant Doe. Had Taylor entered Monrovia there seems little doubt that, as with Museveni in Uganda, his *de facto* rule would have been recognized internationally, pending elections he would have been strongly placed to win.

The Taylor–Johnson split had far-reaching consequences, since it marked the beginning of the factionalization of the Liberian conflict. Groups opposed to Taylor began to copy NPFL youth-oriented guerrilla tactics and media-smart presentation of war for international audiences. This also set the pattern for the Sierra Leonean conflict.

The Sierra Leonean rebel movement was formed from among political exiles and economic refugees in Liberia. Some had learnt the Johnson-style or Renamo-type tactics as recruits to the NPFL. Others seem to have decided to go home with the RUF rather than be shunted around Liberia as refugees. It was in Taylor's interest to support the destabilization of the Sierra Leone government, firm supporters of the international peace-keeping effort in Liberia. Encouraged and supplied by Taylor, and supported by Liberian and Burkinabe mercenaries from the NPFL, the RUF leadership waited its moment to launch an NPFL-style holiday-time incursion from across the Liberian border into Sierra Leone.

The invasion of Sierra Leone

The RUF entered eastern Sierra Leone at Bomaru in Kailahun District from NPFL-controlled Liberian territory on 23 March 1991, a little early for Easter that year. A second flank was opened in Pujehun District by a contingent entering from the Mano River bridge linking Liberia and Sierra Leone. Until this moment the RUF was unknown in Sierra Leone, though according to some sources it dates back to 1982.[6]

---

[5] Doe was negotiating with the ECOMOG peace-keepers when Johnson's forces struck. The incident was reported 'live' by the BBC West Africa correspondent, Elizabeth Blunt, who was in ECOMOG headquarters when the fire-fight broke out.

[6] I am so informed by Lord Avebury, chair of the UK parliamentary human rights group. This is the same year in which a Pan-Africanist organization, PANAFU, was launched in Freetown. PANAFU denies formal links with the RUF, but shares some radical ideas (see p. 53 below).

The RUF was at this stage a small force of no more than about 100 or so guerrillas, made up of Sierra Leonean exiles, plus Burkinabe and Liberian mercenaries. The mercenaries may have been in the majority. The RUF's announced political programme was to overthrow the All People's Congress (APC) one-party regime of Joseph Saidu Momoh and restore multi-party democracy to Sierra Leone. The credibility of this programme was severely compromised in the eyes of local civilians by mercenary terror and looting.[7]

The basic tactic (as with the NPFL) was youth conscription, to constitute a viable fighting force and suggest a credible 'popular uprising' against the APC. Conscripts were tattooed as military identification, and, perhaps intentionally, to discourage escape. The tattoos served to identify RUF deserters to the RSLMF. Some RSLMF troops unwittingly consolidated RUF membership by summary execution of rebel suspects (Amnesty International 1992). Conscripts were also snared by enforced participation in RUF Renamo-style atrocities against local leaders; youngsters were deterred from returning to their villages for fear of revenge.

With poor external communications and little support other than from conscripts, RUF political ambitions were at first unclear. Only as recently as November 1995 have these aims been made explicit at any great length to reporters (*Focus on Sierra Leone* 1995). Most Sierra Leoneans assumed that the RUF was no more than a Taylor-inspired project to undermine Sierra Leone for its involvement in the Nigerian-led peace-keeping operation in Liberia.

At one stage, in June/July 1991, the RUF controlled up to a fifth of the country in southern and eastern Sierra Leone, along the border with Liberia, but was then pushed back by the combined operations of the Sierra Leone army and a Liberian militia force, ULIMO (the United Liberian Movement for Democracy). ULIMO was an anti-NPFL armed faction recruited from among refugees driven by Taylor into Sierra Leone. ULIMO re-entered Liberia and wrested much of the Liberian side of the border zone from NPFL control. As a result, the RUF lost its tenuous grip on several small towns in the border region.

In April 1992 the RUF was further threatened by a military coup of young RSLMF officers from the war front. The coup removed the APC one-party regime, the RUF's reason for existence. Half-hearted offers of amnesty and cease-fire came to nothing,[8] and a re-equipped army went on the offensive, causing the RUF serious losses. It was rumoured that RUF leader Foday Sankoh had been killed or seriously incapacitated in the fighting.

---

[7]The RUF now claims to regret this assistance by persons it terms 'veterans of the Liberian civil war' since 'it became a nightmarish experience for our civil population.' (RUF/SL 1995 p. 8). Most rural Sierra Leoneans consider the nightmare to be unabated.

[8]The RUF insists, at length, that the offer was genuine, but that the Nigerian and Ghanaian military presidents persuaded the infant NPRC to refuse negotiation and crush the movement (RUF/SL 1995).

Later, in 1993, the movement re-consolidated. Avoiding established settlements, it built a series of bush camps to train and indoctrinate conscripts in forest reserve areas towards the centre of the country. Beginning in November 1994 hit-and-run raids launched from these camps affected all corners of the country, and new forward camps were established, including one only a few miles from the capital Freetown.

In secure control only of its camps, the RUF used a tactic (favoured by Shining Path in Peru) of sending out letters predicting advances and threatening prominent figures with death. It 'fulfilled' these predictions through hit-and-run raids on remote and undefended communities, but always seeking to imply it had the strength and organization for 'the big one'.

Rumours spread like wildfire, between January and April 1995, that Freetown was about to be attacked. Both the RUF and NPFL used holiday periods to stage their major attacks. It was widely believed that Foday Sankoh would be carried in triumph into the capital at Easter 1995. People fled from villages along the route he was supposed to follow (the old railway line through Moyamba District). (The significance of the old government railway in the dramaturgy of Sierra Leonean politics is explored more fully in Chapter Two.)

The problem of understanding the basic political aims of the RUF is sometimes exaggerated. The leaders have made few *published* statements of their aims, but in large measure the political aims of the movement are manifest in its actions. RUF threats and acts of violence are dramatized messages to the people about its view of the world, as well as military tactical ploys. Burning of houses and cutting off of villagers' hands and fingers inscribe, on the landscape and in the bodies of village people, a set of political messages rather more firmly than if they had been spoken over the radio.

The chopping off of women's hands in villages between Bo and Moyamba in September–October 1995 was widely understood throughout central Sierra Leone as a warning to village women to cease the rice harvest in full swing during those months. The harvest threatened the RUF since hungry conscripts, courted by government amnesty, were threatening to defect or surrender. Villagers have had hands or fingers amputated to deter others from voting in forthcoming elections. 'Now you have no hands with which to cast your vote' one rebel is alleged to have told his victim. A man was sent into Bo, after his hand had been hacked off by rebels, to warn of impending RUF attacks over the Christmas holiday period 1995. The message is also directed at conscripts, warning them to stay loyal to the rebellion. Mutilation of villagers adds up to a message that there is no longer any functional home to which waverers might return.

Opportunists have joined the war. The RUF denies responsibility for many of the outrages committed against villagers. Public opinion in Sierra Leone believes that some soldiers change by night into rebels. It is hard to judge how widespread a phenomenon this is, since the concept of 'sobel' (soldier by day, rebel by night) fits an enduring cultural notion that all social action in a multi-cultural society is two-faced (Murphy 1980), reinforced by the capacity of some operators to engage in 'shape-shifting' (Richards 1995c). But there seems little doubt that in a climate of general insecurity and breakdown of law and order in the war zone groups of bandits imitate rebel tactics, in pursuit of loot and diamonds. This follows the pattern in Liberia, and recapitulates aspects of the early, mercenary-led, RUF. Conciliators attempting to establish peace negotiations believe that the RUF has remained a coherent movement under single command, but this by no means rules out the idea that silent defections from both RSLMF and RUF have fed freelance operations.

Part Two: Events

RUF Phase 1 (1991)

Early in April 1991 Foday Sankoh contacted the BBC African Service in London (*Focus on Africa*) to proclaim the aims of the RUF: to overthrow the APC government, and restore multi-party democracy to Sierra Leone. Sankoh disclaimed personal presidential ambitions, stating only a desire to supervise free and fair elections.

Villagers in Kailahun were ordered to cut palm fronds 'in support' of the rebels. The palm was a symbol of the opposition Sierra Leone People's Party (SLPP), banned under the One-Party Constitution of 1977, but being re-formed in 1991 following a referendum on multi-party democracy. The SLPP drew much of its support from the Mende people of the south and east. The palm frond incident seems to have been an invitation to the political authorities in Freetown to consider the invasion an ethnic uprising. In the war zone itself it was quickly understood that the RUF was dressed in borrowed clothes. On hearing Sankoh speak with a Temne accent, the typical reaction of some youths in Bo was to ask why his group had not invaded a part of the country where a northerner might expect better support. Other young people, however, were waiting for 'big brother' (Gaddafi) to intervene in Sierra Leone politics and felt this might be the looked-for event.

The RUF was mainly concerned to round up and conscript young people, including children. Youth military training camps were established in captured settlements, some in village primary schools. An RUF group overrunning Pujehun town attacked the hospital and demanded access to the pharmacy stores, shooting dead the store keeper. Some of the young raiders claimed to be removing medicines because they had Aids. Medicine, and other looted items (shoes, dresses, etc.) were taken to rebel camps. These were distributed to young conscripts freely.

Arriving in villages with lists of names of petty government officials, extension workers and merchants they intended to kill, RUF commandos also sought teachers and health workers to join the movement, especially where they were known to have radical sympathies as students. The main victims of the violence were senior figures in the village hierarchy. Seemingly, this was calculated to 'knock out' the group otherwise best positioned to offer patrimonial support to the young people the RUF had a mind to convert. Some migrant (Mandingo and Fula) traders were tortured and summarily executed by the RUF for economic crimes (apparently for activities as money lenders). In other cases cooperative chiefs paid ransom to save long-established village merchants from death.

Populist lessons in revolutionary economics were offered to villagers and conscripts alike. In Joru, Gaura Chiefdom, young fighters priced cups of rice according to the rate of inflation under 22 years of APC rule and told sceptical villagers that under the RUF rice would be given free-of-charge. In an insightful glimpse of RUF didacticism at work, one of the movement's representatives recently described RUF fighters shouting ideological instruction to government troops across battle lines, and claimed that without these bizarre battle-front lectures NPRC junior officers would never have known enough to mount a politically popular coup against the APC in 1992 (*Focus on Sierra Leone* 1995).

RUF groups received some local support from civilians (Atkinson *et al.* 1992). Losers in a local land or chieftaincy dispute might sometimes side with the insurgents to secure revenge. The beheading of a Paramount Chief, Gboney Fyle, in Bonthe District is thought to be one such case. Local support for the RUF may have been strongest in Pujehun District because of the mid-1980s Ndogboyosoi movement (see p. 22 below).

Liberians and Burkinabes, recruited by the RUF to take Bo and Kenema, the main urban centres in the south and east, carried out numerous atrocities against unarmed civilians. Looting (a mercenary preoccupation) slowed down the RUF advance.[9] The Liberians and Burkinabes were withdrawn early in 1992, after wrangling between Taylor and Sankoh about payment of benefits.[10] RSLMF efforts to contain the RUF advance were augmented by Liberians opposed to the NPFL, living as refugees in Sierra Leone. Refugee volunteers were armed by the APC government to support operations by regular government troops. These Liberians understood the tactics of the war

---

[9] Eye-witnesses describe a Burkinabe commando being carried in triumph down an unmotorable bush path to a rebel camp, at the wheel of a looted Peugeot car, headloaded by 16 strong local conscripts. The same man is said to have read out the RUF political programme to bemused villagers in French.

[10] Bonuses were in any case small – US$5000 each to capture Bo and Kenema.

better than RSLMF regular troops. Blue-headbanded irregulars were apparent on road blocks from April 1991. Later most of the Liberians were absorbed into ULIMO, an alliance of mainly Krahn and Mandingo volunteers opposed to Taylor and the NPFL, led by Alhaji Kroma and Roosevelt Johnson. ULIMO was particularly involved in fighting the RUF in Pujehun District and the border zone south of Kenema. By late 1991 the combined operations of ULIMO and the RSLMF had all but driven back the RUF into Liberia.

The NPRC coup (1992)

In late April 1992 a group of junior officers mutinied over pay and conditions at the war front (Zack-Williams and Riley 1993). Reuters News Agency in Abidjan reported the mutiny as a coup attempt by war-front commander Colonel Yaya Kanu. Later that day, Kanu, a Momoh loyalist, denied over BBC *Focus on Africa* that he had accepted an invitation from the young officers to be their leader, and claimed instead to be negotiating a compromise between government and mutineers. Held as a political prisoner, allegedly for involvement in efforts to organize a counter-coup, Kanu was later executed. President Momoh fled to Guinea, and the mutinous soldiers appointed Captain Valentine Strasser, from Teko Barracks, previously serving with ECOMOG forces in Liberia, as Chairman of a National Provisional Ruling Council (NPRC). Counselled by Ghanaian president Jerry Rawlings, and assisted by Israeli security advisers, the NPRC suspended the constitution, political parties and elections earlier announced by the Momoh regime, and formed a military government with the priority of bringing a rapid end to the war and reforming the state after years of APC mismanagement. In his coup broadcast Strasser came straight to the point: 'our schools and roads are terrible'.

The coup was widely welcomed by the majority of Sierra Leoneans, especially by the youths, as offering the country a new start. This enthusiasm was later expressed in episodes of popular wall painting (Illustrations 1.1 and 1.2) and practical street cleaning (1.3) aimed at some of the most obvious signs of state neglect in Freetown and urban centres up and down the country (Opala 1993).

The picture of a pay revolt by patriotic war-front officers spontane-ously escalating into a full coup, carried by a wave of popular support, may not be correct, however. The mutineers may have drawn on more contingency planning than was at first apparent. Seemingly, this planning involving a young army officer, Captain Prince Benjamin-Hirsch, from Daru in Kailahun District, killed in an ambush (some say laid by his enemies in the army, not by the rebels) shortly before the coup took place. His brother, a civilian businessman, John Benjamin, became Secretary to the NPRC (in effect, Prime Minister). Benjamin-

1.1   Freetown wall paintings to celebrate the NPRC coup (1992): military leaders (Photo: Esther Yei Mokuwa)

Hirsch and fellow junior officers, together with a like-minded group of young eastern intellectuals, seem to have understood well the significance of the youth conscription tactics of the RUF. Benjamin-Hirsch recruited youth militia in the battle zone similar to those trained and deployed by the RUF, thereby aiming to deny the rebel movement its principal resource – the youth of the diamond fields neglected by the state.

Sensing an older generation of corrupt politicians had lost touch with young people, the NPRC then invested heavily in youth mobilization and anti-corruption drives to consolidate its own grip on power. Several of the key activists within the NPRC were from the south and east of the country and had a close understanding of the details of the rebellion. Some had lost family and friends during the mercenary-dominated RUF terror campaign in 1991 and may also have had revenge on their minds.

The RUF has subsequently claimed that it was ready to do a deal with the NPRC after the coup (*Focus on Sierra Leone* 1995). But despite the promise to end the war quickly the NPRC paid more attention to capital-city priorities – the possibility of an APC counter-coup and the need to secure a credible position with the international community – than to the nature and predicament of a rebel movement hanging on by its finger nails along the Liberian border. The NPRC considered that it needed a decisive military victory as a step on the road towards a Rawlings-like transition to democracy. The rebels were offered amnesty in return for unconditional surrender, but the NPRC leadership showed

1.2 *Freetown wall paintings to celebrate the NPRC coup: national heroes*
(Photo: Esther Yei Mokuwa)

1.3 *Bo suburban street*
repaired by youth
volunteers after the
NPRC coup

little sympathy for the predicament of a small insurgency movement that had seen its enemy, the APC, snatched from its grasp, and its line of retreat into Liberia cut by hostile ULIMO fighters. Underestimating the impact of its unopposed mercenary terror on civilian attitudes in the war zone, the RUF was naive to expect to be invited by the NPRC to share in the task of post-APC national reconstruction. Better supplied than under the APC, government troops hit the RUF hard, and the movement lost several leading figures. It was even rumoured that Sankoh himself had been killed. Offered nothing concrete beyond amnesty, the RUF saw little option but to fight on.

Later in 1992, Michael O'Neill, an American Red Cross worker supervising food relief distribution in Kailahun and Kenema Districts, was seized as a hostage by the RUF. A former Peace Corps volunteer, and long-term resident of Sierra Leone, O'Neill provided clear descriptions of the RUF camps and youth-oriented training programmes, establishing beyond doubt that the RUF was more than a mercenary rabble sponsored to serve Taylor's purposes in the Liberian war.

In September–October 1992 the RUF pushed from Kailahun into the diamond-rich Kono District. They may have been aided by military indiscipline. Young officers posted to the war front were often those with least 'pull' in Freetown. Under the NPRC, Freetown-based officers with powerful patrons in the APC now found themselves posted to the war front to find out for themselves what the young coup plotters had experienced. Alleged incompetence, 'sabotage' and fraternization with the enemy resulted. Some soldiers, jealous of benefits enjoyed by groups in the army close to the NPRC, sought their own reward from a war they thought might soon come to an end. In diamond areas local populations were displaced for 'security' reasons, and military groups engaged in diamond mining. RUF bands infiltrating Kono slipped past a security cordon otherwise engaged. This infiltration showed signs of long-term planning. In one Kono village, local people discovered that a young refugee offered land to farm early in 1992 was in fact an RUF spy ('movement officer') who then proceeded to identify the leaders of the town civil defence group to the insurgents.

More young people were captured during the push into Kono, and new training camps established. The RUF was driven out of Koidu, the main centre of the Kono diamond fields, only after fierce fighting in October 1992. The area was closed to civilians for much of 1993, and has been intermittently under threat of re-incursion ever since.

In December 1992 the NPRC claimed to have foiled a counter-coup by APC elements, allegedly (and implausibly) directed from Pademba Road jail in Freetown by the detained former head of the police force, Bambay Kamara. The 'counter-coup' was used as a pretext for the execution, after a token legal process, of 28 political prisoners detained for their role and alleged corruption under the APC.[11] Those executed included

Bambay Kamara, Colonel Yaya Kanu, and the former army quarter-master, Colonel K. M. S. Dumbuya. It seems possible the regime seized the opportunity to rid itself of some of its most influential enemies. But international outrage had to be addressed. Accordingly, the forceful coup-maker and Vice-Chairman of the NPRC, Solomon Musa, was relieved of his post and sent on overseas leave.

'Sobels' and the RUF reborn (1993–4)

Government troops recaptured Pendembu, Kailahun town and Koindu late in 1993. Shortly after the fighting a hunter reported meeting a wounded Sankoh, in a hammock, being carried out of Kailahun along bush paths towards the Kangari Hills, a forest reserve in the centre of the country. Other eye-witnesses speak of a small, battered convoy of broken-down vehicles leaving Kailahun, loaded with RUF leaders and their effects, heading south, perhaps to carve out a new sphere of operations in the relative security of the Gola Forest reserves. It was widely assumed that the recapture of Kailahun signalled the end of the war. But any planned victory celebrations were cut short by renewed ambushes and fighting in the Kenema area. Clashes also occurred between local civil defence forces and the army.

Kaplan's article was published in the American journal *Atlantic Monthly*, February 1994. Photo-copies soon started to circulate in Sierra Leone, intensifying the view that the rebellion had collapsed, leaving only anarchy in its wake. In the same month up to 400 disgruntled troops from Teko Barracks, excluded from rich pickings at the war front and fearing peace was in sight, absconded and headed east. According to reports, they either built their own RUF-style camp as a base for raiding activities in the Kangari Hills forest reserve or were absorbed within the RUF.

Raids and ambushes began to be a major problem on the Kenema–Bo highway, close to Blama, and between Makali and Masingbi on the Makeni–Koidu highway, overlooked by the Kangari Hills. An Irish priest (Fr. Felim McAllister) and a Dutch medical missionary family (Dr Elko Krijn, Mrs Karen Krijn and their 3-year-old daughter Zita) were killed in an ambush at Panguma, seemingly the work of an RUF contingent at Peyeima Camp in the Panguma Saw Mills logging concession area. The committee of investigation brought out evidence, deemed inconclusive, of dereliction of duty and possible collaboration by RSLMF troops (Committee of Investigation 1994). Soldiers may have feared Fr. McAllister was collecting a dossier of evidence about looting of civilians.

---

[11] Some sources place the number as high as 48 persons.

Public opinion was now more than ever persuaded that most of the violence in Sierra Leone was the work of 'sobels' (soldier-rebels)[12] involved in 'sell game' (i.e. looting disguised as rebel activity, Keen 1995). One army officer is said to have confronted soldiers returning from operations carrying looted items with the remark that 'RSLMF troops do not carry television sets in battle' and opened fire on the group. The political programme of the RUF dropped out of sight.

It became visible again in November 1994 when two British volunteer aid workers were abducted in an attack close to Kabala, in the far north of country, in an area hitherto untouched by war. There were immediate doubts about whether this could be the work of the RUF. Security experts, concerned that the abductors made no ransom demands, contemplated the ominous possibility that the young volunteers, like Fr. McAllister, might have been killed to ensure silence about 'sobel' raids.

A person claiming to be Foday Sankoh established radio contact with British diplomats in Freetown concerning the hostages, 12 days after their capture. Sankoh successfully proved his identity by reference to the details of his army service in the 1960s. He then demanded that the British government recognize his movement and supply it with arms in return for the release of the hostages.

The hostage crisis was prelude to a major campaign by the RUF beginning just before the Christmas holiday, 1994. On 23 December the road junction settlement at Mile 91 on the Freetown–Bo highway was attacked by about 100 insurgent fighters, some wearing the latest pattern of RSLMF combat fatigues. Many houses were burnt and a road-works repair vehicle destroyed. Graffiti proclaimed the attack the work of the RUF. The lightly armed attackers then disappeared into the vast grassy 'boli' plains linking Mile 91 to Makeni and Kambia, the main towns in the north and north-west of the country. Subsequently, a series of ambushes were mounted on the Freetown–Makeni highway, apparently from a rebel camp in the forested Malal Hills. A rebel contingent attacked Kambia town, on the Guinea border, on 24 January 1995, seizing weapons from a small army store and rounding up some hundreds of young people as new captive recruits. A small group of expatriate nuns was also taken hostage.

A separate RUF group began to attack villages north of Bo in early December 1994; reports indicated that the Kangari Hills camp was being evacuated and that RUF personnel were moving (perhaps with the international hostages) across the northern part of Bo District towards a base camp in the forests above Potoru.[13] Another training camp ('Camp

---

[12] Also see p. 7, sometimes glossed as 'soldier by day, rebel by night'.
[13] Peyeima Camp, in the rich diamond districts north-west of Kenema, under pressure from government troops after the earlier Panguma incidents, may also have been abandoned at about the same time.

Lion') had been established in the Gambia oil palm plantation at Mattru Jong, near Sumbuya. With the border closed, and Charles Taylor under pressure from ULIMO in Liberia, the RUF may have been able to import supplies from Côte d'Ivoire by sea through Camp Lion.

A third RUF group launched a substantial attack on Kenema town, on 24 December, from the forested Kambui ridge, using a heavy machine gun captured from government troops. The leader of this group, 'Black Jesus', was said to be fighting to control the compound of the Kenema secondary school of which he was an old boy.

A fourth group, disguised as civilian refugees, infiltrated Gondama Refugee Camp near Bo 'to enjoy Christmas with relatives', while Nigerian troops stationed in Gondama were policing a Christmas carnival for the refugees at the town football stadium in Bo. Unpacking hidden weapons and donning stolen RSLMF fatigues the group then headed for Tikonko, and attacked Bo from the south on the morning of 27 December.

This group of about 100 lightly armed fighters, stopping to preach to the crowd on entering Bo, was dispersed by a spontaneous counter-attack of civilians armed with whatever sticks and knives came to hand. Rapidly organized in the aftermath of this surprising event, a Bo civil defence movement attempted to wrest control of the town from the army. A curfew was announced but the army was forced to back down. For a week the streets of Bo at night were patrolled by civilians, and army looters apprehended. Rebel attacks were limited to the smaller villages around Bo. The camp of the Italian construction company resurfacing the Bo–Freetown road was also attacked, and heavy equipment destroyed. The Bo–Taiama road, the last leg of the highway from Freetown into Bo, had long been a pot-holed disgrace, with materials for repair regularly misappropriated. The resurfacing project was intended to be a major statement by the NPRC of its commitment to the speedy repair of the physical fabric of the country. The RUF attack on the road construction camp was a considerable propaganda coup.

Raids on the rutile and bauxite mines in the south of country led to the capture of more international hostages early in 1995, and to the closure of the mines, the NPRC government's most important source of revenue.

Steps towards negotiation (1995)

Released to representatives of the International Red Cross, two RUF hostages confirmed that the other hostages were being held together in an RUF base camp, and were well looked after. A human rights group, International Alert, then established contacts with Akyaaba Addai-Sebo, a Ghanaian revolutionary, friend of Charles Taylor, and publicist for the NPFL. Addai-Sebo was well-known to the RUF, and offered to undertake an arduous journey on foot to the RUF base camp, to escort the international hostages to Guinea. Negotiations were made through the International Red Cross. The NPRC agreed the release attempt should go ahead, and Addai-Sebo, and an Ivoirian medical doctor, reached Sankoh's base camp, and returned with the hostages. The march through the forest to the Guinea border in April 1995 took 17 days.

Addai-Sebo made a film of Foday Sankoh and the RUF, some of which was shown on UK TV (Channel 4 News), helping to establish internationally that Sankoh was alive and fit, and in charge of a real 'bush' insurgency. The NPRC complained that the film was propaganda for the rebels. A rumour circulated that Addai-Sebo took diamonds from the rebels to arrange new supplies of arms, as their price for releasing hostages. Addai-Sebo was understood by the RUF to be working as a journalist, and the rebels cooperated in the hostage release on the grounds that they would at last gain publicity from his film. The footage includes a long farewell speech from Sankoh to the hostages, for the benefit of the camera, in which the rebel leader claims the RUF is fighting to bring peace and democracy to Sierra Leone, and insists (with melodramatic emphasis) that the hostages had been seized for their own protection in a chaotic country. Why the chosen few, among all the foreigners in the country, had been so favoured was not clear. Nor did Sankoh appear abashed about the RUF's own leading role in creating the chaos in the first place. The film then documents the journey of the hostages to safety, via 'Cuba Camp', and a war-damaged Bunumbu, ending with the crossing of the Moa into Guinea. The footage also includes a lengthy rendition of the RUF anthem.[14] This is useful evidence concerning the social composition of the RUF. The singers number several hundred, divided into three roughly equal groups – pre-teenage boys, young women from about 14 to 30 years, and older teenage boys/young adults. Older adults are absent.

The hostages, speaking about their experiences in captivity, were then able to confirm that the RUF was not the kind of bandit organization hypothesized by proponents of New Barbarism. Considerable rapport and sympathy had developed between the hostages and their captors.

In an attempt to reverse RUF gains in early 1995 the NPRC recruited Gurkha mercenaries to assist government troops. The Gurkhas were quickly withdrawn after suffering severe losses.

Chairman Strasser then announced a return to democracy, and made unconditional offers to the RUF to talk about a cease-fire and the

---

[14]'RUF is fighting to save Sierra Leone . . .' The chorus is:
   'Go and tell the President, Sierra Leone is my home
   Go and tell my parents, they may see me no more
   When fighting in the battlefield I'm fighting for ever
   Every Sierra Leonean is fighting for his land.'
   Verses 2–4 all demand that Sierra Leonean minerals 'be accounted for'.

movement's participation in elections. The Gurkhas were replaced by Executive Outcomes, a South African security firm with mining interests. The contract with Executive Outcomes appears to have offered a diamond concession in Kono valued at $US30 million. Executive Outcomes also bought shares in Sierra Rutile. Executive Outcomes trains and assists RSLMF soldiers in operations. The company is reported to have ring-fenced its mineral concessions in Kono with land mines. International concern was voiced about the involvement of 'South African mercenaries' in the conflict.

The NPRC insisted that there must be a cease-fire as a condition for peace talks to begin. Rejecting Strasser's terms for negotiation the RUF demanded, instead, the withdrawal of all foreign troops from Sierra Leone, and a hand-over of power to an interim sovereign national assembly, pending a negotiated end to the war and eventual elections. The RUF then announced its refusal to participate in the election announced by the NPRC. This decision appears to be based on a judgement that any election would result either in the return to power of one or other of the old political parties or a civilian government formed from NPRC elements. But it was not clear if the RUF foresaw that such a sovereign interim assembly would need some kind of democratic test, or how they imagined they might fare if their own participation in the assembly was put to such a test.

With potential negotiation bogged down before it started rebel raids continued. Villagers had their hands cut off to deter thoughts of voting. But a serious attack on a major relief convoy to Bo may have been 'an inside job'. The NPRC concluded as a result that convoying vehicles on the Freetown–Bo road was 'asking for trouble' and opened the road to any vehicles willing to risk the journey in their own time.

Government troops backed by Executive Outcomes then reversed some of the RUF's gains. An advance around Serabu was halted by RSLMF troops and Executive Outcomes in October 1995. The army then claimed to have dislodged the RUF from some of its key camps – in the Malal Hills in the north and 'Camp Lion' (in the Gambia Oil Palm Plantation behind Mattru Jong) close to the coast. Small groups of hungry and disillusioned RUF captives began to surrender, and were well-treated by the army, after a government decision to crack down on beatings and summary executions. This threat to the survival of the RUF was followed by a chilling spate of rebel atrocities against civilians, including the decapitation of 15 women, reported from villages between Bo and Moyamba, apparently to halt the rice harvest and deter further defectors. A spokesman denied RUF responsibility for these attacks, but it was not clear who might otherwise have carried them out, unless the rebel movement had split, or (as in Liberia) freelance copy-cat groups were at work.

During the last few months of 1995 some progress was made towards establishing a peace process. Two members of an RUF delegation attempting to make its way to Abidjan for preliminary negotiations were arrested in Guinea and handed over to the authorities in Freetown on 13 November 1995. Madam Isatu Kallon, a trader born in Makeni, but long resident in Liberia where she met Sankoh, was described as an arms dealer for the RUF. She is said by Freetown authorities to have stated that the RUF latterly obtained supplies of cheap Chinese-made weapons by bribing soldiers on the Guinean border with rough diamonds. James Massallay, from Pujehun District, was once a Lieutenant in the Sierra Leone army, until dismissed and jailed in 1971 for alleged involvement in the same coup plot against Siaka Stevens as Foday Sankoh. Released from jail in 1982 Massallay later worked for the National Diamond Mining Corporation. Described as RUF Chief-of-Staff and head of RUF arms and ammunition procurement, he appears to have been recruited during early attacks on the diamond area known as Tongo Field.

Four other members of the same RUF delegation (Agnes Jalloh, Philip Palmer, Fayia Musa and Dr Mohamed Barrie[15]) reached Abidjan and, assisted by International Alert, held discussions with UN and OAU representatives. Two of the delegates also met three London-based Sierra Leoneans (Ambrose Ganda, Omrie Golley and Oluniyi Robin-Coker). A version of discussions at this meeting is the first detailed published account of the RUF philosophy (*Focus on Sierra Leone* 1995). The two RUF delegates contributing to this published discussion are not named in the account. One is described as an engineering graduate from Fourah Bay College, and combatant member of the original insurgent group, now holding the rank of Captain. The other is an agriculture graduate from Njala University College, and RUF 'minister of agriculture'. The agriculturalist was working as a teacher in Kailahun District when the RUF invasion took place. Sympathizing with the aims of the movement he joined as a volunteer.

Both delegates had experienced violence as student protestors against Siaka Stevens in the late 1970s and early 1980s. They justify their own resort to violence by claiming all other avenues of democratic protest were blocked: 'The plight of families, friends and ordinary people around us and the evidence of our own experiences convinced us to take up arms to redress injustices'. The second representative then repeats Sankoh's view that the RUF is 'fighting to enforce peace'. . . 'we could not contain our anger at the lack of social justice in the country'.

[15]Dr Mohamed Barrie is identified as a German-trained medical doctor working for the Sieromco bauxite mine. He was seized in the RUF attack on the mine in January 1995. His membership of the delegation appears to be a tacit way of releasing him from captivity in return for his efforts to secure supplies of drugs and other relief materials for the RUF. He is not to be confused with an Issa (?) Barrie, described by Freetown sources (perhaps on account of his Fula name) as Foday Sankoh's 'juju man' and RUF chief diamond valuer. Agnes Jalloh, from Bonthe District, apparently represents RUF women, and is older sister to NPRC Vice-Chairman Julius Mada Bio, who replaced Valentine Strasser as head of state in a palace coup, 16 January 1996.

He then states that 'it was not helped when ex-President Momoh once said in Kailahun that education is not a right but a privilege' (*Focus on Sierra Leone* 1995). The discussion confirms that the RUF intended to halt the struggle when the NPRC took over, but revised its decision when several of the movement's key figures were killed in renewed attacks by the army. The RUF leadership then decided that the NPRC revolution was fake, and that the military was incapable of breaking free of the corrupt patrimonial politics they had inherited from the APC.[16]

Part Three: Interpretations

Factors proposed as causes of the crisis in Sierra Leone will now be reviewed. Some key issues are flagged for more detailed examination. A specific refutation of the environmental aspects of the New Barbarism thesis is reserved for Chapter Six.

Explaining the war: desiderata

Greater Liberia
NPFL leader Charles Taylor now seeks to deny his involvement in the war in Sierra Leone, but is on record earlier as promising that Sierra Leone would 'taste war' for supporting ECOMOG and openly boasted over the BBC in 1991 that his own fighters were operating '15 miles inside Sierra Leone'. RUF peace delegation member Isatu Conteh stated in November 1995 that the RUF earlier obtained its arms and other logistic support from Taylor, but that this support ceased when Taylor came under military pressure from rival factions in Liberia. The RUF rebellion was launched from Taylor-controlled territory, and it seems likely that rebel communications with the BBC in the early weeks of the war came through Taylor's satellite telephone link in Gbarnga. The Sierra Leone border region was rich in resources (most notably diamonds) of potential interest to the NPFL (and other Liberian factions). A deeply destabilized Sierra Leone would serve to undermine the international peace-keeping effort Taylor claimed was hostile to his interest.[17]

Some insist on a more Machiavellian interpretation, by taking Taylor's term for the provincial entity controlled by his movement – Greater Liberia – literally, and assuming it to represent a revival of

---

[16]In the preliminary peace negotiations with the OAU (December 1995/January 1996), the RUF is reported to have confirmed that the NPRC was not its target, but 'corruption, which is the ideology of the APC' (*West Africa*, 18 January 1996).

[17]The ECOMOG peace-keeping forces in Liberia were dominated by the Nigerians. President Momoh was a close friend of Nigeria's military leader, General Babangida, and Freetown served as an important base for ECOMOG.

Liberian territorial claims to parts of south-eastern Sierra Leone. Some Liberians believe that, historically, 'Greater Liberia' should include the rich diamond and timber resources of the border region of Sierra Leone. Taylor's backers included the late President Houphouët-Boigny of Côte d'Ivoire and some French and Lebanese business interests based in Abidjan (Tarr 1993). Destabilization of eastern Sierra Leone would make the region's trade more readily exploitable from this major francophone centre of commercial interest.[18] A legitimate Taylor-led government in Monrovia would have little scope to press any such territorial claim internationally but trade might flow in the intended direction were a Taylor-friendly RUF eventually to establish a regime in Freetown.

This Machiavellian interpretation makes heroic assumptions about Taylor's political foresight, given what is known of the messy realities of the Liberian civil war. Even so, Nigerian reactions to Taylor, and Nigerian support for the Freetown authorities in their struggle against the RUF, may be based on general suspicion of a growth of francophone influence in a region French commentators sometimes refer to as 'Guinée anglais'.

Regional competition

As already noted, the Libyans and Israelis have both dabbled to some extent in Liberian and Sierra Leonean politics.

Gaddafi appears to have blown hot and cold over events in Liberia and Sierra Leone (Tarr 1993), and has enough problems of his own to constrain further sub-Saharan Africa ventures. But he may retain some residual sympathy for the RUF as one of the more sincere African attempts to apply aspects of his youth-oriented revolutionary philosophy. Sankoh is said to have learnt his guerrilla skills in Benghazi.

The Israelis monitor and perhaps try to control flows of wealth from Sierra Leone's diamonds into Lebanon. In the past, Sierra Leone-based Lebanese diamond merchants have channelled resources to both Shiite and Maronite factions in the Lebanon civil war. Under the Momoh presidency an Israeli company supplied the APC government with urgently needed rice imports and bought diamonds in Kenema. The Israeli government was quick to recognize the NPRC government following the military coup against Momoh in 1992, and supplied the new regime with arms and security advice.

Nigerians troops have protected key sites in Sierra Leone from mid-1991, and their presence in the country is treated as a necessary extension of their heavy involvement in the peace-keeping venture in Liberia. Nigeria's former military ruler, Ibrahim Babangida, was a close

---

[18]French newspapers have commented quite extensively on the role of francophone business interests in supporting the NPFL in Liberia (cf. Tarr 1993). I am most grateful to Jean-François Bayart for supplying me with press cuttings on this topic.

friend of President Momoh, but Nigerian involvement in Sierra Leone has survived the ending of both Momoh's and Babangida's regimes.

It has been suggested that Côte d'Ivoire and Nigeria are both interested in the fate of rebellions in Liberia and Sierra Leone because mineral resources may be important to their longer-term industrialization strategies. It has recently been fashionable, internationally, to write off Nigeria's military leaders as a self-interested clique. Another view suggests the Nigerian military might be the 'party' in Nigeria that has seriously invested, over the longer term, in a united Nigeria, rather than a Nigeria factionalized by ethnic politics. Nigeria's future status as a regional industrial power (a Brazil of West Africa) may depend on being able to link Nigerian oil, gas and hydro power with regionally abundant minerals, notably iron-ore and bauxite from Liberia and Sierra Leone. The staunch opposition of the Nigerian military to an Ivoirian-backed Taylor regime, beginning under Babangida, but continued by Abacha, might be seen as a long-term investment in mineral supplies for the twenty-first century.

Student revolutionary populism
Student activists in Sierra Leone during the 1970s and early 1980s were strongly influenced by the revolutionary language of Pan-Africanism and Gaddafi's *Green Book*, and the Third Wave futurology of the American pundit Alvin Toffler (cf Toffler and Toffler 1994). The RUF leadership includes some of these former activists, and appears still to be seriously committed to aspects of this revolutionary heritage, and to the populism of *The Green Book* in particular.

Public statements, by representatives based in Accra and Abidjan, attacking the APC, and then later rejecting the NPRC regime's offer of a place in a multi-party electoral process, reflect *Green Book* language (with its insistence on the need for a third way between One Party rule and an electoral process in which a 51 per cent majority dominates a 49 per cent minority). The suggestion that the leader (Foday Sankoh) is 'above politics' and the requirement that the issues of the war should be resolved through a national assembly of ordinary Sierra Leoneans are also strikingly Green-Bookish in tone.

Accounts by young captives speak of being ushered into an Aladdin's Cave of looted clothes, shoes, medication, etc. free for the asking, in RUF forest camps. Perhaps intended to rebuild confidence among deeply shocked captives, this is also consistent with the strong emphasis in *The Green Book* on a simple needs-based redistributive populism. According to *The Green Book*, food, personal effects, accommodation, and access to transport should be allocated as of right. Only the accumulation of assets beyond the needs of the individual is rejected (Gaddafi, n.d.).

The influence of Pan-Africanism and the Toffler theory of the Third Wave is briefly reviewed in Chapter Two.

Rebellion from below

For reasons detailed in Chapter Two the border between Liberia and Sierra Leone is a region with several long-standing social and political tensions. There seems little doubt that the RUF attempted to exploit some of these tensions.

One local set of grievances stands out in particular. Under the APC regime, Pujehun politics was dominated by Francis Minna. Minna sought to impose his own choice on Pujehun East constituency in the 1982 elections. Thuggery triggered a reaction among supporters of the rival candidate (SLPP veteran Mannah Kpaka). This escalated into a substantial rebellion (named after the mysterious 'bush devil' of Mende folklore *Ndogboyosoi*). This revolt was put down with considerable force by the army. Some Pujehun settlements were burnt, and villagers were still living scattered in bush camps when the RUF first arrived.

Subsequently, Minna, a Vice President under Momoh, came into conflict with a powerful group in the Momoh regime led by Bambay Kamara, head of the police force and, like the President, a Limba from north-western Sierra Leone. The issues at stake have never been made fully explicit but control of smuggling activities along the border with Liberia seems to have been at the centre of the dispute.

An anti-smuggling patrol had been set up, commanded by Gabriel Kaikai, a policeman from Pujehun, and close associate of Minna. Participants in the force have described the anti-smuggling squadron as a freelance paramilitary group that in operating to control diamond flows in the interests of its principals often engaged in acts of arbitrary violence against border-zone villages. Kaikai was discovered by Bambay Kamara to be planning a coup, and six alleged plotters were eventually pronounced guilty and executed in 1987. Minna was the fifth accused, executed for misprision of treason (having knowledge of the coup but not reporting it).

After Minna was executed Ndogboyosoi supporters were free to regroup. But by this time APC fortunes were at a low ebb and no one seems to have been able to fill the political void in Pujehun. Little was done to 'make peace' after the dislocations of the Minna era. Rallying Ndogboyosoi supporters in 1991 the RUF seems to have found fertile ground for recruitment to the revolutionary cause. After subsequent ULIMO successes against the RUF, the rump of rebels surviving in Pujehun District, especially around the village of Fanima and in forests surrounding Zimmi in 1992–3, assumed more the aspect of 'Ndogboyosoi II' than 'RUF I'.

The tendency of rural insurgencies to be taken over and reformulated 'from below' is a theme pursued by Kriger (1992) in her analysis of the Zimbabwe war of independence, and the same approach may also help explain some of the features of the conflict in Sierra Leone (cf. Young 1990).

The economics of war

When the rebel war continued in 1993 after the RUF was driven out of Kailahun, attention turned to the economic interests combatants might have had in prolonging conflict.

It was suggested that the NPRC was itself fostering war to reinforce its political interest. If true, it was an inept strategy, since much of the NPRC's prestige and legitimacy was bound up in its promise to halt the fighting quickly. By the end of 1995 failure to end the war had gathered many potential votes for opposition groups in promised elections. There may have been rogue elements in the NPRC, but prolongation of the conflict might owe more to military incompetence. Foot-dragging by disgruntled officers still loyal to the former regime has been offered as one explanation. The army, like other state organizations in Sierra Leone, serves as a major instrument of patrimonial favour. The institutional values of clientelism are widely respected throughout Sierra Leone (Richards 1986), and good clients stay loyal to their patrons and sponsors through temporary set-backs. It is to be expected that some officers would remain loyal to the presidents, or other senior governmental figures who gave them their chance.

At times, rival groups within the RSLMF quarrelled about the support they got from the NPRC, and failed to combine effectively on operations. Some groups of soldiers shamelessly concentrated on garnering the rich pickings available in the war zone. The NPRC admitted that sections of the army were not fully under its control. But the 'sell game' phenomenon (Keen 1995) is complex, and arises from social and political conditions in the war zone itself.

A central tactical strength of the RUF rebellion is that it takes place in remote and ill-defended rain forest areas. Foday Sankoh learnt from his days as an itinerant photographer in Kailahun District that bush paths were sometimes the best way of moving around dissected, forested terrain where dirt roads soon wash out in heavy rainy season downpours. Given the state of neglect of the road system in Kailahun under the APC (Chapter Two), it is hard to imagine that even if the regime had wanted to keep its war-front troops better supplied much could have been got through to soldiers in forward positions in a hurry without access to helicopters.

These ill-supplied, ill-paid war-zone soldiers are especially vulnerable to ambush from determined youngsters, high on fear-inhibiting drugs, and well-drilled in forest combat. It would be understandable if some RSLMF soldiers took à safety-first approach, and made informal contact with the enemy, to negotiate local deals on supplies, so minimizing the risk of being cut off in surprise attack.

When an NPRC government, angered by APC neglect of battle-front troops, took over, and established well-supplied forward ammunition and weapons stores, these proved attractive targets for forest-based rebels. Drawing troops forward towards the Moa river in mid-1992, a rebel group based at Fanima encircled Potoru and captured enough weapons to keep the RUF supplied for up to two years (according to the estimates of the officer commanding Potoru at the time).

Local people in remote rain forest environments have little option but to adapt to the presence of armed insurgents who can move through the forest at will. Potoru people found that it was not in the interests of the nearby RUF camp (perhaps the RUF headquarters camp known as Zogoda) in the Kambui South forest reserve to menace local villages on which they had come to depend for supplies of rice and other essentials. Uneasy coexistence was threatened only where government troops threatened to put pressure on the rebel camps. It was no surprise to find that in 1992 local Paramount Chiefs were sometimes as well if not better informed about the position and plans of rebel groups than the local military command.

In other cases, the locals 'joined' the RSLMF instead. In a patrimonial polity, where clientelism is a major means through which inter-generational transfers of knowledge and assets are achieved, young people are always on the look out for new sources of patronage. Where they joined the rebels with any degree of enthusiasm it was to seek training (Chapter Four). The arts of war are better than no arts at all. The army was simply seen as a new form of schooling. Where recruits were gathered together for training in the field, in advanced positions, the commander in question would take young volunteers as personal 'apprentices', rather than as formal recruits. A war-front officer might also have to organize a large farm to feed the local war widows and orphans attaching themselves to him as the only viable patron in sight (Chapter Four). The social logic of life in the battle zone forces such officers to become self-sufficient 'war-lords' whether they intend it or not.

War as social process
The phenomenon of the field commander's farm introduces us to the idea of war as social process. The basic *socio*-logic of rural life in forested southern and eastern Sierra Leone is not destroyed, or even suspended, by the advent of war. Life goes on, and people adapt their cultural skills to higher norms of violence – transforming, unwittingly supporting, and in due time domesticating these patterns of violence. There is a constant interaction between this socio-logic of everyday life ('habitus' to use the term proposed by Pierre Bourdieu (Bourdieu 1979) in a war zone and the ideas, plans and operations of the belligerents. Belligerent schemata (strategic plans, political aims, ways of interpreting violence to captives) are as likely to be ensnared and transmuted by the 'habitus', as the 'habitus' is to be disrupted by extreme acts of violence. The extremity of the violence, it might be

argued, is indeed at times a desperate attempt to burst free of 'habitus' – to disrupt this process of 'normalization' where it threatens to swamp a rebellion whose perpetrators still have a point to prove. But it is a two-edged sword. These acts of violence may signal desperation not terror. Civil values may be strengthened by the realization that horrors intended to shock are signs of weakness, not strength. (Some of these points are elaborated in Chapter Three.)

Understanding the RUF: excluded intellectuals?

Events during 1995 confirmed that the RUF had survived as a single movement, and remained at the heart of the turmoil in Sierra Leone, whatever other opportunist side-shows might have grown up around it. Although spread of violence depends on factors that are independent of the wishes of insurgent activists it makes a logical starting point to consider the ambitions of the leadership.

The RUF when it first appeared was a small group of exiles, with a common experience of being driven to the margins of Sierra Leonean society and beyond by experiences under the All People's Congress government of Siaka Stevens (1968-85). Living as exiles in Liberia when the civil war started, several preferred to accept the chance to fight their way back home than remain in Liberia as refugees. The War Council in 1995 represents the rump of the group surviving nearly five years of war. Leading figures were killed in the fighting, but have since been replaced by sympathizers recruited after the war began. Some of these newer recruits share the same background – social exclusion for political protest and student activism.

RUF leader Foday Sabana Sankoh, a native of Magburaka in Tonkolili District, was once a corporal in the signals section in the Sierra Leone army. Cashiered and jailed for seven years under suspicion of involvement in a coup plot against Siaka Stevens in 1971, Sankoh set up, on release, a photographic business run from a shed in front of the Public Works Compound in Bo. He later shifted to the diamond districts, basing himself in Segbwema, Kailahun District, for several years.

During his Segbwema period Sankoh was noted for trekking the back paths leading from bush-mining camp to camp, rather than using the roads and public transport. Living the reality of state recession in Kailahun he would have acquired a good working knowledge of both the forested terrain and the lifestyle and political sentiments of the diamond tributors of this border region so crucial to the economic fortunes of the state. Senior figures in government, army and civil service had interests in small diamond mining operations and logging operations in the border zone. Sponsorship ties linking the diamond diggers of the region to the Freetown political elite, smuggling, and arbitrary acts of the 'anti-smuggling' services are hardly likely to have escaped the notice of this itinerant recorder of day-to-day life as he scoured the nooks and crannies of the border zone in embittered internal exile.

Other figures in the RUF share Sankoh's background (rustication from a state institution under the APC). Philip Palmer, a combatant in the Pujehun sector in 1991, identified himself to eye-witnesses as a Liberian-based exile radicalized by the APC response to student protests against Siaka Stevens. One of the RUF's senior military figures, ex-Lieutenant James Massally, was jailed for his alleged involvement in the 1971 coup plot. Some RUF recruits worked as rural teachers prior to the rebellion. Some graduates enter teaching only for lack of other preferment and see a rural secondary school as a punishment posting. Other recruits were rusticated student protesters or workers living on, unemployed, in the environs of the institutions from which they had been sacked. Early attacks on the Teachers' College at Bunumbu in Kailahun District may have provided a small 'crop' of such disgruntled educators. Later raids on Njala University College and the Sierra Rutile mine at Mobimbi (both in southern Sierra Leone) seem to have been spurred by plans to 'liberate' other 'internal' exiles.

Once rescued, activists seemingly plan revenge against the institution that has shamed them. One attack on Njala in 1995 targeted only the university records for destruction. Leaders of the attack identified themselves as sent-down former students. They may have been seeking to disguise the fact that they never graduated. The university authorities were warned not to try to re-open the institution while 'the war of liberation' continued.

Only at first sight do these revenge-inspired attacks seem pointless. An attack on the rutile mine at Mobimbi in October 1995 left many buildings burnt. The rutile and bauxite mines, among the very few large-scale solvent ventures in the Sierra Leone countryside, were frequently milked on an *ad hoc* basis by government ministers, unable to persuade the govenment to negotiate proper mining agreements, fair to all parties.[19] In periods of economic crisis mine managements sometimes provided the then APC regime with the foreign exchange or fuel oil necessary to keep the country running on a week-to-week basis. Such deals frequently turned out to have been to the private advantage of the politicians in question.[20]

---

[19]The management of the rutile mine had been anxious that government should replace these informal arrangements with an up-dated mining act and transparent royalty agreements fair both to government and mining interests. There was much foot-dragging on the government side, since the existing *ad hoc* arrangements were advantageously opaque.

[20]A documentary made for BBC TV in 1991 on the environmental consequences of mining found plenty of local voices ready to testify against the companies. But the programme makers failed to press the question of the government's role in such abuses. The documentary was seen on video throughout the country.

The NPRC had promised democracy, but a democratically elected leader would be no guarantee that such patrimonial abuses might not return. The attack on the mine was prefaced by a message to the NPRC government that there would be no mine left for any incoming, democratically elected, president 'to enjoy'.

The abuses thus being flagged are real. It is the rebel response that provokes amazement. Why destroy? Why not take over the facilities and run them in the insurgent interest? Multinational miners in Africa are political realists and would soon come to terms.

What I want to suggest is that these dramatic gestures of protest are a typical academic response. They serve to illuminate (in flames, as it were) widespread patrimonial abuses linked to mining and other forms of resource appropriation in the Sierra Leone countryside in which national political elites and international interests appear to have connived. The point about such protest is that it makes satisfying sense on paper, or in the mind. It is the lack of regard for the practical consequences in a country of such great poverty that is so shocking. It is not at all clear how the RUF would propose running the country without mining revenues, or do they believe in their heart-of-hearts that they will never come to power? This is why it seems Mary Douglas (1986) may be right. The irresponsible destructiveness of excluded intellectual elites can be very great. What could be a more perfect illustration of her point than to attack a university, not for loot, but to destroy its record system.

According to the New Barbarism thesis, the attacks just described are evidence that a mindless or criminal element is at work in Sierra Leone. Just the opposite interpretation is offered here. This is not barbarism, but the product of the intellectual anger of an excluded educated elite.[21]

Parallels with Shining Path?

It seems some useful parallels might be drawn between the RUF leadership and the embittered marginalized group of Andean intellectuals who formed the core of Shining Path in Peru (Palmer 1992; Tarazona-Sevillano 1992; de Wit and Gianotten 1992). Shining Path was formed by teachers and university lecturers, and recruited Andean peasant children sold on the idea of progress, and on education as key to that progress, but then cheated of jobs and success by more powerfully entrenched elites of European origin in the capital.

Like Shining Path, the RUF seeks to build up the self-respect of its young captives through the skills they learn in the movement,

---

[21] This is certainly the tone of the recently published RUF pamphlet *Footpaths to Democracy*, with its protest at 'the raping of the countryside to feed the greed and caprice of the Freetown elite and their masters abroad' and its talk of a 'liberation theology consistent with our pride in ourselves as Africans'.

especially the violent skills of guerrilla bush-craft (Marks 1992). This has provided youngsters at the bottom of the social pile with the responsibility of command, and a sense of their own violent powerfulness.

The confidence reposed in young commandos, both boys and girls, also gives the movement (like Shining Path) considerable strategic flexibility, despite its small size and lack of heavy weapons. When centres of operations are attacked the young guerrillas have the craft and courage to soldier on regardless, knowing, for example, how to re-arm themselves through 'fake' attacks on the ammunition stores of isolated contingents of government troops, and how to re-build their forest camps in new sites.

An obvious difference is that Shining Path is dogmatically Maoist in political philosophy, but the social circumstances feeding both movements – an educated but embittered leadership, and a large pool of modernized rural-based youth with few prospects of continuing education and progressive employment through established channels – seem broadly comparable.[22] Both movements are incorrigibly didactic. Far from barbarism, both movements are precisely what one might expect when a group of embittered pedagogues decides to go to war.

Capture: why the rebellion expands

The RUF has expanded through capturing the kind of young people it considers potential recruits to its cause. There is a calculated judgement that dislocated youths in mining-wrecked countryside will come to see the world like the RUF, even when forced to join the movement against their will. But how is this loyalty induced?

In the short term fear must be a factor – especially fear of what government forces will do to any young person suspected of association with the movement, if re-captured. Certainly, summary execution of rebel suspects (as carefully documented by Amnesty International since 1992) has served as a powerful aid to the RUF's retention of its captive youngsters (Amnesty International 1992, 1993).

But the rebels have more positive inducements to loyalty as well. Some are straightforwardly material. One young girl, asked why she came to identify with the people who had seized her from her home, answered frankly: 'they offered me a choice of shoes and dresses – I never had decent shoes before.'

It is also important to realize that the rebels consider their bush camps an alternative to the failed schooling found in the wider society.

---

[22]Or as RUF/SL (1995) puts it:
   'a society has already collapsed when majority [sic] of its youth can wake up in the morning with nothing to look up for' (p. 19).

State recession means dysfunctional schooling. Teachers' salaries, pittances at best, were paid late or not at all. Conditions worsened under the financial austerity programmes imposed on the country by the IMF and World Bank from 1977 onwards. Rural teachers' salaries were paid last of all. I have vivid memories of the time and money rural teachers in schools around Gola Forest wasted in journeys to the provincial headquarters in Kenema to enquire whether long back-dated pay had yet arrived. Sometimes they could only obtain amounts 'on account' by paying heavy 'interest' to the authorities ('bribes' by any other name).[23]

For many seized youngsters in the diamond districts functional schooling had broken down long before the RUF arrived. The rebellion was a chance to resume their education. Captives report being schooled in RUF camps, using fragments and scraps of revolutionary texts for books, and receiving a good basic training in the arts of bush warfare. Many captive children adapt quickly,[24] and exult in new-found skills, and the chance, perhaps for the first time in their lives, to show what they can do. Stood-down boy soldiers in Liberia have spoken longingly of their guns not as weapons of destruction but as being the first piece of modern kit they have ever known how to handle [Hodges 1992].

The RUF is clearly limited in the weapons at its command (being restricted mainly to supplies obtained through ambush of, or deals with, government troops or troops in neighbouring countries) and, boy-scout-like, the youngsters in the movement carve wooden replicas to create the impression of greater strength than they actually possess.

Mention should also be made of the role of fear-inhibiting drugs in getting under-armed and inexperienced captive youngsters to fight. Marijuana has long been widespread among tributors digging diamonds in the forest. But over the past decade crack cocaine and other substances have become more common in the mining districts. Insurgents in both Liberia and Sierra Leone seem to have made widespread use of crack cocaine, and possibly other substances (e.g. 'angel dust'), for what are believed to be their confidence-boosting properties. Eye-witnesses, reporting the rounding up of rebel forces, describe RUF fighters fearlessly provoking their captors to kill them there and then. This, they assumed, was the drug talking.

---

[23] One of the leading figures in the RUF in 1995, Fayia Musa, a Njala graduate in agriculture and participant in student protests against Siaka Stevens in 1977, was recruited in 1991 while working as a secondary school teacher under these kinds of conditions in isolated Kailahun District.

[24] It is relevant to note what psychiatrists term the Stockholm Syndrome. This is the condition in which terrified captives subsequently identify with their captors – perhaps because to their surprise they are treated with respect, even kindness – and become loyal supporters of the hostage-takers' cause. A famous example was the case of an American newspaper heiress seized by an urban guerrilla group, the Symbionese Liberation Army; the young woman later became an apparently willing participant in the group's armed operations.

Cultural resonances: camps and initiation

The RUF knows how to manipulate to its advantage the cultural 'infrastructure' of rural life in Sierra Leone. Two aspects require brief introduction here – forest camps and initiation.

The RUF believes it is fighting to save Sierra Leonean society from itself. Cut off from that society by exile, and five years of forest-based combat, the leadership sees devastation all around it. This vision, reinforced by 'sobels' and bandits, is a self-fulfilling prophecy. Attacks on civilians and atrocities against women 'prove' that wider society is as the RUF believes it to be – dangerous and corrupt. The burning of villages and the killing of villagers make concrete the assertion that captives have no home to return to, at least until larger victory is won. Even the international hostages were told that their capture was necessary 'for their safety'. As in the chaotic days of the overseas slave trade, security is to be found in isolated camps deep inside the forest.

The main idiom of transition from childhood to adulthood in forest society is that of initiation, followed by instruction in adult ways in the 'bush school'. The Poro Society 'devil' comes to town to seize young boys from their mothers. In the colonial period, before the value of Western education was fully appreciated, the state, in effect, did the same thing when seeking to fill its schools. But now the educational 'devil' no longer calls. In a state near to collapse, with teachers no longer regularly paid, the RUF 'devil' steps into the breach.

With initiation already deeply etched in the lives of many young people in the Upper Guinean forests, capture may serve to recapitulate aspects of the experience. Villagers apply an initiation 'model' to the disaster that has befallen them; they perceive that their children have been taken from them by force (as in initiation) and turned into alien creatures by the power of rebel magic. Offered rudimentary schooling in the bush, and instruction in skills of guerrilla warfare, many captives quickly readjust to their lot.

The larger implications of this argument will be pursued later. Here, however, the point to stress is the military strategic consequences of a rebellion that spreads through captive reaction to this experience of rebel 'initiation'.

In a society and economy in which decline has been accelerated by the destructiveness of the war itself, rebel 'hold' over the minds and imaginations of young captives should not be underestimated. Even where youngsters, unconvinced by rebel claims of revolutionary advance, seek to give up an enforced struggle they are deterred from quitting through fears for their personal safety. The single biggest strategic mistake of the Sierra Leonean army over the war years has been harsh treatment of rebel suspects. There can be little doubt that many captives have been kept from thoughts of surrender by the possibility of summary execution.[25]

In mid-1995 the national security council finally accepted the argument that a steady policy of amnesty for young rebels was best, and instructed troops in the field accordingly. There were doubts about whether the NPRC had sufficient control over the army to make this policy stick without lapses. But enough RUF conscripts surrendered and reported positive experiences (over the radio) to encourage others to think of doing likewise. So long as the RUF lacks extensive spontaneous political support in rural Sierra Leone, and is forced to expand by conscription, it must remain vulnerable to a policy, unswervingly applied, of offering amnesty and rehabilitation to captive youngsters.

The leopard has come to town: the dramaturgy of forest war

Sierra Leone is a compact ring of forested or once-forested territory gathered around a coastal primate city. Freetown, containing today about 20–25 per cent of the country's total population, was founded as an early outpost of Empire, and became a noted centre for mission and educational activity reaching up and down the western African coast. The country has a long history of violent opposition between 'bush' (the forest) and 'town' (established patrimonial authority linked to overseas trade).

Spreading from a heavily forested periphery from which a weakened patrimonial state was seen to be withdrawing, the present war recapitulates aspects of that history in intentionally dramatic terms.[26]

The crisis of patrimonialism is seen by protagonists of the war as a crisis of 'bush' come to 'town' (or as a saying puts it, *lɛpɛt dɔn kam na tɔn* – 'the leopard has entered the city'). The leopard is a long-standing and powerful symbol of malign, and illegitimate, political agency in Sierra Leonean life. According to one local theory it is the animal form assumed by weakened political elites seeking, by stealth, to rebuild their political fortunes (Richards 1993). The rebel leadership stalks the enfeebled patrimonial state to reverse and revenge its earlier banishment from political light into outer forested darkness.

But the crisis of bush come to town has international resonances as well. Sierra Leone was one of the first places where the Western world came into exploitative contact with the great African rain forest.

---

[25] Amnesty International's first report on the summary execution of rebel suspects in the Sierra Leone conflict (1992) may have unwittingly exacerbated the situation by focusing only on abuses by government troops and not examining the wider context, including the possibility that the rebels were marking captives in such a way as to provoke their harsh treatment if and when any tried to desert the movement.

[26] 'No more shall the rural countryside be reduced to hewers of wood and drawers of water for urban Freetown' (RUF/SL 1995, p. 14).

Freetown's great natural harbour was touched early by the fifteenth-century European voyages of discovery, and then became an important staging post for the first global sea-borne trading system raised upon the Atlantic triangular trade (trade goods to Africa, slaves to the Americas, sugar and cotton to Europe). The Sierra Leone river was an early, and late, centre for the slave trade, based on the fort at Bunce Island. Sierra Leone was a source of slaves favoured by South Carolina planters because of their knowledge of rice agriculture, and Bunce Island was at one stage under joint American and British commercial management. Many of the slaves shipped through this outlet came from the interior forests of today's Liberia–Sierra Leone border region.

A tradition of meeting Atlantic maritime service needs survived until very recently. Freetown harbour was a major staging post for Allied forces fighting in North Africa during the Second World War. The bush around the village of Grafton still bears the scars of its war-time encampments. Many Sierra Leonean men were recruited for military service in the Burma campaign. In a last gasp of empire, Freetown harbour was used for bunkering purposes by the British Falklands fleet.

Shaped by its involvement in the violence-laden Atlantic world, Sierra Leone has also felt the impress of comparably violent attacks on local forest resources. Elephant hunting close to Freetown and along the coast of Sierra Leone supplied an abundant ivory trade that was one of the early factors attracting international trade to the region. Timber along the Sierra Leone river was removed at a slightly later date to supply the British Royal Navy with timber for its ships of the line.

By their actions the rebels make a rhetorical point deeply rooted in this troubled history of resource extraction. First you used our harbour and took us as slaves, and then you took our timber, ivory and valuable mineral resources. But now we have been dumped in the darkness of the bush. This darkness comprises both reduction in the educational opportunity for which the country has long been famous, and the physical darkness that frequently afflicted the two rural higher educational establishments from which some of the rebel leadership comes.

The insurgents use the forest, then, as a stage on which to enact a drama of state recession. But with their stage opening directly onto the Atlantic world the rebels hoped that this might make the drama visible even to the international community as far away as New York and London. Only after five years of conflict has this been achieved.

Despite intensive depletion from the harbour side there is heavy forest much closer to Freetown than might be imagined. In fact, along the inaccessible ridges of the Peninsula Mountains it is very close indeed. Leopards and rare antelopes no longer found in the interior forests of the Liberian border still roam these thickly forested ridges a few miles from State House (Davies and Richards 1991). In January 1995 the rebels achieved their greatest success and threatened to establish camps in these ridge-top forests to attack Freetown, spreading terror and panic in the town. The world's media and the international agencies finally noticed the 'bush devil' at the city gates.

Conclusion

It is now clear that the RUF is a coherent movement and that its political project cannot be ignored. This chapter has painted a bleak picture of a vengeful movement of exiles wrecking the countryside and expanding through youth capture. What sense does it make to wreck the countryside in this way? In a market-driven world we tend first to look for an economic rationale. But this may be less important in Sierra Leone than some commentators think. We need to consider to what extent, also, the war makes sociological sense. The present chapter has characterized the rebel leadership as an excluded intellectual elite. Their violence is an intellectual project in which the practical consequences have not been fully thought through. Attention has been drawn to the ways in which, with anthropological cleverness, the insurgents have manipulated practical and psychic security concerns of the mass of ordinary rural Sierra Leoneans living in an environment stamped by violent processes of forest conversion over many years.

A main aim in the following chapters is to explore this longer-term history of violence and wider societal search for peace and security. If war has spread 'from within', making its own cultural sense as it goes, then the search for peace may have to trace out similar paths. This implies a reliance upon the capacity of ordinary Sierra Leoneans in war-affected regions to figure out culturally smart ways to contain further outbreaks of violence and invent peace. It may be important to protect what Mary Douglas (1986) calls 'the shared prejudices of [local] society'.

2

State Recession & Youth

The Political Culture of Patrimonial Decline

Introduction

This chapter discusses the recession of the state in Sierra Leone, and its impact on the lives of young people targeted by the rebels. The RUF first attacked the heavily forested region bordering Liberia. Poor communications made it difficult to find out what the rebels were up to, and to supply defending troops. The weakness of the Sierra Leone state in the border region was largely a self-inflicted wound, reflecting economic mismanagement in the 1970s and 1980s and earlier political miscalculation. The rebels also exploited the ambiguous national identity of some border-zone groups, playing on tensions dating from the imposition of the colonial boundary. The chapter considers the plight of young people working in diamond mining on the border, trapped by economic recession, corruption and lack of educational opportunity. Youth culture in Sierra Leone reflects some of these dilemmas of state recession. This is seen especially clearly in interpretations of the Rambo film *First Blood*, viewed locally as a charter for self-empowerment under conditions of patrimonial decline. The rebels have tried to build on this legacy. As self-declared revolutionaries rebel leaders have also drawn upon a common pool of student radical debate in Sierra Leone. The ingredients of this debate – *The Green Book*, Pan-Africanism and Toffler's theory of the Third Wave – are briefly discussed.

Patrimonialism in Sierra Leone

Patrimonialism involves redistributing national resources as marks of *personal* favour to followers who respond with loyalty to the leader rather than to the institution the leader represents. Patrimonialism is a systematic scaling up, at the national level, of local ideas about patron–client linkages, shaped (in Sierra Leone) in the days of direct extraction of forest resources, about the duty of the rich and successful to protect, support and promote their followers and friends (Richards 1986).

In patrimonial systems of government 'big persons' at the apex of political power compete to command some share of the 'national cake' which they then redistribute through their own networks of followers. The leader is the ultimate patron – i.e. the politician with the most resources to redistribute. The leader uses these resources to resolve conflict between rival networks by out-bidding the lesser patrons. Under Siaka Stevens' rule in Sierra Leone, for example, State House, the President's office, had a number of mobile generators that could be installed as temporary electricity supplies in towns or on college campuses where local politicians were unable to obtain the money and parts to fix a broken supply. Students angry at interrupted study would then be told by the President – see, if you had come to me first, without rioting, I could have fixed this thing for you earlier (as your 'father'). This is a typical power play in patrimonial politics.

Patrimonial rule is often considered a pre-modern form of government. But in fact it is quite compatible with various institutions in modern state and society, e.g. cabinet-style government and some of the informal networking and brokerage activities of global 'big business'. Patrimonialism thrives in countries where the main revenues come from rich natural resources such as minerals or timber, since mining or logging companies will carry out many of the more complicated tasks of the state (like organizing communications, schooling and medical services) in enclave areas, and state officials need do little more than collect rents for access to concessions. It is often in the interests of both parties for official rents to be set at well below market values with unaccountable sums disappearing into patrimonial pockets.

It is widely misunderstood that this money, quietly salted away from kick-backs on contracts, concessions and export deals, is for personal enrichment. In fact patrimonial accounts are political resources. The 'personal fortunes' of patrimonial leaders are political bank accounts used to fund the workings of what Reno (1995) terms the 'shadow state'. It might be better to think of the 'shadow state' as the substance of patrimonial politics, but hidden from scrutiny by a carefully constructed film-set-like structure approximating Western theoretical notions of the 'modern state'.[1]

As much as possible, this façade-like 'official', visible, state is propped up by aid appropriations.

---

[1] If this seems too cynically 'post-modern' I shall later argue that, as elsewhere in the world, Sierra Leoneans use films as an imaginative prop to thinking about the future. The modern state may only be a film-set-like façade, but it has given young Sierra Leoneans some definite ideas about the kind of modern state they really wish to have (cf. Chapter Eight).

African patrimonial systems of rule grew vigorously under Cold War conditions, since skilful leaders could use geo-political position (as in Siad Barre's Somalia), or a threat to switch allegiance between communism and capitalism, to chisel increased aid resources from the Western and Soviet systems.

Patrimonialism in the 1990s faces a double crisis. World recession has reduced prices of many raw materials. Countries like Sierra Leone have also seen the exhaustion of some of their best sources of minerals. Meanwhile the ending of the Cold War caused sources of aid money to dry up. There is less money around to maintain the crumbling façade of the 'official state'.[2]

This throws patrimonialism into a crisis of legitimacy. The state shrinks – both physically (in terms of its communication facilities) and sociologically (in terms of the groups it can afford to patronize). The regime's priority attention has to be given to maintaining loyalty among the security services. Entire areas, e.g. education and social services, may find themselves bereft of the extra resources from quiet patrimonial deals they need to survive. Official salaries for civil servants, doctors and teachers in Sierra Leone, for example, are hardly living wages. The system depends on the *ad hoc* support of president or other senior figures in government to secure supplements, e.g. an extra allocation of subsidized or free imported rice and other food items, sometimes extracted from food aid sources, without which a professional's family budget fails to add up.

The next generation suffers especially from the recession of the patrimonial state, since one end point of much patrimonial redistribution is the payment of school fees. President Momoh admitted the depth of the crisis in the patrimonial state in Sierra Leone when he made a speech in Kailahun stating that education was a privilege not a right.

In a nation built up for two hundred years or more around systems of schooling in which Western models have been held out as the ideal, educational issues are one of the key aspects of the present crisis (and also a reason why the New Barbarism thesis seems so out-of-place when applied to the Sierra Leone case). NPRC leader, Captain Valentine Strasser, justified the coup, in his first broadcast, by calling for the repair of roads and schools. One rebel leader, Fayia Musa, recently cited Momoh's speech about education being a privilege and not a right as a turning point on the RUF road to violence (*Focus on Sierra Leone* 1995).

This crisis of the patrimonial state (often invisible to outside agencies – since so much redistribution is *ad hoc*) is one of the main consequences of the ending of the Cold War in Africa. A dangerous vacuum has been created around the edges of many African states into which

---

[2] Between 1982 and 1985 government revenues, as a percentage of GDP, declined from 8.3 per cent to 5.5 per cent, while GDP itself was static (Conteh 1996).

some of the wilder elements in civil society are drawn to try their hand at alternative forms of political organization.

The advance and decline of the Sierra Leonean nation-state

The modern constitutional history of Sierra Leone dates from 1787, when the Black Poor first settled on the northern end of the Sierra Leone peninsula (Braidwood 1994; Fyfe 1962; Peterson 1969). The Black Poor were mainly ex-servicemen from the British army living in London. It was their wish to be re-settled in Africa. The British government owed them support in return for service to the Crown in the American war of independence. Newspapers at the time confused the preparation of their expedition with the expedition being fitted out to ship convicts to a penal settlement in Australia (Braidwood 1994). New Barbarism insists that the problem in Sierra Leone today is not war but crime (Kaplan 1994). It is ironic to note that over two hundred years ago ill-informed journalists bracketed the original settlers with the criminal classes even before they became Sierra Leoneans.

After many vicissitudes, Sierra Leone became a Crown Colony in 1807, and the base for a British anti-slavery squadron operating in western African waters. Subsequently the population of Freetown and the peninsula came to be dominated by 'recaptives' (Peterson 1969). The recaptives were not returned ex-slaves from the New World but recently enslaved West Africans released in Freetown from slave ships arrested on the high seas. Fresh from their homes, and freedom, they brought into mid-nineteenth-century Sierra Leonean society a rich mixture of technical ideas and social influences from up and down the western African coast, greatly boosting a process of African 'cultural creolization' already several centuries old at this western end of the Upper Guinean forest. This is how ideas from the Niger Delta and Yoruba country (e.g. about self-government in spiritual matters, and cooperative trading ventures) became elements in a modern 'creolized' national self-awareness, and helped foster a local intellectual climate that contributed significantly to global movements of Black consciousness such as Pan-Africanism (Gilroy 1993; Peterson 1969; Richards 1990).

Equipped with a cross-section of West African ideas and commercial resources Sierra Leonean traders were active in penetrating the interior. At first they tended to follow the better established trade routes through Port Loko into the savanna, or shipped along the coast into British Sherbro. But by the end of the nineteenth century Freetown traders had also penetrated the forested and more inaccessible parts of Mendeland in the south and east. These trade developments were sometimes seen as socially and politically threatening by interior rulers.

Colonial rule was imposed over the interior in the 1890s followed by a proposal to levy a house tax. This provoked widespread discontent among interior peoples leading to uprisings in 1898. Violence was directed against missionaries and creole traders, seen as harbingers, if not representatives, of colonial rule, and agents of economic instability, especially in communities experiencing intensified lumbering, rubber tapping and exploitation of a range of hunted and gathered forest commodities.

Mende warriors carried out violent attacks on creole traders and missionaries (notably at Taiama and Rotifunk). The British moved swiftly to contain the rebellion, and later hanged ninety-six persons, including prominent Mende chiefs. Governor Cardew then pressed ahead with the building of a railway, to ensure better military control of the interior. It was envisaged that the railway would be paid for through the trade with the interior it would help stimulate.

A proposed destination for the railway was Bumban in the savanna north of the protectorate, on the old trade caravan road to Falaba in the Guinea highlands and the Upper Niger basin. It was soon realized, however, that the economic potential to pay for the line was much better in the forested south and east of the country, and the destination was changed to Pendembu, in Kailahun District, on the Liberia border. A branch line was later built from Bauya in the south to Makeni in the north.

The railway from Freetown through Moyamba (the westernmost Mende town) to Bo, Kenema and eventually Pendembu (all within Mende-speaking districts) was henceforth the main axis of up-line development and 'cultural creolization' in Sierra Leone (Illustration 2.1). The country's main provincial secondary schools tended to be clustered along the line of rail, beginning with the Bo government school for sons of chiefs (1906) and Harford School (1900), the first provincial secondary school for girls, relocated to Moyamba in 1911.

By the 1940s when the idea of internal self-governance was first taken seriously up-country Sierra Leone had a small educated 'creolized' elite to challenge the Freetown-based creole political classes. This conservative provincial elite was led by a doctor, Milton Margai from Gbangbatoke in Bonthe District, skilled in bridging the gap between European officials and traditional chiefs (Cartwright 1970). Dr (later Sir Milton) Margai was able to back a claim to inherit power from the British with democratic weight of numbers. Committed to the idea of representative democracy the British authorities handed over power to an administration led by Milton Margai. Drawing much of its leadership from along the line of rail, Margai's party, the Sierra Leone Peoples' Party (SLPP), was henceforth seen (to some extent correctly) as being especially committed to the interests of people in the south and east of the country. To some , it was without doubt the political party of the Mende people (Kilson 1966).

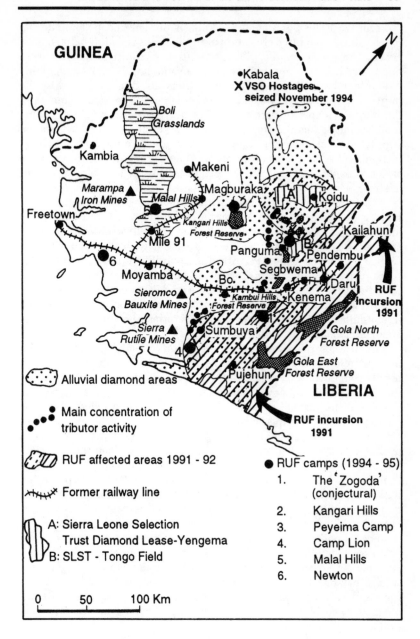

2.1   *Sierra Leone:*
     areas of conflict and main
     mining zones

From the 1930s the economic emphasis in Sierra Leone shifted from forest products and tree crops grown in the forest zone (oil palm, coffee, cocoa) towards minerals. By the 1960s the country's exports were dominated by diamonds, iron ore, bauxite and, later, rutile. Much of this new mineral wealth was found in districts not directly served by the railway. A mineral line was built to evacuate iron ore from Marampa in the north to a special port at Pepel on the Sierra Leone river. At one time Marampa was the world's largest iron mine, much of its product supplying steel makers in Scotland. Diamonds, mined by industrial methods by a De Beers subsidiary at Yengema in the north-east, were easier to export. All that was necessary to ship diamonds was a small airstrip.

A new type of provincial politics emerged somewhat rooted in mining trade unionism at Marampa and Yengema. One of the trade union leaders was Siaka Stevens, who had spent time at the trade union college in Oxford, Ruskin College. Breaking with the SLPP Stevens formed a new party, the APC, drawing upon this union background for some of its socialist rhetoric (Stevens later flirted with the idea of a Soviet-style workers' one-party state). The APC appealed to the young and drew much of its mass grass-roots support from districts off the line-of-rail. These were less developed in terms of secondary education and commercial opportunity.

The APC narrowly won a general election in 1967, against the ruling SLPP then led by Sir Milton Margai's half-brother Sir Albert Margai. The results were disputed, and the army intervened briefly. Civilian rule was restored in 1968, and power handed to Siaka Stevens and the APC.

Once in power APC 'workerist' associations soon faded. The APC made pragmatic attempts to forge an alliance of political support from among largely rural, and often educationally disadvantaged, groups. The upshot was the further extension of a conservative 'patrimonial' state that had already begun to take shape under the SLPP.

From the late 1970s the mineral economy went into steep decline (Luke and Riley 1989). Marampa mines closed in 1975, and De Beers quit Yengema in 1982, many of the best deposits having been worked out. The APC became more and more dependent on aid support to balance its budget. Donors worked to secure a more open and account-able use of state resources. The major target for reform was the inflated state budget for salaries, and Stevens was required to reduce the civil service pay-roll, with consequences for the smooth working of patron-age politics. But no direct attack was made on the principle of patrim-onialism as such. This would have seemed a 'neo-colonial' interference in internal politics.

The scope and effectiveness of the Sierra Leone patrimonial state depended on two conditions in particular:

First, there was the long-established political legitimacy of patrim-onialism in the eyes of a largely rural and conservative electorate, to whom state sponsorship was but a village-level moral economy writ large, in which patron–client relationships were essential to survival in a harsh and capricious agricultural environment (Richards 1986).

Second, after expatriate-owned mining of iron ore and diamonds ceased, mining of alluvial diamonds by informal pre-industrial methods emerged as the main source of wealth in the economy. This is a type of economic activity that lends itself extraordinarily well to patrimonial politics, depending very much on quiet deals, *ad hoc* licensing arrangements, and political protection from 'on high'. Diamonds are pocketed and smuggled across the country's porous borders at will. The product is almost invisible to bureaucratic inspection. In an emergency a stone can even be swallowed. It would appear to be a fact of political life in Sierra Leone that all political leaders must have a stake in the clandestine diamond trade. Without this source of 'magic money' they would lack the political charisma necessary to keep the patrimonial 'shadow state' afloat.

In 1978 Stevens introduced a one-party state after a dubious referendum. Stevens had faced intense opposition from students in 1977, but his move may have been also intended to stimulate a more intensive Cold War auction among aid donors, to make good some of the short-fall from mineral wealth in a country of little global strategic concern.

In 1985 an ageing Stevens handed over to a hand-picked successor from the army, General Joseph Saidu Momoh. Momoh was later confirmed in office by a presidential election. The Momoh regime made some attempt to align the official state with new international priorities (improving its human rights record in particular, and supporting the American-led coalition against Iraq in the Gulf War), but failed to reach an agreement with the International Monetary Fund over economic restructuring. The APC was caught between the urgent need for international credit to fund pressing patrimonial demands (e.g. the need to supply the army, police and other state organizations with cheap rice) and the longer-term 'developmental' needs of the shadow state (having a pool of jobs and educational opportunities to reward client loyalty).

The following example well illustrates the dilemma. The World Bank offered money to 'restructure' the Ministry of Agriculture, and provide an operating budget (the Agricultural Sector Support Plan). This money could only be tapped at the price of a substantial redundancy programme. These redundancies were aimed mainly at lower cadres of ministry employees – precisely the people who had been given jobs under patrimonialism, rather than for their technical skills.

To gain some relief the APC organized a referendum on return to multi-party democracy, with an eye to improving the country's status with the aid donors. Multi-party elections were pending when the RUF incursion began. But a lethargic Momoh was unable to resolve the major contradictions, now increasingly apparent, between an official aid-supported state on the one hand and a shadow state largely funded from clandestine diamond operations on the other. The war was the last straw, and the angry young officers from the war front found they were pushing at an open door. Momoh fled to Guinea.

In the early days of the NPRC, enthusiasm for the renovation of the official state was high. Young people in urban centres gave vent to their desire for a transparent, accountable, modern state by physically cleaning up the street environment, and painting murals, largely featuring strong educated leader figures from Sierra Leonean and West African history, in palpable opposition to the graffiti of the destructive rebels (Opala 1993, cf. Illustrations 1.1 to 1.3). But the logic of diamonds and the shadow state soon began to reassert itself. Rebels and soldiers have become the main figures in the diamond fields. Smaller fry mainly line their own pockets. Those (on both sides) pursuing political agendas are more concerned to secure diamonds to pay for arms and ammunition to continue the war. Civil aspects of the patrimonial system are on hold, creating dangerous currents of urban instability. Both sides seek to use the war, and the threat of generalized collapse, as a way of riding these dangerous currents to victory.

Unable to solve the contradictions that faced Momoh, or to end the war, the NPRC announced presidential elections for February 1996, even while attempts to establish a peace negotiation with the rebels continued. Political legitimacy in Sierra Leone, however, remains rooted in patrimonialism, and it is hard to see which, if any, of the thirteen political parties contesting the elections have new and effective ideas for bringing the shadow state to heel while the clandestine extraction of diamonds in the forest remains such a large factor in the political economy of Sierra Leone.

Beyond the State? The Sierra Leone–Liberia border region

When the APC came to power in 1968 one of Stevens' first acts was to up-root the railway. It was slow and inefficient. Economic advisers from the World Bank suggested closing it, and German aid money was offered to build a replacement network of tarred roads. A German-managed bus service was intended to reach all parts of the country (especially those places disadvantaged by their distance from the line-of-rail). However, no good roads were built to replace the railway along the far eastern section from Kenema through Daru to Pendembu, the railway terminus in Kailahun District, on the Liberian border. This seems to have been a deliberate decision by Stevens (see below) to undermine the power of the SLPP in the east (Abraham and Sesay 1993). Kailahun District was a hotbed of opposition to Stevens.

In a BBC radio interview at the time of his retirement in 1985 Stevens remarked that if he had his time again there was one thing he would do differently; he would not close the railway. Stevens, always a canny politician, anticipated that by withdrawing from the border the APC regime had shot itself in the foot. But it was too late. Border loyalties were always somewhat ambiguous. The RUF leadership, Liberian-based, equipped and funded by Charles Taylor, and embittered by its own exclusion from the fun-and-games of the shadow state, seized its chance to pursue political dreams of its own, incommunicado, in this resource-rich region well beyond the scrutiny or easy reach of the Freetown authorities.

Let us now look at this border zone in closer detail. The Liberian border stretches from Koindu in the north to the mouth of the Mano river in the south, a distance of about 220 km. At its northern extremity Gissi (Kissi) people (mainly Mende-speaking today) are found in Guinea and Sierra Leone. The remaining northern third of the border divides Mende people in Kailahun District in Sierra Leone from Mendes and speakers of Gbande (a closely-related language) in Lofa County in Liberia (Dennis 1972). The middle third of the border, roughly from Pendembu to Zimmi, is a boundary wilderness – the Gola Forest – dividing Mende speakers in Kenema District (Sierra Leone) from Gola speakers in Lofa and Cape Mount Counties (Liberia).

The Gola National Forest on the Liberian side of the border is the more extensive of the two components of this boundary wilderness, but the three Gola Forest Reserves in Sierra Leone, first delimited in the 1920s, are the single largest area of closed-canopy rain forest remaining in Sierra Leone (Illustrations 2.2 and 2.3). From Zimmi (Pujehun District) to the coast, villages on both sides of the border are mainly Gola or Vai in origin. Throughout the border zone – from Koindu to the coast – Mende is the *lingua franca* in rural communities.

Unsupervised through much of its length, the border was, until the outbreak of the Liberian war, regularly crossed by smugglers seeking better prices for diamonds in Monrovia (cf. van der Laan 1965). The Liberian dollar, supported by large injections of American aid ($400 million between 1980 and 1985 alone), was at par with the US dollar, so that smuggled exports were paid, in effect, in hard currency, during a period of rapid inflation and systematic over-valuation of the official exchange rate in Sierra Leone.

Clandestine cross-border trade was also encouraged by heavy producer taxes, in Sierra Leone, on coffee and cocoa. The relatively greater vigour of the Liberian economy drew in specialist food items from eastern Sierra Leone, such as an illegal trade in protected animal species (e.g. the Red Colobus monkey) in heavy demand on the bush-meat market in Monrovia (Davies and Richards 1991). Some smuggled trade passed in the opposite direction. Border mining communities in Sierra Leone found it easier to acquire high-value electronic items, and US-subsidized white rice, from Liberia than from distant Freetown.

Much of this cross-border trade passed through or around the main recognized border crossing points between the two countries, in

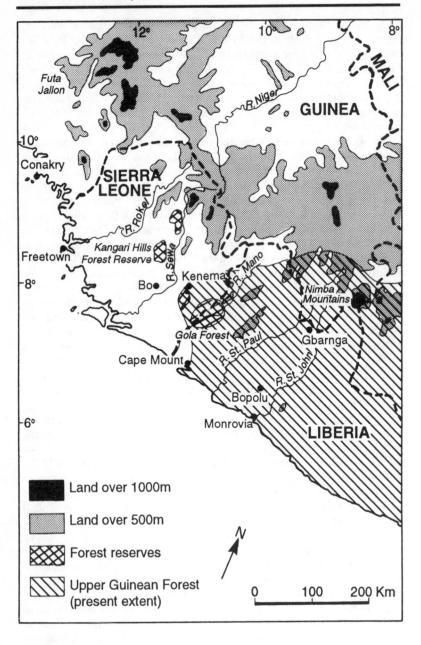

2.2   The western end of the Upper Guinean rain forest

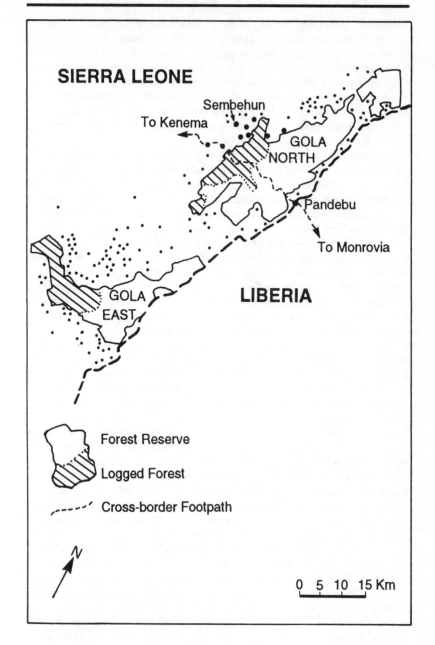

2.3   The Gola Reserves and the Liberian border

Kailahun District and via the Mano River Bridge in the south. Diamond smugglers, as van der Laan (1965) noted three decades ago, prefer to travel by road and bribe border officials, rather than suffer the tedious bush paths that cross the Gola Forest. These major crossing points were used by the RUF when it mounted its incursion in March 1991. At first the Freetown authorities found it hard to sort out news about the invasion from reports of petty bickering among border guards over smuggling deals gone sour. Many looted items from Liberia were being sold in border settlements at the time.

Initially, and then again after being pushed back to the border by government troops and Liberian irregulars, the RUF 'dug in' around the Gola Forest. The small towns and villages between Gola North and Pendembu were a particular focus for RUF activity, and Foday Sankoh seems to have been based in Pendembu, the former railway terminus, during much of 1991–2. The remote forest paths crossing into Liberia may have served as supply and escape routes *in extremis*. But revisiting the Gola North Reserve in September 1992, in a lull in the fighting, showed that the main 'smuggling path' to Liberia, which our research team regularly used during field work in 1989 to cross the reserve from Lalehun to Pandebu (Chapter Seven), was so overgrown that it would have taken weeks of work to open it again. The villages on the far side of Gola North were wrecked by fighting and abandoned.

Chiefs and their communities in the border zone have a long history of ambiguity about their attachment to state administrative structures. Isolation and central government inertia have not helped, but some of the ambiguity stems from the way the border, and the colonial system of indirect rule, were imposed (Brownlie 1979; Wyse 1977; Wylie 1967).

Colonial administration in rural Sierra Leone was at first *ad hoc* rule through traditional chiefs. But following the reorganization of Native Administration in Nigeria in the 1930s, most chiefdoms in Sierra Leone were subjected to a comparable process of reform. Paramount Chiefs were stripped of some of their powers. Attempts were made to secure financial accountability, and generally to 'modernize' indigenous political institutions along bureaucratic lines. Perhaps most notably, chiefs lost the power to try cases in chiefdom courts, for which purposes court chairmen were appointed. But this process of reform was incomplete at Independence. Barrows (1976) records the fact that one border chiefdom, Nomo, was still 'unreformed' as late as 1973.

Nomo Chiefdom is one of the smallest and most isolated administrative units in eastern Sierra Leone. Its villages (including Pandebu) extend along the Moro River trench deep into the Gola Forest. The river is the international border, and can be forded at low water in the dry season. But none of the villages along the Moro has access to the road network of either country. Lacking schools or any other state facilities these communities are a law unto themselves. They are populated by diamond diggers with identity papers for both Liberia and Sierra Leone, and useful family connections and political protection on both sides of the border. Many miners operate alluvial diamond workings without licences (see Illustration 7.5, p. 131), and hunt at will in the forest reserve. Life in one of these 'off limits' settlements, Pandebu, in the depths of the Gola Forest, is described in Chapter Seven.

The northern segment of the border between Liberia and Sierra Leone, north of Pendembu, was the part that proved most troublesome to the colonial authorities to delimit. The nub of the problem was Luawa chiefdom, a polity forged by the powerful late nineteenth-century Mende warrior Kai Londo (McCall 1974). In reviewing events the Sierra Leonean historian Arthur Abraham (1978) notes that 'in all probability state formation in this [part of Sierra Leone] was a historically recent phenomenon' (p. 202). Kai Londo forged Greater Luawa when the chiefs of towns ravaged by Ndawa of Bandajuma promised to recognize him as their paramount if he would deal with the Ndawa menace. Ndawa defeated, Kai Londo then built Kailahun as his capital, and carried on his military exploits by extending war into what is now north-west Liberia, defeating the Gbande at Popalahun, and making them submit to his rule.

Kai Londo was a firm ally of the British, but his enlarged polity did not survive his death in 1895. In 1896 Governor Cardew, on tour in the interior, began to seek opportunity to exclude from Luawa Chiefdom various Kissi towns, east of Kailahun, paying allegiance to Kai Londo. According to Abraham, Cardew's reasons were somewhat complex. He doubted the Kissi chiefs would transfer their support to Kai Londo's successor (who that successor might be was far from clear at the time), and (perhaps more urgently) it became apparent to him that at least two of the Kissi towns (together with the eastern part of Luawa) fell within the Liberian sphere of influence already agreed by the British and the French. Meanwhile, the chiefdom elders had decided upon Fa Bundeh as Kai Londo's successor. Cardew informed him he would only approve his appointment 'if he gave up his claims to the more distant parts of the state . . .' with the result that by 1896 'the state of Kai Londo was . . . contracted virtually to the core from which the king had expanded his authority' (Abraham, 1978: 205).

The difficulty over delimiting the border arose as follows. The British and French had agreed that from the source of the Niger to the Liberian frontier they would partition their spheres by adopting a straight line, 13 degrees west of Paris. This had the effect, as Cardew had apprehended, of assigning a large section of Kailahun District to Liberia. Cardew campaigned for a border in which 'tribal limits should be followed as far as possible'. Perhaps motivated partly by respect for a pro-British chief, his main objection to the proposed partition of Luawa was that the area immediately east of Kai Londo's domain had, for several years, been a battleground between Kai Londo and Kissi and Gbande chiefs. The warring parties rejected Liberian rule and a weak

Monrovia government had little or no capacity to quell continuing violence. In February 1896 'Momoh Bahoni, a Gbandi chief from the Liberian side, attacked and burnt two towns in Kpombai, part of which was in Liberian territory, but the greater part in the British sphere' (Abraham 1978: 207). Cardew was powerless to intervene since this would have meant operating beyond the agreed line '13 degrees west of Paris'.

The situation of a divided Luawa chiefdom remained unresolved for a number of years. A more permanent solution was found when Liberian officials attempted to take over the chiefdom headquarters, Kailahun, in 1906. This caused Fa Bundeh to petition for British Protection (Abraham 1978). A Liberian District Commissioner, a Lieutenant Lomax, established himself in Kailahun in 1907, but 'recurrent maladministration led British officers to eject Lomax at the end of 1907 and the British were left in de facto occupation of Luawa' (Abraham 1978: 209). A temporary boundary agreed between Freetown and Monrovia in 1908 gave the whole of Luawa to Britain. 'In 1911 this was officially recognized . . . but Kissi Tengea remained under Liberia' (Abraham 1978: 209). A portion of the Sierra Leonean Gola Forest, the (so-called) Moro-Mano Triangle, was assigned to Liberia in compensation, and a joint commission demarcated the present boundary of Kailahun in 1913 and 1914, confirmed by the Anglo-Liberian treaty in 1917 (Brownlie 1979). Abraham notes that the Kissi chiefs (once tributary to Kai Londo) petitioned to be brought under British protection, but took care to assert their independence of Luawa. Some leading families opted for the Liberian side of the border.

During fieldwork in the Gola Forest in 1989 I met a number of educated young men from Liberia apparently chaperoning village chiefs. One of them gave me a well-informed but hostile lecture on the perfidy of the British in establishing the border and siding with Kai Londo's successors against 'Liberian' interests. Just prior to the launching of the NPFL rebellion into Nimba County his language was already that of 'Greater Liberia'. Conceivably these young men were an advance guard for the NPFL, the RUF, or both.

The political economy of a rural slum: rice, diamonds and youth

The political economy of Sierra Leone is dominated by two contrasts – between the capital Freetown and the more isolated rural districts, and between the mining sector of the economy (the country's main source of foreign exchange) and the stagnant semi-subsistence agricultural sector to which many young Sierra Leoneans return when urban life and mining employment fail (cf. Illustration 2.1).

Abandoned by trans-national mining interests in the 1980s, Sierra

Leone diamonds are now mainly mined by small-scale tributors using non-industrial methods (Zack-Williams 1990, 1995). This type of mining would not be easy to tax even under the most favourable political circumstances, but it must be doubted whether it has ever been in the interest of a patrimonial regime to try very hard. As a result the formal state has suffered a revenue crisis over the past 15–20 years, starving key public sector services such as education and public health.[3]

The mining economy was largely a product of the later colonial period. Alluvial diamonds were first identified in Kono (in eastern Sierra Leone) in the 1930s, but serious mining did not get under way until after the Second World War. The richest alluvial deposits (at Yengema in Kono District and Tongo Field in Kenema District) were mined industrially by Sierra Leone Selection Trust, a De Beers sub-sidiary, and later, as a joint venture, by De Beers and a state mining enterprise. Elsewhere along the main rivers and many side streams in eastern and southern Sierra Leone diamonds could be mined simply by digging pits in alluvial gravels during the dry season (see Illustration 7.5, p. 131). Young men flocked from all over Sierra Leone to these areas in the early 1950s (van der Laan 1965). Many sites lay within areas already mapped out as concessions to expatriate mining interests.

To prevent creaming of the deposits, the government of Sierra Leone (independent in internal affairs from 1950) attempted to control the influx of diamond tributors. Later, the industrial concession was reduced and a licence scheme introduced to regulate mining activities by tributors (van der Laan 1965; Zack-Williams 1990, 1995). At peak periods for diamond mining there are 30,000 or more tributors, from all parts of the country, mining diamonds in rural (and often very remote) parts of eastern and southern Sierra Leone (Zack-Williams 1990). In addition, many young people moved to the diamond districts to meet the demand for services (entertainment, sex and drugs, cooked food, items of petty trade, equipment repairs).

Life in the mining districts was much more lively than in non-diamond rural districts, but at times dangerously violent. The young men who do the actual mining work under very primitive and arduous conditions, and make little money in the long run. Many diamond diggers *average* little more than they might make in a more humdrum occupation, such as cash-crop farming. They depend for their sub-sistence and protection on a complex network of sponsors, fixers and political patrons (Zack-Williams 1995).

No educational qualifications are needed for work as a diamond tributor. In the earlier stages of the diamond boom, many tributors were

---

[3] Diamond exports declined from 31 per cent to 21 per cent of total export earnings during the period 1984–92 (Conteh 1996). These are official figures based on transactions by licensed dealers. The order of magnitude of the percentage smuggled is sometimes reckoned to be about one third to one half of the total but no one knows if the figure remains the same year on year.

farmers, opting out of rice production for a time; others were more urbanized youngsters lured into leaving school early by the excitement and promise of fast money from diamonds. More recently, it has become noticeable that many of the tributors are no longer mining by choice, but because they lack the money or sponsors to pay school fees, or because after School Certificate or university graduation no better work could be found. Few if any Sierra Leoneans willingly imagine for themselves a future in diamond mining (see Chapter Eight).

In one village on the Liberian border tributors were desperately concerned by the lack of educational prospects for their children (Chapter Seven). The world of the tributor has matured. The best deposits are exhausted and exciting vistas of fame and fortune have receded. Many tributors, increasingly, feel trapped in what is now, in effect, a rural slum.

Their feelings of no longer being in control of their fate are intensified by the opaqueness of all transactions in the world of diamonds. This opaqueness starts at the top, where De Beers maintains a global buying operation that monopolizes supplies and artificially boosts world prices. At national level, diamond buying is largely in the hands of about 30 main licensed dealers (mainly Lebanese) and 15–20 major unlicensed dealers (mainly of Guinean extraction). Diamonds are so easy to secrete that smuggling is rife. When state authorities step in, it is not to ensure the state exchequer its fair share of revenue, but to take a 'cut' in return for protection from political or bureaucratic harassment.

Under such conditions, it is hardly surprising that tributors find it hard to assess the real value of their labour, or to work up much enthusiasm for free markets and democratic competition. The Libyan-inspired message of the RUF strikes a chord.

Before the war many Sierra Leone diamonds were sold through Liberia, though others passed northwards to Europe via Guinea and Senegal. Under conditions of insurgency it is more than usually difficult to see where the diamonds have gone, but the national rumour mill supplies many stories about diamonds and war.

The underlying assumption, that soldiers and insurgents are now the main diamond miners in the war zone, and that this has determined the course of the fighting, is probably accurate enough. Both the RUF and the United Liberation Movement (ULIMO) in Liberia, conscripted and recruited heavily in diamond districts. Captive tributors in Liberia (some reportedly working as slaves) raised at least some of the revenues that kept ULIMO armed and fed (Ellis 1995). Isatu Conteh testified that the RUF bought arms from Guinean troops stationed on the border and paid for them in rough diamonds. As explained in Chapter One, the NPRC engaged the South African-based security firm, Executive Outcomes, to train troops and fight against the rebels, by granting it a diamond-mining concession in Kono district.

Under the APC regime, alluvial diamond mining was the milch cow, and the government sought to sustain and expand a tributor system in which its own ministers, allegedly, had a direct stake. A major state intervention was to ensure supplies of cheap rice from overseas.[4] Rice is the main staple of the country, but diamond mining made worse a chronic shortage of agricultural labour. Mainly through the exchange controls necessary to support an over-valued currency, the government facilitated a flow of cheap imported rice to feed the diamond districts and damp down political trouble in urban areas. Some ministers then made money in the food importation business (Abraham and Sesay 1993). Allocating licences to sell government-imported rice provided further scope for patrimonialism.

Sierra Leonean small-scale rice producers respond to price signals, and in the past have several times quickly eliminated national rice shortages given suitable price incentives (Richards 1985). However, the country lacks the right kind of marketing and processing infrastructure readily to sustain the tributor system. The sponsors of tributor teams are mainly politicians, government officials and large-scale Lebanese or Guinean merchants. They have little time to organize the purchase, bulking and milling of country rice, but prefer instead to acquire white rice, bagged and ready from the docks, by the lorry load. Government control over foreign exchange allowed them to do this easily. Only had there been a steady policy to support local producers over the years, with the attendant risk of politically expensive periodic rice shortages in the diamond districts and urban areas while the system adjusted, would the necessary in-country purchasing, transportation and milling infrastructure have emerged.

The APC government became locked within a cycle of dependency on diamonds and white rice, and agrarian life declined into semi-subsistence stagnation. Young people, modernized by education and life in the diamond districts, are reluctant to revert to this semi-subsistence way of life; many treat it only as a last stand-by. The APC regime hoped to fend off political trouble by paying attention to the food needs of the urban poor (especially Freetown youth). But in recent years, with structural adjustment forcing the price of rice upwards, and reducing prospects of a government job, many young people in Sierra Leone have seen themselves locked out of the urban areas, perhaps permanently. Life is a stressful shuttle between bouts of digging in a rural diamond-mining slum and bouts of even harder labour digging in the farm.

This puts in place the main pieces of the political economy jigsaw necessary to understand the context in which the RUF invasion took place: a patrimonial state running out of resources (especially resources to support education), emergence of rural slums in diamond districts,

[4]Abraham and Sesay (1993) estimate that the price of rice to producers (farmers in Sierra Leone) declined in real terms by 67 per cent over the period 1976–87, making a mockery of formal agricultural development initiatives in the food-crop sector.

and the agrarian failures of an urban- (and mining)-biased development policy.

Evidence that the political mood of blighted youth had soured can be seen as early as the 1977 student demonstrations against Siaka Stevens and in riots and strikes by school children in the 1980s.[5] Student leaders were rusticated and often harshly treated in detention. Students and pupils from Njala mounted a protest against government in 1987, marching on, and burning down, the provincial secretariat building in Bo (a ruin to this day). A Catholic missionary priest, seeking to intercede on behalf of the ring-leaders, quietly reminded senior government figures that as beneficiaries of the fruits of political office under a one-party regime they had safely installed their own children in expensive private schools overseas. This contrast replenished a deep pool of bitter discontent since mobilized by the rebels.

When the RUF invaded Sierra Leone it sensed a potentially receptive audience among the many *dregman dɛm* (youths struggling for their livelihood and living by their wits) in the diamond districts of eastern and southern Sierra Leone. Some youths in the diamond districts along the border are reported to have rallied voluntarily. But even conscripts soon discovered that RUF political analysis addressed their sense of social exclusion from the games being played by the diamond elite along the border.

With motivated followers, and poorly trained opponents (the result of the years in which the APC treated the army as a vehicle for the disbursement of political patronage), the RUF found it easy to destabilize large areas of the border zone. The NPRC coup was a major set-back for the RUF, since the coup was very widely supported by urban youth throughout Sierra Leone. But the political transformation led by Chairman Strasser, a Krio, concentrated on urban issues, and on repairing the formal state visible to the donor community. In refusing to surrender, the RUF, in effect, shifted the emphasis back to the unresolved contradictions of patrimonialism and the distinctive problems of the *rural* slums that have emerged in Sierra Leone's mining districts. The strategic opportunity for the RUF was the extent to which the NPRC failed to re-think patrimonialism, and its inability to recover ground in border regions from which the APC had withdrawn.

Youth radicalism: PANAFU, Toffler and *The Green Book*

This section is a brief introduction to the ideological 'mix' of youth politics in Sierra Leone under state recession.

---

[5]'And what happened to these [protesting] school children who life had taught that if they did not stand up then they would be the next victims of a collapsing society where their seniors graduate without hopes of job and any form of social security' is the way the RUF, rhetorically, now refers to these events (RUF.SL 1995: 23).

Radical student groups in Sierra Leone in the 1970s and 1980s found relatively little appeal in Revolutionary Marxism. The main debates centred on three other sources of radical ideas: the writings of Nkrumah and other Pan-Africanists, the Libyan leader's *Green Book*, and the work of American 'futurologist' Alvin Toffler. PANAFU is the Pan-African Union of Sierra Leone, launched at Fourah Bay College in the early 1980s. *Green Book* radical ideas were debated by the 'Gardeners' Club', (allegedly, it met in the patch of rain forest reserved as a botanical garden on Mount Aureol behind Fourah Bay College). At Njala the 'Future Shock Club' was named from the title of the Tofflers' book (Toffler and Toffler 1970).

RUF spokespersons at times use some of PANAFU's uncompromisingly radical language. Although this language is common property among youth-oriented political movements in Sierra Leone, a number of people have taken the view that there might be links between the rebels and PANAFU. This is vehemently denied by one of the organization's founders, Ismail O. Rashid, who describes PANAFU as a legitimate and peaceful mass-based organization of youth, workers, students and women, running various educational and campaigning activities, and properly registered with the Department of Social Welfare.[6] It was founded in 1982, and claims inspiration from the veteran Sierra Leonean radical I. T. A. Wallace-Johnson (see Illustration 1.2, p. 11). PANAFU's declared position on the war is that it should be ended by a national democratic conference of all parties, including the armed factions, and that conflict only benefits the belligerents at the expense of the suffering masses of ordinary Sierra Leoneans. PANAFU leaders have been subject to police harassment from time to time.

Toffler, an American exponent of globalization theory, stresses electronic revolution as the key to what he terms the Third Wave – a world in which computers and global telecommunications liberate us from the material and geographical constraints of the first, agrarian, and second, industrial, waves of change (cf. Toffler and Toffler 1994). The idea is especially appealing in a small, marginal country where prospects for conventional industrial development look remote, but where educated citizens may be better informed about global events and cultural trends than their peers in the West.[7]

---

[6] PANAFU has an office at 56 Dundas Street, Freetown.

[7] It is interesting to note that Alvin Toffler also has a strong following in the Philippines. At a recent lecture he noted that his audience of 850 was equally divided between men and women and contained many young people – 'This', he said, 'was a first for him in his lectures around the world'. An advantage of the Philippines in preparing to meet the challenge of the Third Wave in the twenty-first century (he told his audience) was that its 'existing diversity of cultures' shows it 'not yet to be truly massified'. Highly industrialized countries, to compete in the information age, will have to demassify. ('Future belongs to nations like RP, predicts Toffler', *Philippine Daily Enquirer*, 11 August 1994). (I am grateful to Sietze Vellema for the press cutting.)

There are a number of hints that the RUF might have inherited some of this Toffler-like techno-radicalism. Like Taylor's NPFL, the movement, however small and ill-equipped, seems to have a keen sense of the significance of the fast-developing world of global, satellite-based, telecommunications and broadcasting.[8]

As noted earlier, the NPFL was alert to the possibilities of new satellite telecommunications technology. The RUF apparently used Taylor's Gbarnga link from time to time, but never acquired a satellite link-up of its own. But Sankoh was once in the RSLMF signals unit, and is said to be skilled in radio repairs. The young RUF captives have been trained to coordinate guerrilla operations with field radios. One of the first conditions laid down by the RUF for entering into negotiations over the international hostages was access to a satellite phone link. When released, one of the hostages, a Russian, reported that the RUF had taken trouble to find him a short-wave radio on which to follow developments in Chechnya.[9] The rebel movement is comfortable with modern technology, and perhaps seeks to make the point that those driven to the margins of society would be a force to be reckoned with, if they had the right kind of technological resources and education.

Many Sierra Leonean students read Muammar Gaddafi's *Green Book* (Gaddafi n.d.) and some teachers transmitted the message to the next generation of school pupils. Statements issued by RUF spokespersons based in Accra and Abidjan echo *Green Book* language.

The Green Book advocates private property, but rejects profit and accumulation. Every member of the community has rights to basic needs (food, housing, health, and transport). It proposes direct democracy (through people's assemblies) to avoid the pitfalls of Western democracy and Soviet-style one-party rule. Divisive tribalism is to be eschewed, as is the spectator mentality of modern consumer society. Stress is placed on the participation and empowerment of all.

RUF internal actions are consistent with such a vision. Surrendered captives report a movement that redistributes food, drugs, clothes and shoes 'liberated' from government sources. Sankoh seeks medical supplies for a popular health programme as part of hostage or peace negotiations. Neatly planned lines of huts in RUF camps speak of a desire to supply model housing for all.[10] The movement attempts mass literacy training with whatever scraps of books and paper it can obtain.

---

[8] A picture in *Footpaths to Democracy* (RUF/SL 1995: 31) shows four young RUF members operating a solar-powered radio, and is captioned 'simple but effective communication centres relying on solar energy'. In several places the booklet stresses the need for Africans to take their rightful place in a technologically sophisticated world..

[9] Quite what this did for his morale during his period of captivity is not clear, but it says something about the sensitivity of the rebels to media events in the wider world.

[10] cf. 'We are fighting for affordable energy, fuel and power including access to appropriate technology so that we can build for ourselves modern housing, health care, educational and recreational facilities' (RUF/SL 1995: 21).

Girls as well as boys are trained as RUF fighters. The RUF, seemingly, has no truck with tribalism. In regard to religion it is vigorously ecumenical.[11]

Sankoh's lack of presidential ambition, and the stress the movement places on collective leadership (the 21-member 'war council'), may reflect *Green Book* emphasis on the importance of decision-making through people's assemblies. RUF representatives in Abidjan have said 'Foday Sankoh is above politics, there is no need for elections, the country will accept him when they see what his programme is about'. This is as Green Book-ish as it is millenarian in tone. Diffidence about the electoral process initiated by the NPRC may reflect the simple pragmatic view that the RUF would be highly unpopular with the electorate at large. But it might also echo a central political proposition of *The Green Book* that Western multi-party democracy based on the tyranny of the (small) majority is as fraudulent as rule by the Party Machine under communism.

It seems possible, therefore, that Sankoh and the RUF are more whole-hearted exponents of the Libyan revolutionary theory than Taylor and the NPFL. Taylor seems only briefly to have been in Libya (Ellis 1995), and Gaddafi soon decided that Taylor's revolutionary credentials were fake (Tarr 1993). The usual idea that the RUF was hastily concocted to serve Taylor's strategic interests and lacks any ideological core needs to be queried. Even comparison of the names of the two movements suggests that the Sierra Leonan insurgents may be the more seriously committed to *Green Book* revolutionary ideas.

Survivalism: Rambo and the dramaturgy of war in Sierra Leone

Shortly after the commencement of the RUF campaign at the end of 1994, the RSLMF commander, Colonel Kellie Conteh, made a radio and TV broadcast to the nation appealing to civilians not to give in to their own worst fears. Rebels, he explained, were flesh-and-blood creatures like themselves, not magic entities able to transport themselves through space and time and materialize at will. If the RUF gave the appearance of ubiquity, it was because the movement had been able to work out a specific strategy to that effect. By using bush paths, by spreading attacks as far and wide as possible, by burning only undefended villages, by never staying long in one place, by avoiding direct confrontation with government troops, and by sending out letters and starting rumours to panic villagers and decoy and divide army defences, they were able to

[11] cf. (Describing life in RUF areas) 'The different divisions in Islam and Christianity . . . worship under one roof and under the guidance of a Chief Imam . . . and a Church Mother' (RUF/SL 1995: 13).

project an image of great power. Whether this image bore any relation to their true strength Conteh begged leave to doubt. If at the end of the day civilians had an impression of the far-reaching and inexplicable power of the rebels then this is exactly the effect the careful stage management of their insurgency was intended to achieve.

Journalistic comment on Sierra Leone, and more so on Liberia, has regularly drawn attention to the carnival-like elements of insurgency in the region, implicitly contrasting, so Mary Moran (1994) has argued, the bizarre battle costumes of young fighters in Liberia (Kung Fu kit, horror comic masks, young men setting off for battle in women's dresses and underwear) with the clean, orderly, rationalistic uniforms and battle order of the allied forces in the Gulf War, the media-oriented show-case for modern combat.

Moran interprets these odd costumes, convincingly, as youthful *jeux d'ésprit* intended to 'attack' the values of the Liberian regime of Samuel Doe. Doe was seen by his opponents, she argues, as the epitome of the ignorant, brutal rank-and-file soldiery whose day-to-day petty brutality served to keep many African post-colonial regimes in power. The cross-dressing, horror-comic-helmeted, young teenage rebel fighter was, by contrast, brilliantly recapitulating an inventive pre-colonial tradition, where dress served to disguise and protect, rather than express, the true character of the warrior. But here we have no simple reversion to the African past. These are post-modern costumes, straight from Hong Kong or an American joke shop catalogue, made mainly from that deeply traditional African raw material – plastic.

As Kellie Conteh's remarks suggest, the carnival element is not without tactical purpose. But perhaps at the same time the costumes are also close in spirit to the international Saturday Night finery of the diamond digger 'on the town' (flares and platform-soled shoes were especial 1970s favourites). The imprecatory graffiti the RUF leave behind in sacked villages relate to the rich stock of slogans adorning the shutters and lintels of the village rooms of school-educated young people throughout rural Sierra Leone. These graffiti are often ironic commentary on the strange juxtapositions of the local and global, as experienced by those at the bottom of the social pile.

When I first prospected possible research sites in eastern Sierra Leone in 1978, I was struck, in a village close to the Liberian border, by a fine cartoon, drawn on the shutters of one young diamond digger's room, of a helicopter hovering low, making a close study of that archetypically essential village activity, two women pounding rice in a mortar for the evening meal; traditional and hyper-modern in the closest juxtaposition.

However brief its attacks, the RUF generally managed to daub at least some handy walls with suitable slogans, for all the world as if its adherents were a street-wise gang in New York. The walls of buildings in Potoru in 1992 were thick with RUF anti-Strasser slogans at a time when many rural civilians were still struggling to recall the Chairman's name and title. Someone with a fine sense of irony, and something of an ear for the nuances of American English, had scrawled 'RUF mass transport' on a clapped-out old blue truck, during the attack on Mile 91 on 23 December 1994. Slogans in praise of 'Black Jesus', a rebel commander, were found plastered over buildings at the rutile mining compound after its recapture by government troops in mid-April 1995.

All warfare has its expressive dimensions. In low-intensity warfare, in poor countries like Sierra Leone, this expressive dimension may be highly visible, for want of more practically functional kit. It deserves proper exegesis, not the 'isn't this bizarre' dismissal it receives in the international media.

One London-based Sierra Leonean journalist expressed the view that Sierra Leoneans ought not to take Sankoh seriously, 'since he is not educated, only a photographer'. This seems to underestimate the photographer's importance in rural Sierra Leone as an 'organic intellectual' capable of posing groups and scenes that overcome the gap between illiterate and educated. The complaint that the Sierra Leone rebels have never articulated their political demands is true only to the extent that the intended audience continues to ignore the expressive poses they strike through their destructive actions.

One of these poses seems to grow out of a widespread interpretation young people in Sierra Leone have made of the 1982 Rambo film, *First Blood*.

Shot in the forested Cascades of the north-western United States, *First Blood* tells the story of a veteran of the Vietnam war, drifting through the American backwoods, with no friends or job. Driven out of town and then beaten up by the police as a vagrant, John Rambo escapes jail and flees into the forest, with the forces of law and order in hot pursuit. To defend himself Rambo is provoked into using the combat skills he has acquired for service to an uncaring country. With nothing but his fitness and wits to draw upon he is able to turn the tables, ambushing his pursuers and capturing their weapons. The ensuing mayhem is beyond the capacity of the clumsy local police to cope with. Finally the officer, Colonel Trautman, responsible for Rambo's military training, has to be called to the scene, and the film ends in the smoking wreckage of the police station where Rambo was first jailed. Here, Rambo and his one-time trainer embark on a mumbled tongue-tied negotiation about possible rehabilitation into a wider community that has paid the price for neglecting the damaged state of mind of its abandoned young veterans.

Video has had a wide impact in the forested diamond districts of Sierra Leone, and this little drama of the social exclusion of the mis-educated is often cited by young people as one of their favourite films, or the film they found most enlightening (significantly, the word they most often use in this context is 'educative'). *First Blood* has several times been compared, by informants, to the impact of studying Shakespeare's *Macbeth* at school. *Macbeth* strips the mask of public service from politics to reveal naked personal ambition beneath. The point that strikes home about Rambo is social exclusion. Ejected from town by the corrupt and comfortable forces of law and order, with only his wits for protection, Rambo is on his own in the forest. The *result* of social exclusion, the film seems to say, is unconstrained violence. That violence is cathartic, since it serves to wake up society at large to the neglected cleverness of youth. The film speaks eloquently to young people in Sierra Leone fearing a collapse of patrimonial support in an era of state recession.

Western media critics see little in Rambo beyond 'American Cold War militarism' under the Reagan presidency. Kellner (1995), for example, entitles one chapter (in a recent book) 'Media culture, politics and ideology: from Reagan to Rambo'. But in fact Kellner's chapter hardly discusses *First Blood*. His attention is focused on the second Rambo film, a depiction of a Cold War-type struggle (based on the conflict in Afghanistan), a cynical attempt to cash in on the first film's unexpected world-wide success suggesting the producers hardly understood why their creation was a hit.[12] To Toffler and Toffler (1994) Rambo symbolizes a passing era in which war was based on brawn and bravery not brains. Young Sierra Leoneans (even those inspired by Toffler's theory of the Third Wave) draw an exactly opposite conclusion from *First Blood*. Rambo suggests that someone young, clever and strong always has a chance to outsmart the well-armed but slow-witted opponent. It is curious to see prophet and disciples at odds over this point. The Tofflers focus on the computer software in 'smart war'; young Sierra Leoneans prefer to note the unbounded potential of the human software.

Rebels in both Liberia and Sierra Leone were alert to the political potential of the Rambo message for their young captives from the beginning. An eye-witness in Gbarnga in the early days of the NPFL reported five generator-powered video parlours running night and day to show such material to young fighters. The young combatant interviewed in Chapter Four attests that all factions in Liberia and Sierra Leone have routinely used *First Blood* and similar videos to inspire, to entertain, and perhaps to orient their young captives towards the ambush skills that are the staple fare of this kind of low-level jungle warfare. The Rambo figure frequently appeared in the murals depicting the war painted by urban youths in Sierra Leone following the NPRC coup. Rebels frequently affected Rambo-style headbands. Some adopted

---

[12] Or perhaps they understood that their long-term sales potential was mainly to be found among Western audiences more interested in violence as entertainment than in epics of self-empowerment. One of my students recently discovered in a survey of video shops in south London that there is no longer any demand for *First Blood* but the second Rambo film still sells well.

the name. One RUF commando in Kailahun – summing up the war in two words – was known as 'Nasty Rambo'.

Perhaps the rebels then added to the unresolved conclusion of *First Blood* a final scene of their own devising, in which they hoped their one-time trainers might own up to the damaging consequences of abandoning their half-educated charges in the bush, while the sons and daughters of the elite were being expensively educated overseas. Secreting in the forest two young British volunteers taken hostage by the RUF, Foday Sankoh refused talks with the NPRC government, seeking direct negotiation with the British government instead.[13] Sankoh had once been on an army training course in the United Kingdom. Did he expect the 'colonel' to express remorse for the miseducation of his rampant charges? Unlike the plays of Shakespeare, *First Blood* counts for little in the Western cultural canon. British diplomats may not have had much idea about the text to which they were supposed to respond.

Rambo is a trickster figure in classic West African mould. His exploits are close in spirit to those of Musa Wo, the youth trickster of Mende tradition (Cosentino 1989). Musa Wo stories serve to remind Mende elders not to neglect the energy and cunning of the young. Rather the challenge is to harness these skills for the greater social good. The RUF rebellion seems at first to indicate patrimonialism at the end of its tether about to be replaced by the violence of youthful self-empowerment. This would suggest that the RUF's ultimate aim is to replace the patrimonial system with a revolutionary egalitarian system of its own devising. But another interpretation is also possible. The *Schadenfreude* of the young rebels may be equivalent to 'wrecking the police station'. The main aim of the destruction may not be to clear away the old system entirely, but to establish a national debate about a new and fairer patrimonialism. Year Zero or an African Welfare State? – this remains the major unresolved question concerning the war aims of the insurgents in Sierra Leone.

Conclusion

Baffled international reaction to the war in Sierra Leone suggests little understanding of the socio-economic and forest-bound conditions under which the RUF has expanded, or why the movement could continue to survive more or less indefinitely beyond the recession-shrunk edges of a weak state. According to outside assumptions, 'proper' rebellions in Africa should have 'people' (an ethnic identity), contiguous territory under unambiguous control of the rebels, and an announced programme

---

[13] Sankoh made radio contact with British diplomats in Freetown concerning the two VSO hostages on 18 November 1990, demanding arms and recognition of his movement by Britain (Tim Rayment, 'Foreign Office turns down ransom demand for hostages', *Sunday Times*, 20 November 1994).

that the world at large can understand. In short, they should be Biafra-like 'mini-states' in waiting. None of these criteria apply to the rebel movement in Sierra Leone, so doubts were entertained about whether it existed at all. External views are still dominated by the notion that African states are arbitrary colonial creations, and that political progress will depend on the emergence of more 'natural' units. Although the RUF might not be out of place as a survivalist movement in Montana, say, there is no place for any such Rambo-style social movement in the mental schemes outsiders have laid down for Africa. If the category does not exist then neither can the phenomenon.

Here, however, a different argument has been proposed. The RUF is much more readily understandable, it is suggested, if the background of state recession is put in place. The movement is a creature of the unresolved contradictions of the post-colonial state. Cold War aid kept alive a façade of international respectability – the official state. Donor pressure in the post-Cold War period has demanded deep reforms – but the reformers are leaning not on a real set of institutions, but on a façade. The real state, much reduced but still fed in significant measure by diamond wealth, remains patrimonial in character. Donors cannot reach that state, and Sierra Leoneans have not yet developed any firm consensus about what they want in its place or how to achieve it. Even shrunken patrimonial states need modern communications. The strategic mistake of Siaka Stevens was to allow the patrimonial state to wither, physically, in the border region, to secure a short-term sectional political advantage. Stevens quickly realized his own mistake. But it was too late. The door was wedged ajar for rebellion.

As a movement operating beyond the recession-shrunk edges of the patrimonial state the RUF manifests two main sets of political motives. The first is its apparent desire for revenge. A deeply embittered group of exiles seeks to reveal the official state as façade and fraud. Their violence trashes a rotten set, flapping in the breeze, of a film epic in which they no longer believe. But in recognizing the hollowness of the patrimonial state the rebel leadership also seeks the ground for experiments in bush education aimed at rebuilding society 'from within'. How these experiments are viewed depends on whether the patrimonial state is adjudged capable of reform. If it is not, then the construction of radically new forms of political association may be an urgent necessity. Civil society may still have something to learn from the challenge posed by the RUF. One lesson is that where patronage fails there are precedents in the history of Upper Guinea forest society for self-help approaches to community renewal built on the shared 'prejudices' (Douglas 1986) of social experience. It is to these precedents, rooted in forest survivalism, that the next chapter turns.

3

Forest Conversion | The Making & Re-making of Forest Society

'Frankly, we were beaten and on the run but our pride . . . would not let us face the disgrace of crossing back into Liberia as refugees . . . We dispersed into smaller units . . . We destroyed all our vehicles and heavy weapons . . . We now relied on light weapons and on our feet, brains and knowledge of the countryside. We moved deeper into the comforting bosom of our mother earth – the forest. The forest welcomed us and gave us succour . . .' (Foday Saybana Sankoh, RUF/SL 1995: 11).

Introduction

To justify walking away from present turmoil in Africa New Barbarism says 'these people have never been like us'. Perhaps this is less racism than a frustrated realization that shallow neo-liberal universalism has been oversold. 'Beyond the miracle of the market' (Bates 1989) more subtle understandings of humanity's common bonds are required.

To appreciate more fully these commonalities and differences is to recognize (as Mary Douglas suggests) that adoption of a social philosophy is inseparable from the making of a social world (Douglas 1986). But the range of possible social worlds is not infinitely large. Shared social predicaments tend to shape similar sets of beliefs about the world. Metropolitan elites tend to think alike. Backwoods communities have their common patterns of thought. Rarely, however, do forest and city see eye to eye.

Trouble starts when intellectuals, driven from the city, but uncomfortable in the bush, take up backwoods ideas and develop them into a universal complaint, but without putting their theories of social exclusion to the test in the making of communities that work. This intellectualism sunders the subtle links between forest ideas and forest community. Community checks and balances go by the board. Backwoods violence of a Pol Pot kind becomes thinkable. To metropolitan elites – who never understood the checks and balances of backwoods society in the first place – this is an abstract and terrible barbarism. But the disdain of the metropolitan elites makes the excluded intellectuals in the forest more than ever determined to flog their idea to death.

The antidote to this kind of fringe intellectual violence may be, as Douglas proposes, to restore the links between theory and community. This is no easy task for forest communities undergoing globalization. The world at large could help by repenting New Barbarism and seeking to understand the subtly interwoven fabric of social philosophy and social life in backwoods communities.

The task of this chapter is to introduce some of the 'shared prejudices' (Douglas 1986), i.e. the linked beliefs and social processes, that have helped backwoods communities in the Upper Guinean forests survive over 500 years of often violent resource exploitation for overseas markets. By mis-reading these beliefs and processes New Barbarism further corrodes the links between forest ideas and forest community, allowing rebel leaders, as excluded intellectuals, an even clearer field in which to pursue their abstract and angry vision to the detriment of ordinary forest folk. The urgent need is to find space for forest communities to re-claim their ideas. If Mary Douglas's argument is correct, this will be a first but very important step on the road to peace.

Primitive accumulation: slaving and forest resources

Sierra Leone is located at the point where two early international trading systems intersected the western tip of the great African rain forest. The hills of the northern borders of Sierra Leone look down into the Upper Niger basin, one of the ancient gathering grounds of the trans-Saharan gold trade. Freetown's great natural harbour opens out into the Atlantic world founded on the Triangular Trade (slaves from Africa, sugar and cotton from the Americas, manufactures back to Africa from Europe). In and around the forests of Sierra Leone merchants from these two worlds competed to acquire slaves and forest resources (gold, ivory, spices, stimulants and medicine). Mande traders from the Upper Niger basin shipped their gold and slaves northwards to the Mediterranean and Middle East. European and Afro-European traders on the coast exported ivory and other forest products to Europe and slaves to the Americas.

Sierra Leone and Liberia loom large both early and late in the story of the slave trade to the New World. But during the high-watermark of trans-Atlantic slave trade from the mid-seventeenth to the end of the eighteenth century the West African coast between the Sierra Leone river and Cape Mount, a sphere of operations, successively, for the Portuguese and then the British and Dutch, was noted as much for conventional exports, especially items of forest produce.

The Liberian forests exported an African pepper, *Afromomum melegueta*, an understorey plant of which the dried, fragrant grains were known to Europeans as 'grains of paradise', and from which (according to some) the coastline between Cape Mount and Cape Palmas derives its name (The Grain Coast).[1] The Sierra Leone river, Sherbro and Cape Mount exported large amounts of ivory. The Portuguese tapped Sierra Leonean (probably Sherbro) artisanal talent in the sixteenth century to produce the so-called Afro-Portuguese ivories (ornamental items and items of European tableware carved in local styles). The dye-stuff camwood (derived from the small forest tree *Baphia nitida*) was a major export for two hundred years, until replaced in Europe by industrially manufactured synthetic red dyes at the end of the nineteenth century. Beeswax and timber were two other forest products that figured prominently in early trade returns from local forests.

Throughout, forest conversion was a process in which the possibility of violence, and violent death, loomed large. Today, Mende farmers and hunters continue to seek the forgiveness of the ancestors for damage they cause in burning the forest. Risk of accidental death felling large trees and protecting farms and villages from wild animals such as elephant and leopard still occupies the local imagination in forest-edge communities. It is Mende etiquette for women and children to walk first on forest tracks since the stealthy and sinister leopard is said always to attack from behind.

Forest conversion thrived on implements with violent, secondary, anti-social uses – guns and cutlasses (Sierra Leonean English for the long bush knife that is standard equipment for persons working in farm or forest). In Nigeria the cutlass is a matchet, as in the title of T. M. Aluko's novel *One Man, One Matchet*. The British media prefer 'machete', a suitably exotic-sounding word that when applied to violence in Africa (e.g., Rwanda) is, in effect, shorthand for 'New Barbarism'. The 'cutlass culture' is as strongly engrained a feature of West African society as (frontier-forged) 'gun culture' is in the United States.

With intensification of overseas trade, much forest exploitation took on the character of 'primitive accumulation' (asset stripping, with little thought for sustainability of resources or local social institutions). Timber extraction, much of it for the Royal Navy, accounted for extensive deforestation along the Sierra Leone (Rokel) river and Sherbro estuary by the early nineteenth century. Elephants were hunted to near extinction throughout southern Sierra Leone, and by the end of the nineteenth century were common only in the extensive forests of the Liberia–Sierra Leone border region.

The international slave trade turned persons into commodities. Slavery within Africa was regulated by some mechanisms of institu-

---

[1] Another explanation is that this referred to rice grains. Rice was the staple of the coast, and an item purchased to victual slave ships.

tional accountability, but the residual civil rights of domestic slaves were totally extinguished by international transportation. Under the demands of Saharan and Atlantic slave trade many civilians from the Upper Guinea forests became slaves through war or kidnapping. In local understanding it was sometimes assumed that Europeans were cannibals, and needed slaves for meat.

Nationalists in the colonial period emphasized the responsibility of foreigners for the violence and local disruption caused by these external trades. More modern accounts include African agency in the story (Gilroy 1993; Thornton 1992). This agency had two aspects:

First, slaves had skills, forged in the battle with the forest, that survived Atlantic transportation, and contributed to the shaping of New World society and economy. Sierra Leone is one of the centres of the slave trade in which it can be shown that recruitment took account of these skills (Opala 1986). Slaves from the Upper Guinea coast of West Africa were preferred in South Carolina, in all probability for their knowledge of rice agriculture (Littlefield 1980). There are technical similarities between the tidewater-pumped rice farming systems of this part of the African coast and those upon which rice cultivation in South Carolina was based (Carney 1993; Littlefield 1980). Richard Oswald, the main partner in the British firm owning the main slave fort in the Sierra Leone river, at Bunce Island, from about 1750, had a business agent in Charleston, Henry Laurens, to whom he shipped several vessels a year during the 1750s and 1760s, each containing about 250–350 slaves (Opala 1986). According to Rodney (1970), many of the slaves shipped through Sierra Leone were Kissi, Gola and Mende from the eastern forests. An *adaptive* orientation to rice agriculture (Richards 1996a, 1996b) was particularly strong in this region where three different streams of African rice cultivation technology met in the process of forest conversion (see below), and it may have been this adaptiveness that made these Africans such effective and knowledgeable workers on New World rice plantations.

Second, 'primitive accumulation' was unsustainable, and more regularized ways of acquiring slaves, ivory and other forest products were needed. Powerful members of forest society collaborated with merchants to organize the trade (Rodney 1970). Trade-oriented cultural 'brokerage' entered forest society as one of its key social skills, but in turn provoked popular suspicion concerning the selfish motives of political leadership (Murphy 1980; MacCormack 1983). This tension (between 'cultural creolization' and 'egalitarian' measures intended to render the powerful accountable to popular opinion) survives in Upper Guinean forest society to this day, and re-surfaces in garbled form in the Neo-Barbarism thesis (Richards 1996c). It is a tension with both negative and positive aspects. As will be argued, perpetrators of recent patterns of violence in the region invoke this tension to their own benefit, but so, too, can the protagonists of peace.

The foundations of forest society: ivory and rice

Ivory and rice play an intertwined role in the history of human settlement in the Upper Guinea forests. The earliest Portuguese visitors to Sierra Leone encountered an abundance of rice (the main staple) and ivory (from the small forest elephant, *Loxodonta cyclotis cyclotis*). Elephant hunters opened forests to rice farmers, and ivory became an important item of trade between local rulers and Europeans on the coast. Local carvers in the forests backing the coasts of Sierra Leone were soon supplying the Portuguese and other visitors with ivory items (goblets, salt sellers and the like) in local style for table use. But rice was (and remains) the political priority in the region. At busy periods in the rice farming calendar local rulers suspended trade in slaves and forest items with the European traders so that farmers might concentrate on their crops (Rodney 1970).

Rice is the staple crop of the coastal region in West Africa from Senegal to Côte d'Ivoire (Richards 1996a). Asian rice is a recent introduction. For perhaps two thousand years or more local populations depended mainly on Africa Rice (*Oryza glaberrima*) and the unrelated 'Hungry Rice', a small millet (*Digitaria exilis*) often grown in rotation. According to Portères (1976) African Rice was first domesticated in savanna riverine wetlands in and around the Inland Delta of the Upper Niger, and reached the forest only at a later date.

Reflecting the Upper Guinea forest's position as part of the Atlantic world, present-day rice agricultural systems in the region represent a synthesis of indigenous and external influences. Richards (1996a) argues that the Asian rices have been inserted into landscape 'slots' earlier developed for the cultivation of the indigenous African rices, much as foreign and local influences combine to make a creole language. Nowhere is this 'agrarian creolization' more intense than in a triangle of land between Freetown, Kailahun and Cape Mount (in Liberia) bisected by the Sierra Leone–Liberia border zone. Here genetic resource streams from three distinct African rice farming ecologies (tidal wetlands, riverine and inland wetlands, and drylands) have converged, and mingled with rices from Asia introduced by the Portuguese and others (Carpenter 1978; Richards 1986). The skilful management of this 'polyglot' array of rice genetic resources by local farmers is the key to understanding the enduring role of rice agriculture in forest conversion (Richards 1986, 1992b, 1996b).

Given the clear felling required, it seems likely that *major expansion* on to forested *uplands* took place only with the advent of iron tools. There is evidence of iron working techniques in the western Upper Guinean forests from c. 1200 BP (Holsoe, 1979). Rice agriculture was firmly established on the *coast* of Sierra Leone and Liberia by the time of first contact with Europeans (fifteenth century). Although rice is now the dominant staple throughout the forest from Sierra Leone to Côte d'Ivoire the frontier of rice agriculture seems to have moved through the Upper Guinean forest from north-west to south-east. Holsoe (1979: 68) considers 'rice production among populations in western Liberia [to be] of greater age than in the eastern portion of the country'.

The presumed wild ancestor of African Rice (*Oryza barthii*) is widespread in West Africa, being found both in savanna wetlands and along streams running through grassy clearings in the forest. Farmers may have first settled around naturally occurring grassy vents in the forest favoured by elephants in the dry season. Elephants are powerful agents of environmental change, and wallowing and foraging among climbers and fruit trees on forest margins may have enlarged these vents (Richards 1993). Atherton (1979) quotes a mid-fifteenth-century description of elephant hunting along the Gambia: 'they seek elephants in woods, for these prefer swampy places, where for the most part they resort, like swine' (Cadamosto, in Crone, 1937). These woodland 'swampy places' on the forest margins may have been among the first sites colonized by rice cultivators.

Ivory was one of the most valuable early West African exports to Europe, sitting (literally) under the fingers of every nineteenth-century drawing-room pianist. The international ivory trade is sometimes represented as the work of 'White Hunters' in 'pristine' Africa. But the relationship between elephants and human populations in the West African forests may be symbiotic. According to the calculations of Prins and Reitsma (1989) forest elephants are ten times more numerous in secondary than in primary rain forest in Gabon. This reflects the greater foraging opportunities provided by a patchy forest mosaic. Rice farms also suit elephants exceptionally well, and Mende rice farmers still today recognize a special category of rice, *helekpoi* (lit. 'elephant dung'), rescued from elephant droppings, and formerly occasionally used as famine food (Richards 1993). This symbiotic relationship is one reason the shy and elusive forest elephant (dangerous to hunters when cornered) assumes ancestral status among many rice-growing peoples of the Upper Guinean forest. The Mende often describe their settlements as being founded where a hunter killed an elephant (Hill 1984). Ideas about shape-shifting between human and elephant form are widespread (cf. Jackson 1989). In the Kpa-Mende village of Mogbuama (Richards 1986) members of the oldest land-owning group are believed to be elephants, and revert to this form of existence when they die. Ivory trumpets speak of a chief's power and ancestral legitimacy.

The more early farmers opened up areas of the forest to rice the more elephant numbers may have increased. In short, there would have been no large ivory export trade to Europe from the seventeenth to nineteenth century from West Africa without local agency in first modifying the forest environment. That prize instrument of Victorian civility – the upright piano – embodies African culture as much as rain forest nature. It seems especially fitting that many a late Victorian and early

Edwardian salon would have clattered to the music of an Anglo-Sierra Leonean composer, Samuel Coleridge Taylor (Richards 1987), in arrangements of his popular settings of Longfellow's ballad of American frontier regret, *Hiawatha*.

Valorization of forest: tree-crop agriculture

Sometimes the picture is painted of forest conversion as the process by which farmers clear trees for farming purposes. This picture is incorrect as far as the Upper Guinea forests of the Liberia/Sierra Leone region are concerned. Farmers on the forest margins protect and plant trees to encourage the spread of forest onto hitherto grassy land. Fairhead and Leach (1996) argue that in some savanna regions the process of human settlement has created extensive forest islands, and that where these begin to coalesce the forest-margin expands outwards. Areas that in the nineteenth century were grassland are today high forest wilderness. Farmers are interested to coax forests to expand because this is the best way they know to improve their soils for farming. Fairhead and Leach (1996) challenge the widespread concern with the shrinking of the Upper Guinea rain forest, and argue that it is largely an administrative misperception inherited by modern conservationists. Documentary evidence and airphotographs disprove it. Although it is true that the forest is changed in terms of species composition, with implications for the conservation of natural biodiversity, their main point is well taken. We should not think of human occupance of the Upper Guinea forests as 'clearing' but as 'conversion' (the usage adopted throughout this book).

A rather similar point about human occupance making as well as breaking forest can be made in relation to cash tree crops. Ford (1992) presents an interesting example concerning the production and trade of the kola nut.

Kola is a stimulant still highly valued by the Islamic populations of the savanna, and has been a mainstay of forest-savanna trade throughout West Africa over many centuries. The nut is harvested from several species of forest tree. The main kola of commerce is *Cola nitida*, but *Cola acuminata* and *Garcinia cola* ('bitter kola') are also locally important, though only the first two are cultivated. Kola is likely to have been one of the first Upper Guinean forest products to pass extensively into regional trade.[2]

The picture usually presented of the development of kola production in the forest is of savanna traders penetrating the forests to induce established subsistence rice cultivators to gather, for trade, an item normally only regarded as of importance in social and ritual exchange.

[2] *Kola* (or cola) must be one of the most widely used Africanisms in daily international use.

Ford's paper, however, suggests a significantly different scenario for some parts of the Upper Guinean forest.

For the Dan (Gio), a rice-cultivating group of the Guinea/Côte d'Ivoire/Liberia border region, kola was both motive and technique for forest colonization. Growing kola, Ford (1992) shows, went hand-in-hand with rice farming in the land-use system of the Dan. By excluding suitable land for food crop production from the rice swidden cycle, kola speeded up the process of forest penetration by farmers.

This changes the normal picture (farmers entering the forests first as subsistence cultivators, later to be connected to a wider commercial world by a savanna trading diaspora). Ford's analysis stresses that Dan kola cultivators contributed to the creation of trading networks on the forest edge not because they were forest food-crop farmers alerted to an economic opportunity by passing Manding merchants, but because they built up sufficient tree holdings in the forest to attract the necessary trading interest. Tree-crop opportunities may have been the reason Dan farmers began the process of forest conversion in the first place.

These new analyses (by Fairhead and Leach, and Ford) support a more general point. By and large, standard accounts of social and environmental change in this part of West Africa have tended to understate the role of forest populations in shaping their own futures. The proven historical capacity of forest populations to 'build from within', as well as to synthesize local and wider cultural and technical influences, are important (as will be argued later) in re-assessing prospects for war and peace. As on the American frontier, forest societies in West Africa generate 'survivalist' political philosophies that lead both in the direction of anti-state violence and also in the direction of sturdy civil self-reliance. If war and peace *both* come from within, urbane outsiders may be among the least well-equipped to understand the issues.

A sixteenth-century invasion of Sierra Leone

War spilling out of eastern forests is not a new experience for Sierra Leoneans. Early Portuguese and English commentators on the coast of Sierra Leone described a country turned upside down in the middle–late sixteenth century by the invasion of warrior bands of the Mane from the eastern forests. Mane war-lords had established themselves as a ruling elite throughout much of Sierra Leone by the early seventeenth century.

Who were the Mane (Northcote Thomas 1920)? And why did they go to war?

Some contemporary commentators understood the Mane invasion to have been a long-distance military expedition conducted over a number of years by a group of warriors from ancient Mali, involving campaigns as far afield as the forests of present-day Ghana. Fage (1978) considers this might not be entirely fabulous, since Manding traders were active across the region.

A more straightforward idea, however, is that the Mane were essentially the product of an internal 'Mandingization' (a social revolution using Mande ideas about the organization of long-distance trade) at the western end of the Upper Guinean forest in the region between Gola Forest and Cape Mount (in present-day south-west Liberia).

Hair (1967) first established (from vocabularies noted by the Portuguese) that the Mane spoke Vai (or, to put it more cautiously, that Vai speakers were numbered among the Mane invaders). A 'Mani confederacy' was based on the Cape Mount region (though its original leadership may have originated further east). If the Mane spoke Vai, then following Jones (1981), the question becomes 'Who were the Vai?'

Jones establishes that they were (and remain) a group of traders and farmers living on the Atlantic coast between the Gallinas estuary and Cape Mount, engaged in long-distance trade with markets further north, in salt, kola nuts and perhaps other high-value commodities such as gold and ivory. The Vai had converted to Islam at a relatively early date, and seemingly were not averse to trade-related politico-military adventures to protect and extend their power and networks of influence in the wider region.

Why did they seek to expand into and control the Atlantic coast territory as far as the Sierra Leone river in the mid-sixteenth century? One plausible answer might be that they were seeking to impose control on a trading hinterland, at a time when new agents, from the Atlantic world, were beginning to appear on the coast, threatening to redirect flows of slaves and forest products away from Cape Mount and towards the Sherbro coast and Sierra Leone river. The Mane had mastered the Manding arts of war (and these, historians have noted, centred on ambush and protection from ambush of trading caravans, with an emphasis on mystical as well as material means).

One of the striking features of the Mane expansion was the way the invaders were soon absorbed within the wider fabric of social and economic life in and around the western end of the Upper Guinean forests. As we have seen, they left behind no clear identity as a people or founders of polities within Sierra Leone. But then this is characteristic of the cultural flux prevailing at the western end of the Upper Guinean forests. In a tight space, where life is hard and uncertain, getting on with the neighbours aids survival. Where new influences flood in from several directions at once, and where everyone has complex cultural origins, identity is situational and highly negotiable. To be firmly flagged as having 'age-old' roots simply makes for difficulties when it is time to adjust to new neighbours, or move on.

The hope for conciliation in the present war in Sierra Leone is that all parties share a heritage of cultural compromise forged over many centuries of social and economic flux. There are many articulate ideas in local cultures about the importance of forgetting the past, the danger of over-defining the present (concisely summarized by the Krio proverb *tɔk af iɛf af* – i.e. don't say all you know) and the positive virtues of political compromise, religious syncretism and the hybridization of material culture (cf. Murphy and Bledsoe 1987; Richards 1996c; Stewart and Shaw 1994). Within these cultural resources it is possible to discern a neglected but positive potential for making peace. It is now time we examined the cultural resources in question more closely.

Talking about war and peace

An obvious starting point is the question of communication. Liberians have lamented that they lack a common language in which to talk peace. Sierra Leoneans do have such a language. Krio, the creole *lingua franca* of Sierra Leone, is now spoken by nearly all members of the younger generation. With the language young people absorb a rich legacy of skills and ideas concerning cultural mixing and social brokerage forged over several centuries of forest conversion. Meta-linguistic syncretic competencies of this kind have been termed 'cultural creolization' (by Hannerz 1987). As a multi-ethnic, Krio-speaking movement stressing its commitment to religious syncretism (RUF/SL 1995) the RUF explicitly acknowledges that it belongs to the world of cultural creolization. Here is one framework within which common understandings might be forged.

The biggest problem the Sierra Leone state experienced with the rebels was to find ways to open contact. Once it withdrew into its forest fastnesses sporadic messages via unreliable short-wave radio sets were the RUF's only form of contact with the outside world. But at issue was more than physical contact. Mental orientation was also an issue. At times leaders ensconced in the capital paid more attention to the international community than to the careful decoding of wild noises and crackly static from the interior.

For their part the rebels were afraid of negotiation, aware that there is a language of international diplomacy and they do not speak it.[3] The fear was expressed that an incomplete education might let them down. RUF leaders told conciliators, frankly, that they had been in the bush for too long and they lacked the clothes, manners and knowledge to sit around a table to talk peace in an international setting.

The RUF's own preferred idea of negotiation is a Gaddafi-style moot in Sierra Leone (perhaps in the forest itself) attended by ordinary Sierra

---

[3] In a letter to International Alert in May 1995 the RUF asked 'if it is written in International Alert's mandate to offer requisite and appropriate technical assistance to . . . help the RUF . . . understand the international system [and to] provide training in negotiation skills' (*West Africa*, 18 January 1996).

Leoneans rather than college-educated city people, and with Krio the medium. The rebels 'dared' the government to find them and hold such a meeting. They doubted the international peace-makers could withstand the many days of hard foot-slog needed to reach their forest bases.

The capital's presumed physical and mental isolation from the forest interior is thus woven into the discourse as one of the key points about the rebellion. Rebel capacity to move along back tracks unknown to city slickers, and attack at will, is one of the main resources of the RUF. Its significance is less tactical than symbolic – power and danger lurk in those inner jungle pathways that link all parts of the country. These paths are the intellectual highways of the poor. They are unknown to a motorized elite.[4]

Thus it should be understood that contact is not just a technical matter. As the RUF sees it, communication is one of the key political issues in the war. This makes it doubly significant that the rebels were denied their first request – an international press conference, and they were later denied a satellite telephone link to negotiate the hostage crisis. Members of the Sierra Leonean business community are said to have been prepared to supply the equipment. The offer was rejected, perhaps on the advice that it would be regarded as rewarding terrorism. If the argument that the rebellion is a domestic siege writ large holds good, then denying the rebels their chance to talk must be counted a major blunder.

It is said the rebels have never put their position to the wider Sierra Leonean society. This may have been more lack of opportunity than intentional silence. They have never turned down an opportunity to be heard on radio or seen on TV. On the contrary, the hostage-taking episode seems to have to been calculated explicitly to achieve such coverage, and so project the movement's picture of Sierra Leone's predicament to a careless wider world.

Electronic media aspects of the conflict are explored more fully in later chapters. Here, I want to concentrate on the issue of language. The RUF's implied preference for negotiation in the local *lingua franca*, Krio, rather than in a language of international diplomacy, English, is a point to ponder. To understand its significance we need to ask how fragmented communities talked to each other in the forest in the past. How did they communicate across the barriers and divisions created by the long and troubled scramble for ivory, gold and slaves?

Black Atlantic: coast hybrids and Krio

Krio is an English-oriented creole (Fyle and Jones 1980). It has been assumed that the origins of Krio and related languages lie in a pidgin language drawing upon Portuguese (a development perhaps attributable

---

[4] Reflecting hard-won knowledge of the inner geography of Sierra Leone, the RUF has chosen to call its recent manifesto *Footpaths to Democracy* (RUF/SL 1995).

to the heterogeneous African and Portuguese populations of the off-shore Cape Verde islands). This pidgin was then largely displaced by a later English-oriented version of the language widely used for intra-African, as well as European-African, communication up and down the West African coast. Kru sailors, from south-eastern Liberia, are numbered among the early users of the language, and probably contributed much to its development and diffusion along the coast.

Linguistic developments along the Sierra Leone coast received further decisive impetus from large numbers of 'recaptives' (Africans from slave ships arrested on the high seas by ships of the Freetown-based Royal Navy anti-slavery squadron) landed and resettled in and around the Sierra Leone peninsula from 1807 onwards. The recaptives, many of them victims of conflict in regions interior to the Gulf of Guinea, or from as far afield as Angola, and intended by their captors for the slave markets in Brazil and the Caribbean, had no local language in common. Koelle (a German missionary linguist working in Freetown in the first half of the nineteenth century) reported two hundred different African languages spoken by recaptive populations on the Sierra Leone peninsula in the 1840s (Hair 1987). The recaptives, soon outnumbering the original Freetown population of freed slaves from the New World, absorbed and developed the coastal English-oriented pidgin, and enriched it with many new terms from their wide spread of African languages. A later generation of Sierra Leoneans on the Freetown peninsula spoke the language as their mother tongue, once Yoruba, Igbo, KiKongo, etc. lapsed at home. Pidgin lapsed and Krio emerged as a fully-fledged creole language.

The recaptive community found commercial and professional success in the later nineteenth century, with the result that Sierra Leonean Krio, closely related to, and to some extent mutually intelligible with, other English-oriented pidgins and creoles of West Africa and the Caribbean, lost (or never gained) the stigma normally associated with 'broken English', and trade languages more generally. It is now readily accepted as the national *lingua franca* in Sierra Leone, and is generally the medium of choice for national political discourse on radio and television, or in election speeches. Addressing an international audience, via the International Alert video of life in an RUF forest camp, Foday Sankoh uses stilted English, but slips into Krio to supervise the head-shaving of a young recruit.

Although the pidgins spoken in Ghana, Nigeria and Cameroon have less status than Sierra Leone Krio, Todd (1984) suggests there may be as many as 15 million speakers of mutually intelligible variants of the language in West Africa today. In scale, the English-based pidgins and creoles in West Africa rival Maninka and Hausa as the main languages of interregional communication.

Pidgins and creoles are among the most characteristic fruits of a 'reflexive' global modernity (cf. Giddens 1989). New languages were once thought to be produced by divergence from a common root stock.[5] But linguists realized that in the modern world new languages were also being formed by convergence, in situations where societies with no previous historical contact were forced to communicate. Aspects of pidgin formation appear to be independent of the historical circumstances of culture contact (Bickerton 1981; Muehlhausler 1986). Some argue, therefore, that pidgins are manifestations of a universal cognitive capacity for language. Pidgin and creole studies moved from being a fringe study of the pathology of culture contact to a central position in linguistic research, raising basic questions about how the brain is 'wired' for language, and how language learning takes place.

The historical argument, however, is not to be discounted entirely. West African and Atlantic basin English-based pidgins and creoles have features, and elements in common, that can only easily be explained by examining their history stretching back to the time of the Portuguese and perhaps earlier. Hancock (1983) makes the interesting suggestion that behind pidgin Portuguese lies an even earlier West African pidginization of Maninka associated with the spread of Mande trade.

The cultural and commercial world of the Upper Niger basin was first centred on two polities known to historians as Ghana and Mali (Fage 1978). But the Saharan gold trade, and later Mande articulation with the Atlantic system, triggered commercial, social and institutional changes far beyond the confines of specific political formations or ethnic groupings. A positive orientation towards trade, Islam, and possession of the linguistic skills and technologies of security (including adoption of a Manding clan identity) that facilitate long-distance mobility can be described as 'Mandingization', irrespective of where along the Upper Guinea coast or in the interior a person might have been born (Linares 1981, 1992; but cf. Launay 1982). Mandingization was a process apparently well-established among forest peoples of the Liberia/Sierra Leone interiors in the sixteenth century. One aspect of Mandingization was the adoption of a simplified trade version of Maninka generally called Dioula (Jula).

Dioula is widely spoken today throughout Mali, Côte d'Ivoire and parts of Burkina Faso, as well as by traders operating in the forests of Guinea, Liberia and Sierra Leone. The concept of Dioula as a simplified version of Maninka has also influenced local perceptions of Krio as a language of trade. Krio speakers in the Gola Forest sometimes still use the term *kangbe* (from Maninka meaning 'clear speech' – i.e. language stripped down to its basics) to differentiate their more strictly functional use of Krio from the richly allusive and proverb-saturated Krio spoken by the natives of Freetown and the Sierra Leone peninsula.

---

[5] It is this 'tree trunk' theory of language change, first developed by German linguistics in the eighteenth and nineteenth centuries, that Vansina (1990) draws upon to track endogenous developments in the agricultural settlement of the African Equatorial Forests.

The suggestion of a Maninka root for Krio, on to which Portuguese and then English elements have been grafted, would explain the otherwise puzzling fact that Krio (like Maninka but unlike Portuguese or English) is a tone language. As in Hausa, there are few semantic distinctions in Krio made by tone alone, but garbling the tones in speech makes sentences incomprehensible to listeners unfamiliar with English.

Hancock's notion of pre-European linguistic creolization in this region is consistent with the picture developed above of hybridization in Upper Guinean forest zone material cultures from a very early date. The coast was undoubtedly important in the story of creolization but not the only source of influence. Positive orientation towards cultural relativism appears to be a long-established and widespread feature of institutional cultures within the Upper Guinean forests themselves, as groups converting the forest from different directions sought cultural accommodation in a relatively tight space.

Creolization and the forest language map

It is likely that forest communities were involved in shaping local trade languages at an early date. The acceptance of Krio as the *national* language of Sierra Leone, and not just the language of the descendants of the recaptives and of the coastal elite, may owe something to such early and perhaps widespread exposure to, and involvement in, shaping regional languages associated with intra-African trade. To understand that 'creolization' is a socio-linguistic process invoked by endogenous as well as exogenous factors we need to examine the formation of the language map of the western end of the Upper Guinean forest.

At first sight, this language map is a patchwork of unrelated elements (Illustration 3.1). According to the well-known Greenberg classification, four major elements can be discerned on the map – Gola, Kissi and Bolem (Bullom), belonging to the Mel/West Atlantic language family; Mende and Bandi (south-west Mande family); Kono and Vai (North Mande family), and Dei, Kwaa and Baso (Kwa family of the Niger–Congo phylum). But grouped by families the pattern is distinctly odd. Why is Vai, a cognate of Mandinka and other languages of ancient Mali, found right down on the coast? Vai and Kono are to a degree mutually intelligible. Presumably they were once together, but if so how and why have they become separated? What accounts for the Kwa outlier in north-west Liberia? How do we attempt to explain the apparent extrusion of South-west Mande languages that appears not only to divide Vai from Kono but to have fragmented the Mel group?

Africanists were once inclined towards bold hypotheses: speakers of languages in the Kwa group were descended from forest autochthons; Mel-speakers inherited an older-established culture once widespread along the forest-savanna transition; Vai and Kono were representatives

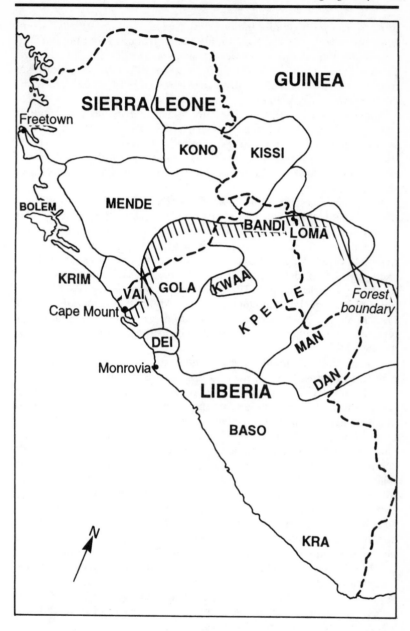

3.1   *The language map of the western end of the Upper Guinean forest*

of an 'advanced' (Islamic, trade-based) savanna culture attracted to the coast by trade in salt and kola (or, alternatively, forced into the forest by changes in the balance of power in savanna and desert-edge medieval polities); Mende and related languages were diffused by warrior clans from the Guinea highlands cutting across the grain of established trade-based north–south relations.

Some elements in this bold picture remain defensible. For example, trade in salt and kola linked forested areas in the coastal zone with savanna markets to the north. But, overall, historians and linguists are now inclined to be more cautious about an implied pattern of superimposed folk wanderings. This caution is the result of two considerations:

First, languages have their own dynamic, and often spread without the speakers moving. During the last hundred years, Mende has become the mother tongue of many forest communities in Sierra Leone where once Gola or Kissi prevailed. This process continued in the early twentieth century, despite the cessation of warrior rivalries between, for example, Gola and Mende war-lords in the border zone immediately prior to colonial conquest. Those who have adopted Mende sometimes point to its perceived convenience, or to stylistic considerations. Like French, Mende is considered to be a very elegant language conferring a reputation for sophistication on those who aspire to use it (Dennis 1972; Sengova 1987).

Second, not all linguists accept the basic assumptions of language classification resulting in discrete higher-order aggregations such as 'Mande' and 'West Atlantic'. Dalby (1977: 10) points out that language classification is often based on the assumption that 'the complex language map of today has evolved from a much simpler language map in the past'. Assuming links of descent between an assumed 'proto-language' and current exemplars, comparative linguists, Dalby charges, sometimes concentrate on 'possible ultimate and most distant relationships . . . before establishing on a sound basis their immediate relationships' (pp. 10–11). This can lead, at times, to dangerously circular reasoning, in which languages are grouped in a family according to assumptions about cultural affinities further supported by apparent but untested similarities between languages in that particular family. Even more pertinent to the present discussion is Dalby's further point (reflecting his background as a creolist) that fixation on the idea of a common (often hypothetical) origin from which groups of modern languages are assumed to have branched leads 'to the neglect of the process of convergence among unrelated languages or of reconvergence among related languages.' (Dalby 1977: 11).

To understand why the Vai today speak a language very close to Kono, while being separated from Kono country by speakers of at least two other main language families, we need to take note of the kinds of criticisms Dalby levels at a comparative linguistics too firmly focused on *divergence* at the expense of *convergence*. Attention should be paid to the role, in common with other Northern Mande languages, of Vai as a language of trade. Rather than consider the territory of the Vai as a linguistic 'block' it might be better to conceptualize the geographical distribution of the language in terms of trade networks, and the routes and nodes in that network. If, as seems possible, the Vai pioneered a salt trade between the coast and the savanna interior, when Saharan salt trade routes suffered disruption, this would explain the first appearance of a savanna language on the coast. Perhaps Vai was spoken only by a handful of merchants. Later, and simplified, it might have become the *lingua franca* of the entire trading system, from north to south, co-existing all the way with the country languages of farmers. But a network is not a region. It is less of a puzzle to explain why some linguistic links in a network structure might drop out and be replaced by other trade languages (when, for example, network junctions are captured by other groups) than to account for a linguistic block being divided, and its borders being rolled back, by the incursion of an alien tongue. Moreover, later, a perhaps not very numerous group of Mande traders, seeking renewed ties with the coast, may have 're-Mandingized' Vai, making it once again more like Kono and other Northern Mande languages (recall Dalby's point about reconvergence) and less like surrounding local languages.

Now we have in place the elements to understand a language flux that appears to be typical of many Upper Guinean forest communities from an early date, especially where long-distance trade was important.

The Liberian traveller Sims, reporting on Bopolu, a forest trading town between Cape Mount and the Gola Forest, in the mid-nineteenth century, offers a relevant example (Sims 1859–60). Bopolu had a mixed population of Mandingo, Gola and Vai traders. Sims thought the inhabitants had invented their own hybrid tongue. The description he offers strongly suggests this was, in fact, a Manding creole (Chapter Four).

The overall point is that by recognizing the possibility of linguistic convergence and reconvergence, in addition to the possibility of divergence, multiple outcomes are possible. The linguistic map may, as a result, become simpler as well as more complex over time. A linguistic patchwork by no means necessarily indicates folk wanderings and superimpositions by conquest. It is just as likely that these complex outcomes are *in situ* socio-linguistic developments. The advent of Mande-speaking traders in the forest may be as much the result of an internal process of 'becoming Manding' as an external process of penetration by savanna traders.

In regard to present dilemmas it is important to realize that the processes of bridging, reaching out and re-making society are as dependent on internally generated capacities for communication, brokerage and social enlargement as they are on syncretic capacities resulting from external interventions in Upper Guinean forest society. RUF ideology, shaped by exile, is one of those external factors. Rejecting this ideology out of hand, or succumbing to it absolutely, may not be the only options. Some of the RUF concerns are resonant with a wide range of local experiences and understandings, and forest communities may yet find ways of putting to positive use some of the ideas upon which the rebels have seized. Conceivably, valuable social 'alloys' are being forged in the crucible of war and destruction. Outside agencies, seeking to assist in conciliation, need to recognize, and find space for, cultural creativity as one of the keys to peace-making. They need to know that in this region of Africa, perhaps above many, cultural creativity has its roots within a socio-linguistic and cultural 'soil' of internally generated, as well as externally induced, 'creolization'.

Concepts of community in Upper Guinea Forest society

We now pass from the topic of communication to a consideration of some of the basic ways in which the forest peoples of the war zone in Sierra Leone engage in 'community making'. The aim is to hint at some of the ways in which, forced into forest incarceration, the rebels have made their own self-conscious (reflexive) analysis of what makes forest society tick. They have become practical anthropologists for tactical reasons. Such analysis hands the rebels a military advantage. But the analysis is not restricted to the rebels alone. RUF 'anthropology' may be provoking wider reflection on forest community dynamics. Later, it will be suggested that this wider debate may have positive, community-enhancing, as well as destructive, consequences.

'Paths towards a clearing'
Vansina (1990) suggests that in the equatorial forests of central Africa distinct communities have been formed by a process of variation from a main cultural stem parallel to the 'branching' of the Bantu languages. Bayart (1993), drawing attention to the deep-seated political values upon which the apparently ramshackle states of the equatorial region depend for their survival, extends Vansina's imagery by talking in terms of the 'rhizome state'. Such states – Mobutu's Zaire, for example – are held together by nothing very much on the surface but by a dense network of cultural roots reflecting centuries of social segmentation underground.

At the furthest western extension of the Upper Guinean forest block in West Africa this analogy is less appopriate. True, Upper Guinea forest society is also a world of villages and small-scale chiefdoms, and centralizing tendencies have been few and far between. But, here, the settlement fission and dispersal Vansina identifies in central Africa are absent. In a much tighter space, and influenced by early currents of globalization, the dominant pattern of social change in the Upper Guinean forests has been one of cultural convergence. Where equatorial communities faced with conflict might split and go their separate ways, pushing off into vast empty sectors of the forest, Upper Guinea forest groups are compelled to draw upon reserves of worldly wisdom to merge differences and resolve disputes *in situ*.

Local commitment to finding a common 'grammar' for distinct varieties of social experience can be conveniently labelled 'cultural creolization', a term that deliberately seeks to invoke parallels with some of the linguistic and material convergences already noted (Hannerz 1987, 1992). Jackson (1989) has a metaphor that sums up this process of cultural accommodation in the Upper Guinea forest region and hints at wider convergences as well; he entitles his book of essays on thought and action among the Koranko of Sierra Leone *Paths towards a clearing*.

Indigenes and late-comers
The social processes associated with this high level of historical acceptance of multi-culturalism in Upper Guinea forest society have been described by a number of anthropologists, following the lead set by D'Azevedo (1992).

One such process is the tendency to emphasize bilateral kinship and 'situational' history in forging viable local political communities. The position of early arrivals in the forest is always worth respecting. Early arrivals may possess reserves of forest lore (medicinal secrets, for example) worth knowing. But equally often, late-comers have reserves of labour power (measured in client numbers and children) and better trade connections. Leaders of these more powerful groups will demand and receive political recognition in proportion to their wealth and social significance.

Realigning the local political system so that it accords with *de facto* distribution of wealth and prestige often requires creative use of the possibilities of a bilateral kinship system. The mother's brother–sister's son relationship is a convenient hinge for many such local political manoeuvres (Currens 1972; Leopold 1991; Murphy and Bledsoe 1987). But real marriage alliances are by no means essential to such adjustments. The political seniority of powerful late-comers can sometimes just as easily be ensured through transfer (or even purchase) of relevant family histories (Richards 1986).

Patrons and clients
In the absence of well-developed markets and palace bureaucracies, Upper Guinea forest society depends to a large extent on patron–client relationships to regulate and integrate loose hierarchies of regional trade and the labour exchange procedures required for forest conversion and village rice production. Young men, in particular, perform a large

number of labour-demanding tasks in self-regulating gangs under the patronage of elders. Trade depends on local 'landlords' (Mende *hotakɛɛ*) whose role it is to provide migrant 'strangers' (*hota*) with hospitality, protection and recourse to local courts when settling trading disputes.

These patron–client networks tend to be unstable, since leading landlords compete, often vigorously, to recruit stranger clients, and establish exclusive control over a section of a trading network. In former times, ambitious chiefs might hire a warrior to cut out rivals. Clients on the losing side would suffer seriously.

Moral panic resulting from such collapse sometimes takes the form of a set of ideas frequently (but incorrectly) translated into English as 'cannibalism' (from the Mende term *bɔni hinda*). This is the belief that weak patrons under pressure sometimes changed to, or disguised themselves as, chimpanzees, Nile crocodiles or leopards (the only three animals in the Upper Guinea forest that kill humans in unprovoked attack) to murder children (the weakest members of society) in order to make a magic medicine that would revive flagging political fortunes.

Episodes in which chiefs and other big people were accused of *bɔni hinda* are associated, in colonial records, with forest communities and contexts most open to the destabilizing influence of overseas trade (Abraham 1975).

One such case involved an American-educated Sierra Leonean missionary, Daniel Flickinger Wilberforce, who had become a local chief in the Imperri District (on the Sherbro coast) in 1899 'because he thought it would give him a larger opportunity to introduce civilization among his people' (US Vice-Consul in Freetown, 1906, quoted in Kalous 1974). Wilberforce had earlier been 'an active supporter of the Colonial Government in stamping out cannibalism' (*ibid.*) but now stood accused himself. Similar patterns emerge for cases in Liberia. These are not beliefs associated with the back-of-beyond but with commercial centres most regularly in touch with the Atlantic economy.

Perhaps the most satisfactory explanation for the incidence of *bɔni-hinda* accusations is that they arise, or seem most believable, when clients become especially sensitive to the fragility of ties that bind them to their patrons. Political reputation and business confidence go hand-in-hand, often vested in the same 'big-man' merchant or political 'broker'. The business – political or economic – dies with the man or woman concerned. There is no institution or on-going concern to be inherited.

Leadership contests are acutely troubling, therefore, since there are no accepted procedures to guarantee the organised transfer of clients between the competing parties. The loser will 'sink with the ship' taking down all hands.

Acutely aware of the extent to which power is personalized, people come to suspect that politics 'feeds' on weak and defenceless persons. This belief in a propensity for 'cannibalism' within politics (or commerce), where personalized networks prevail, is not, however, a reversion to any set of inherent primitive urges. It is a way of expressing concerns over the ambiguities of personalized power in weak patrimonial political formations. The problem of personalized power would abate in communities regulated by institutions that outlive their incumbents.

Boni hinda is exactly the kind of material that feeds New Barbarism. A sociologically informed reading suggests that the nub of the problem is patrimonial leadership and lack of institutional continuity. This in turn is linked to short-term (unsustainable) resource extraction procedures. These short-term processes may be 'primitive' but they are also procedures in which the outside world has long played a prominent part (Richards 1995b; 1996b). New Barbarism tries to hide this fact.

Initiation
A central historical feature of the Upper Guinean forest world is the near universality of the male and female associations, Poro and Sande (Bellman 1980; Butt-Thompson 1929; D'Azevedo 1962; Ferme 1992; Gittins 1987; Jedrej 1976; Little 1949; MacCormack 1979; J. V. O. Richards 1974). Initiation marked the ending of childhood and allowed for re-birth into a world of adult responsibility. Childhood was a period of dependence on the expertise of one's parents. The Poro 'devil' seizes boys from the family home, and in symbolically breaking the family tie, opens up membership of a wider social world. The rigours of initiation create bonds among peers, life-long respect for the expertise of elders, and commitments beyond the web of kinship. The RUF leadership, after near-defeat in 1993, withdrew into the forest and today uses the language of initiation to justify its attempts to rebuild society from within. It even explicitly terms its forest camps '*sowo* (i.e. sacred groves for the initiated)' (RUF/SL 1995: 11.)[6]

Many commentators have noted the judicial and military aspects of Poro (Fulton 1972; Little 1965–6). Perhaps a more basic feature of initiation in Upper Guinea forest society is that it is a process for creating social bonds 'from within' (Hoejbjerg 1995). Only initiates create initiates. This gives initiation comparative advantage over means of establishing social bonds dependent on external reference (e.g. to King or Country) in social landscapes where trust has been shattered by civil war or primitive accumulation. Initiation is a way of beginning again where larger frameworks for social trust lie in ruins, or perhaps never existed. This would be one way to explain the importance and spread of Poro and similar institutions among largely 'stateless' Upper Guinean forest communities (D'Azevedo 1962).

Whether Poro and Sande have ever acted as single organizations there is considerable reason to doubt. Initiation rituals and practices,

[6]The second line of the chorus of the RUF anthem also directly alludes to initiation: 'Go and tell my parents, they may see me no more' (RUF/SL 1995).

and the knowledge handed on in the course of initiation, probably vary widely across the region. But this does not diminish the force of the fact that initiation as institutional culture was common to almost the entire Upper Guinean forest region in the pre-colonial period. Civil society and initiation were in effect coterminous on the eve of the colonial intervention.

Colonialism introduced other forms of socialization for youth – most notably Western-style schooling. However, schooling tended to adapt itself to the prevailing institutional climate. Entry to school soon began to be treated as another form of society initiation. Bo School, founded by the British authorities for the sons of chiefs in 1906, and still one of the premier secondary schools in the Sierra Leone provinces, assigns an entry number to all its pupil intake. This number stays with a Bo old-boy throughout life, determining precedence and seniority among the members of the politically influential Old Bo Boys Association (OBBA).

But the institutional culture of initiation has been eroded little by little during the twentieth century. Sande initiation is still practically universal for girls from the Sierra Leone provinces, but elsewhere in the Upper Guinea forest region traditional initiation has declined in importance, for boys especially. This decline was brought about not through lack of interest, but because the Americo-Liberian leadership in Liberia, and Marxist dictator Sekou Touré in Guinea, feared this key institution of provincial civil society as a challenge to the supreme authority of the state. After Sekou Touré died, initiation underwent a strong revival among groups like the Toma in south-east Guinea (Hoejbjerg 1995). Members of some Islamic trading diaspora in the Upper Guinean forest refuse to join Poro or similar societies, or allow their children to be initiated. Manding traders, often married into local communities, frequently join, but Fula traders from Guinea regularly refuse on religious grounds. But those resident before the war in the small towns ringing the Gola Forest (places like Daru, Mendekelema and Joru) frequently sent their children, secretly, to be initiated in out-of-the-way villages on the forest edge (Davies and Richards 1991).

Tension between trade and initiation as a means to rebuild local society in ruined forest landscapes is a central factor in the RUF's own understanding of the present violence in Sierra Leone. The RUF is explicit that it is a social movement seeking to repair the damage caused by mineral extraction and other forms of 'primitive accumulation' in the Upper Guinea forests (RUF/SL 1995). Historically, initiation has been one of the few social resources capable of withstanding the externally induced social dislocations of 'primitive accumulation' from the time of the slave trade onwards. In its own eyes the RUF, having been driven back into the forest,[7] was forced to re-examine its aims and renew itself

---

[7] 'The forest welcomed us . . . We regained our composure and engaged ourselves in a sustained period of intensive self-examination and self-criticism . . .' (RUF/SL 1995: 11).

(RUF/SL 1995). It offers the same chances of renewal to the children it seizes. These captives are being 'rescued' from the 'family' clutches of a failed patrimonialism. But the exile leadership of the RUF pursues initiation with an intellectual fervour that disables other more broadly-based attempts at social renewal from within. The RUF's only means to attack a patrimonial elite is to terrorize *rural* communities that have gained little or nothing from patrimonialism. This pits the power of new initiation against the old. Existing institutions forged through initiation are apparently in the process of revitalization as a result of the war (Keen 1995; cf. Ellis 1995). They may yet force a rethink of the more narrowly sectarian plans of the insurgents.

Killing the ones you love – the puzzle explained?

Throughout the centuries social creativity in the Upper Guinea forest has repeatedly risen to the challenge of making communities that work, despite appalling difficulties. The ideas and processes on display – creolization, initiation, fear of 'cannibalism' – seem 'wrong' to outsiders, and especially so to metropolitan elites who have other self-styled 'civilized' ways of making the world work. To write off backwoods social philosophy as a bizarre cultural essentialism is a neat trick, since it hides the role of outsiders in helping create the unstable conditions against which local 'world making' has to work. But the essentialism of New Barbarism will not wash, since many of the ideas and processes involved in community formation in the Upper Guinea forest are found widely distributed across the globe.

The creation of social bonds through initiation, where there is no trustworthy wider social frame of reference, or where there is special need to separate from that wider frame, is a commonplace of the comparative ethnographic literature (Bellman 1984; La Fontaine 1985). For an example of 'agrarian creolization' in forest backwood conditions comparable to the case of Upper Guinean rice agriculture outlined above (cf. Richards 1996c) look no further than the Upper Delaware valley in seventeenth-century North America, where Finns and Swedes, with a background in shifting cultivation, were not too proud (unlike immigrant peasant farmers from better-favoured parts of Europe) to learn backwoods survival techniques from the Delaware Indians, and thereby lay a functional foundation for a hybrid Euro-North American low-intensity woodland agriculture on which later generations of Irish and German immigrants were happy to build (Jordan and Kaups 1989).[8] Fear of shape-shifting 'cannibals' is far from unique to the forests of Sierra Leone and Liberia. Beatty (1915) thought he had discovered an

---

[8] It is hard to resist pointing out that according to a map in Jordan and Kaups's study, one of the family names in the seventeenth-century Upper Delaware valley serving to identify the settlers as Karelian Finns and Swedes is 'Rambo'.

Africa-wide freemasonry of 'cannibal' secret societies. Much more likely, the belief regularly recurs where, as so often in recent African history, unstable mercantilism and weak patrimonialism have collided. Creole languages share grammatical features across the globe (Bickerton 1981; Muehlhaeusler 1986), and there is reasonable consensus that these common features reflect *both* the way the brain is wired, *and* the regular recurrence of creole-forming socio-linguistic contexts under conditions of maritime 'culture contact'.

The RUF – as a rain forest insurgent movement – makes strategic use of elements in this generalized (rather than place-specific) forest cultural heritage. Creolization (it is a multi-ethnic rather than 'tribal' movement) and initiation stand out. But let us forget the idea that in so doing it is a movement re-asserting an age-old Africanism. Creolization and initiation are products of 'culture contact'. If creolization and initiation, along with a deep dislike of shifty metropolitan politicians, are symptoms of New Barbarism, then the New Barbarism is as common in Montana as in Kailahun.

Harder to explain is why the RUF insurgents connive at the destruction of forest communities whose predicament they share and whose interests they claim to want to protect.

This is where Mary Douglas's comments about the irresponsible world of the excluded intellectual seem really to come into their own (Douglas 1986). West African history offers some examples of localized 'peasant intellectual' movements (cf. Richards 1992c) but the RUF is, seemingly, not one of them. The social characteristic of the RUF leadership that seems most clear is a shared history of exile. The leaders are a town-oriented excluded elite, not a group with strong place-specific community links. I hazard the guess that their main focus was, and remains, to take over at the top; perhaps they seek to square the circle by implementing a 'bottom-up' view of the world in a 'top-down' way. The rural mayhem is intended to teach a lesson to those who sit pretty in the capital. The suffering of the masses is an idea in which they have come to believe. They are blind to its reality all around them, except as proof that they were right all along. This is academic talk – the world view of the lonely and disregarded intellectual – not the practical wisdom of those who know that forest beliefs must work for the community, or there will be no one left to inherit the vision.

'Footpaths to Democracy'

Since the draft of this chapter was completed the RUF has produced a pamphlet – its first published statement of its aims and objectives – *Footpaths to Democracy*. According to this document, the RUF saw itself initially as a conventional insurgency movement, fighting to control towns and territory, using vehicles and heavy weapons. Near-defeat in 1993 drove the survivors into the forest and caused a rethink. The RUF re-emerged as a forest survivalist movement. The new RUF stresses a closeness to nature and a respect for forest resources and the knowledge and social institutions through which forest communities have long survived.

A cynic might be inclined to detect, in this pamphlet, the hand of professional conciliators, anxious for the rebels to tell a coherent story – environmental if not political – to their enemies and the world at large as a basis for negotiation. But there is evidence that the RUF was well-embarked on this forest survivalist course before the near-defeat in 1993. Bush initiation of rural youngsters was a feature of RUF activity from the outset, and it was in terms of initiation that the RUF was understood by villagers in Pujehun District in 1992 when I interviewed survivors of the original invasion. Foday Sankoh was known for his bush-trekking and survivalist interests even before the war. An awareness that syncretism and multiculturalism are long-established social responses to asset-stripping environmental flux in the forest of eastern and southern Sierra Leone, and could be used for strategic purposes, crops up in the earliest reports of rebel attempts at social mobilization in Pujehun and Kailahun in 1991.

What *Footpaths to Democracy* argues is that being forced back into the forest has intensified these awarenesses. This leads it into contradiction. Although it is frank about earlier mistakes – notably the mercenary terror violence – the document cannot justify (other than in terms of its hostility to metropolitan elites) a terror campaign directed against precisely the people and communities who embody the indigenous eco-knowledge that life and circumstances have taught the movement to respect.

The problem seems to be that 'exile' and 'wilderness' have become conflated in the minds of the RUF leadership, with a peculiar love–hate relationship emerging as a result. The wilderness is a tactical shield, but it is also a powerful symbolic and practical reminder of the leadership's social exclusion from the patrimonialism of national politics. Unless it respects the forest, and bush knowledge, the movement cannot survive; but at the same time the leadership hates being where it is. It has engaged in a complex and dangerous political game of brutalizing the villages in order to terrorize the city, through involving some of the city's own fears of the barbarity lurking in the bush. This is war as a dramaturgy of social exclusion, not war as business, as envisaged by von Clausewitz (1832).

But is the situation as hopeless as outsiders assume? Bush knowledge is not barbarism. It is a way of making ends meet in harsh circumstances. The rebels are pointing to practical lessons of survival in the wilderness of potential value to a wider audience of urbanizing young people. The RUF helps validate indigenous knowledge and the value of forest resources even while it is mired in the contradictions of wanting to defend but escape wilderness existence. It is of interest to ask what the wider audience of young people is learning about the bush as a result of the war, and this is a topic taken up in later chapters (notably Chapter Eight). The war has focused attention on the forest, but not always with negative consequences (as these later discussions will show).

Secondly, the RUF has discovered (or invented) its own reflexive anthropology, and this too is a discovery worth noting for its potential value to the wider society. Initiation, for example, is a resource that the rebels have revitalized. In focusing on how to mobilize youth for its project, the RUF directs attention to the crisis of youth in Sierra Leone more generally, in ways that are already beginning to provoke useful peaceful debate.

Traditional initiation values have been boosted by the requirement for civil defence. But perhaps more importantly, the rebel challenge will have had a seriously useful impact if it directs attention to the urgent issue of how a poor country, experiencing globalization (and concomitant heightened social expectations), can meet the demands being placed upon it for social services, especially education and health (Fyle 1993). Self-help (with teachers paid 'out of school') is already a large element in education in Sierra Leone, and peace-making will have to address how this type of community self-reliance can be enhanced to ensure that the young are less vulnerable to capture by future disgruntled opportunists with a box or two of guns and a basic knowledge of bush craft. In the end, it may be possible for the majority of Sierra Leoneans to come to terms with war as a drama of social exclusion if it helps force the pace for reform and the discovery of alternative more peaceful solutions to the underlying problems of the social exclusion of youth.

Conclusion

The present chapter has attempted an outline history of ideas and community in the Upper Guinean forests under forest conversion (cf. Guyer and Eno Belinga 1995). Creolization and the forging of social bonds through initiation are two of the ways in which multi-cultural forest communities have made and re-made society despite dislocations fostered by outside interests. The Sierra Leone rebels have invoked some aspects of this intellectual heritage of sturdy forest independence. But perhaps because theirs is a city movement at heart, bush ideas are explored at the expense of bush communities. The quintessential African demons proposed by the New Barbarism thesis are beside the point. The phenomenon of frontier sectarianism in Sierra Leone is an exile appropriation of ideas at the expense of community. Peace requires that forest communities reclaim their intellectual heritage of creolization and initiation.

4

Bush War & Primitive Accumulation

The Voices of Young People

Introduction

The war in Sierra Leone is a tussle for the hearts and minds of young people. How do young people experience and react to war in contemporary Africa? This perspective has been neglected in the New Barbarism debate. The present chapter describes bush war and primitive accumulation in the forests of eastern and southern Sierra Leone from the standpoint of youth. First, we meet an under-age fighter: a 14-year-old Sierra Leonean boy describes two years spent as an irregular, fighting the RUF in Pujehun District, telling us what he has learnt about the forest, fighting, drugs, and himself. Second, *njɛpe wovɛ* (a Mende historical narrative) performed by an elderly hunter from a Gola Forest village on the Liberian border in 1989 takes us back to a time (perhaps mid-nineteenth century) in which young men in the Gola Forest encountered world market forces directly, in the form of slave raiding and the ivory trade. Violent struggle to command scarce natural resources, this account reminds us, is nothing new in Africa. To understand local violence we must begin to see behind it the external agents of primitive accumulation – the slavers and ivory traders, and their latter-day equivalents, the diamond smugglers, drug pushers and arms dealers. The Malthusian arguments of the New Barbarism carefully screen such figures from view. In a third account we hear the voices of the *drɛgman dɛm* – young people, often with little or no formal education, who scrape a living on their wits in the diamond-rich border-zone forests. Two young Sierra Leoneans who peddle a portable video set showing war films to diamond diggers and smugglers in the border region describe their life, explain their attitudes, and review their films. They 'read' Rambo-style texts not as a charter for violence, but as a stimulus to youthful cunning in a life full of nasty surprises (cf. PEA, 1989). No more or less than their stocks of Indian love epics, Rambo and other videos of violence are a spur to the imagining of new and more

87

spacious worlds of social and economic opportunity. They freely admit that at the first news of the RUF insurgency they were tempted to join the rebels and live their dream.

Charlie's Tale: fighting with ULIMO

Charlie (not his real name) is a Sierra Leonean teenager from Pujehun District recruited in 1992 (when he was 12 years old) by ULIMO in their attempt to wrest control of the Sierra Leone–Liberia border from the RUF and re-enter Liberia to fight the NPFL.

The ULIMO forces were recruited mainly from among the 500,000 or so Liberian refugees in Sierra Leone who fled the NPFL advance through Liberia in 1990. Young NPFL fighters carried out many atrocities against Krahns and Mandingos, seeing these two groups, the one from rural eastern Liberia, the other a long-established trading diaspora with historical roots in the Upper Niger basin (cf. Chapter Three), as among the principal supporters of their enemy, President Samuel K. Doe. Doe himself was a Krahn, with close business and personal ties to members of the Monrovia-based Mandingo business elite.

Among refugees streaming into Sierra Leone in early 1990 were a number of members of the Armed Forces of Liberia, fearing NPFL reprisals. These ex-AFL troops formed the nucleus of a band of irregulars recruited to help Sierra Leonean government troops repel the RUF, July–September 1991. Many then joined ULIMO. ULIMO was a Krahn–Mandingo alliance, led by Alhaji Kroma and Roosevelt Johnson. The alliance was later sundered in early 1994, when Krahn elements broke away to form a separate armed faction (ULIMO-J). ULIMO achieved a major strategic objective in wresting control of much of the Liberian side of the border from the NPFL in 1992. Only subsequently, however, was it recognized as a party to the Liberian peace negotiations.

Charlie was swept up into the ULIMO forces during their cross-border operations in 1992. His guardian, his grandfather, was killed by the RUF. The practice of recruiting war orphans as under-age 'shock troops' was introduced by the NPFL, but later became general among all factions in Liberia, and among parties to the dispute in Sierra Leone, not excepting the Sierra Leone army, where under-age 'vigilantes' were selected and trained by battle-front commanders to 'fight fire with fire'. Under-age boys are good soldiers, slipping through the bush with ease and little fear, treating battle as an extension of play.

The practice may first have arisen in the context of the need to provide material assistance to war widows and orphans, where regular relief activity is impossible. In a brief visit to a genial and experienced RSLMF war-front commander in the Pujehun sector in 1992 I discovered, to my amazement, he was responsible, each day, for feeding up to 40-50 orphans or children abandoned or lost during flight. To meet the drain on his regular supplies he had organized one of the largest upland rice farms in the district that year. Village young men came to him to work on the farm and (because Sierra Leonean youth is always keen to acquire skills via apprenticeship) receive elementary military training. Detailing several of these young men to go off into the bush to sleep inside our broken-down vehicle, he carefully cautioned them, in a fatherly sort of way, about what to do if they woke in the night to find people gathered outside. Their response was that they would shoot on sight. After warning them he did not want, in the morning, to meet the corpses of concerned villagers who had stopped off from their farms to offer help to the broken-down visitors, the youngsters cheerfully scampered off into the night, firing into the air to scare any ghosts or rebels standing in their way.

Charlie saw his recruitment by an ULIMO commander in similar terms. The RUF had killed his own patron, his grandfather, and he had fled into the bush. Back in the village after the RUF withdrew he had no one to feed him. He took the first offer that came along.

Large numbers of under-age fighters have been deployed in the wars in Liberia and Sierra Leone (Furley 1995; Goodwin-Gill and Cohn 1994). It has been estimated that 10 per cent of NPFL fighters were under-age. Charles Taylor had a praetorian guard of under-age fighters. Under-age soldiers, without family (many were war orphans), have less reason than most to be disloyal to their leader. Some as young as eight and nine belonged to the SBU (Small Boys Unit). Girls also became combatants, but they tended to be older. Some were field commanders, in fact. Women figure quite prominently in the leadership of both NPFL and RUF.

In a positive development for human rights in the region the NPRC government in Sierra Leone signed and implemented the UN convention on under-age combatants in 1993. This meant that under-age fighters on the government side were stood down, to undergo rehabilitation (Amnesty International 1993). Charlie is unusual only in being a Sierra Leonean volunteer within ULIMO. As such he was not stood down, but left ULIMO voluntarily, probably because as a Sierra Leonean he was deterred by the prospect of leaving his home area when ULIMO pushed on into Liberia.

Charlie's account speaks for itself. It confirms several points made earlier about the modern (even post-modern) character of insurgency in Liberia and Sierra Leone (the significance of videos of violence, the importance of drugs like 'crack' cocaine). Charlie's comments on chimpanzees remind us of discussion in Chapter Three, where it was suggested that chimpanzee 'cannibalism' is not an 'Africanism' from the remote and barbaric past, but one of the complex imaginative processes through which forest communities have attempted to adjust to the more destructive side of the global spread of 'market forces'. Charlie (unlike proponents of the New Barbarism thesis) is quick to point out that violence in Africa does not just 'happen' but involves outside agents who provoke war in pursuit of financial gain. His comment on the Ndogboyosoi conflict in Pujehun District (cf. Chapter One) points up the apparent ease with which war can become endemic in a region with a prior history of community instability and violence.

A positive aspect of Charlie's story is that he recognizes the instability inherent in the world he has left. He has chosen instead to return to secondary school, determined to succeed in formal education. His gravelly, recently-broken, voice speaks with pride at his new-found enthusiasm for mathematics, a subject where calculable outcomes contrast strongly with his magic-drenched experiences in the dark and impenetrable bush. In a war of tricks and terrible surprises, nothing was ever what it seemed.

The most poignant moment in the story, perhaps, is when Charlie expresses enthusiasm for the school's Boy Scout troop – as near now as he can get to fulfilling a desire for proper military training. It changes the picture somewhat to know that the 'loose molecules' of Kaplan's frightening account might be harbouring a secret desire to join the Boy Scouts. Or that some of them, desperate for education by whatever means, are thinking not so much in terms of unbridled anarchy but of a period of National Service.

Charlie's Tale[1]

I. [In Mende] Charlie, where are you from?
C. Pujehun.

I. You are now in secondary school, but what were you doing before that, in Pujehun?
C. I was there with my grandpa, [continues in Krio] the rebels [RUF] came and killed grandpa.

I. Was this why you joined ULIMO?
C. I really wanted to join.

I. When you joined what exactly did you do?
C. We would go to those villages [and fight] and when we came back we would sing.

I. Are you able to use a gun?
C. Yes.

I. When you were with ULIMO did you ever realize that you had shot and killed somebody?
C. Yes

[1] The interview with Charlie was carried out in Krio and Mende, in Bo Town, April 1994, by Samuel Mokuwa; I am responsible for the translation.

I. *Why did lots of Pujehun people join the war?*
C. The earlier Ndogboyosoi War made them join.

I. *Why?*
C. Because lots of people were killed, and the others were unhappy. This way they could gain revenge on their enemies.

I. *Do you think the present war will be soon over, even though people are still disgruntled about Ndogboyosoi?*
C. Yes, because there are now [RSLMF] soldiers in the area.

I. *When you fought with ULIMO did you loot property?*
C. No, because ULIMO said they would shoot us if we looted [Mende, *kapu*] property.

I. *How long were you with ULIMO?*
C. I was with them for two years – they taught us.

I. *How did RUF fight?*
C. They went to villages where there were no soldiers, and threatened the people to make them give their property to the rebels.

I. *Did ULIMO dig diamonds in the area?*
C. No, but rebels and soldiers did, in areas where no vehicles could reach.

I. *How did they sell diamonds?*
C. They didn't – they would keep them on hand. They had no road to transport them.

I. *When ULIMO trained you did they give you anything to make your heart strong to go to the warfront?*
C. Yes. We would 'eat' cocaine.

I. *What is that like?*
C. The smoke . . . inside the thing . . . you open the thing and smoke, you put it on wood . . . then you are afraid of nothing . . . for one or two days.

I. *Did they show any films?*
C. Yes, when we came out of the warfront we would watch films on video.

I. *What films did you watch?*
C. Rambo films.

I. *Do you like Rambo films?*
C. Yes, they show you the tactics.

I. *How do you think they can finish this war quickly, now it has gone to the Northern Province where there is no background of Ndogboyosoi?*
C. There is the hand of some 'bigmen' inside that.

I. *How exactly?*
C. They carry food to the rebels.

I. *What do the rebels give the 'bigmen'?*
C. Nothing . . . only the 'bigmen' support them.

I. *Do you know the name of any 'bigman' supporter?*
C. Yes [names a high-ranking officer in the army], but there are others also . . .
more than thirteen.

I. *That's why they have been sacked?*
C. Yes.

I. *Why do these rebels still attack the Bo-Kenema highway, what do they
really want?*
C. They want to stop people coming from Kenema, and giving news to the
army.

I. *Do you know how the rebels entered Boajibu?*
C. Two people went ahead, without arms, to spy out the place for some days.
Then they went back to report.

I. *What do they do with the women they capture?*
C. They turn them into rebel women, and then they cook for the rebels.

I. *Did you ever see babies that the rebel women had given birth to?*
C. Yes. But if a woman wants to escape she must first split the baby . . . they
cut the baby in half . . . she takes the head and the rebel keeps the body.
Some rebels cook humans.

I. *Have you ever eaten humans?*
C. No.

I. *When you were in the bush did you ever see human flesh in the pot?*
C. No . . . but I heard victims crying in the bush.

I. *Are you happy you have left the fighting?*
C. Yes.

I. *Now you have returned to school have you joined any clubs?*
C. Yes . . . the Boy Scouts.

I. *What makes you like Scouts?*
C. The way they perform is fine.

I. *When you go out with the Scouts do they teach you tactics?*
C. Yes. They show how to lay ambush.

I. *Do the other boys provoke you?*
C. Yes, they call me 'kɔndo bl[r]oke' [destroyer of food prepared for the

workers] . . . because of the amount of food I eat. They also call me '*tɔf boi*' [tough boy] because they think I am the strongest [most thick-set] boy in the class, and afraid of no one.

I. *Do you have problems in school?*
C. They say I eat two plates of food, and step out of line!

I. *Do you ever meet up with your friends at the camp [for under-age ex-fighters]?*
C. Yes, I can go there every Saturday and Sunday, and we talk about what we did at the warfront.

I. *Do the boys still smoke marijuana and cocaine?*
C. Yes, they still smoke cocaine.

I. *Why do they still take cocaine, even though they are no longer fighting?*
C. Because that way they are afraid of nothing.

I. *What can we do for those boys who still have these bad habits?*
C. They should be given places in the army . . . because that is where they fit . . . but they can do farm work even as soldiers.

I. *Where is your mother . . . is she still alive?*
C. Yes. She is at Gondama refugee camp . . . I can visit from time to time. My father is in Freetown . . . he treats me fine.

I. *What is your age?*
C. I will be fifteen next October.

I. *Do you have any other friends who fought with ULIMO?*
C. Yes, one . . . but he hasn't come yet.

I. *When you go to your friends at the rehabilitation camp do they give you food . . . what exactly do they do there?*
C. Yes, I can eat with them. They do anything they want...they give them money, medicine, and they train them not to steal.

I. *But why do some of the boys there want to go back to the warfront? Some have escaped, even.*
C. It is because they don't see their people [kin] . . . that makes them want to escape.

I. *Who was your commander in ULIMO?*
C. His name was 'Bush Devil'.

I. *Where did he come from? Is he still alive?*
C. From Liberia . . . yes, he's at Buyea.

I. *When he sees you is he happy? What can he do for you?*
C. Yes, he tells people 'this is one of my boys'.

I. *How can government encourage the refugees to go back to their areas?*
C. They should help them . . . build houses for them . . .

I. *What can we do to make sure war never comes back to this country?*
C. They should check everyone for identity cards. Then also they should stop white men coming to the country. They make blacks turn into slaves. They go to some parts and give the chiefs tobacco and other things, and then the chief gives to them all the stubborn [*tranga yes*, lit. 'strong-eared'] kids and tells the white men to take them away.

I. *Do you believe government should clear all the forest, so rebels cannot hide?*
C. Yes, but it will soon grow back.

I. *If they clear the forest do you believe you will suffer?*
C. Yes there are some good things there . . . like diamonds.

I. *Do you think the forest will soon be finished?*
C. Yes, but it will grow back.

I. *What do you like and dislike about forest?*
C. I like it because there you get diamonds, timber for boards . . . people can make farms for food when they clear forest. But I don't like wild animals . . . chimps, and monkeys.

I. *Why is the chimp a bad animal?*
C. Because it can grip human beings, and begins to beat you . . .

I. *Chimps, leopard and Gaboon Viper – which is worst?*
C. [Without hesitation] Chimpanzee . . . if you are passing through the forest to another town it will grip you and beat you until you are exhausted . . . but if you succeed in beating the chimp, it will salute you so that you can carry it off to town . . .

I. *[In Mende] Of leopard and viper, which is worse?*
C. Viper [*tupui*], because it eats [bites?] people.

I. *If you had the choice to care for one of the three – chimp, viper and leopard – which would you take?*
C. Chimp. The other two cannot be trained [*makε* – to train up a child or apprentice].

I. *When you were with ULIMO what did they pay you?*
C. Thirty dollars [?a month]

I. *That was plenty of money then!*
C. Yes.

I. *Did you ever experience an attack by the RUF?*
C. Yes, at Blama Massaquoi [Gallinas-Peri Chiefdom, Pujehun District]. The rebels came into the town singing an insulting song – 'Sierra Leone

soldiers, your mothers' private parts' [speaking in Mende, but Charlie quotes the Liberian English phrase 'Mammy Pussy' in the words of the song, then reverts to Krio] They passed inside our ambush, there was firing, but no one was killed on either side . . .

I. *Do you like agriculture?*
C. [In English] Farming is a method of producing crops.
[Charlie's stilted response to this question is in a style Sierra Leonean school pupils call 'cram talk'!]

I. *What were you asking for the other day?*
C. I want the revision notes, but they are Leones1000 for two – I don't have the money.

I. *Which subjects do you like best?*
C. Maths, it is a good subject...at times I can get 60–70 percent . . . I also like agricultural sciences.

Njɛpɛ wɔvɛi: nineteenth-century primitive accumulation in the Gola Forest

This Mende oral history records the social and historical consequences of trade in slaves and forest products – principally ivory – in the nineteenth-century Gola Forest. Its performer, Bemba Gogbua, was a hunter of Gola descent, about 80 years old in 1989. Recorded in the village of Sembehun on the western boundary of the Gola North Reserve, the text was given as a formal recitation (*njɛpɛ wɔva*, lit. 'talk about former times'). Such recitations are a literary genre, and Cosentino (1982) warns us that they are influenced both by formal requirements and the speaker's current preoccupations. However, they are distinct from *dɔmɛi* (a Mende genre of performed but clearly fictional story), and may be assumed to convey lessons thought to be based on real incidents, even if, in the telling, more modern concerns shape the selection of incidents. In Bemba Gogbua's case, his specific reason for reciting this story was a stated desire to 'correct' more established versions of the political history of the Sierra Leonean side of the Gola Forest. These orthodox versions first gained currency as a result of administrative changes in the border region under British colonial rule.

Nineteenth-century communities in the border zone had links both to the east and west of the Gola Forest (Davies and Richards 1991). There was no general concept of community-wide ethnicity. The ordinary population was generally of mixed descent, though different villages would be recognized as 'Gola' or 'Mende' according to the origins of the warrior chief. These chiefs strove to maintain the peace through marriage alliances, many across linguistic lines. But the colonial border created its own ethnic identity. From then on the 'Mende' were those living in Sierra Leone, the 'Gola' those in Liberia. The Mende language became a regional *lingua franca* during the nineteenth century and many communities on the Sierra Leonean side of the border, perhaps originally Gola-speaking, rationalized their identity to fit colonial administrative norms, and downplayed the significance of earlier contacts with Liberia. Bemba Gogbua, from a Gola-speaking family, was supplying a dissident account that resurrected some of these forgotten links.

In outline, his tale describes how elephant hunting for the international ivory market was first organized in these remote communities on the edge of Gola. It alludes to the significance of firearms and strong drink in extending this trade. Forest-edge West Africans have access to two sorts of palm wine, but the technique of making distilled spirits was introduced only by ex-soldiers after the First World War. Prior to that time 'trade gin' was an important prestige item for chiefs engaging in the Atlantic trade, and grave sites in Gola sometimes produce broken bottles of Hamburg or Dutch gin (Illustration 4.1). Another feature of the story is the way that young men from the community were engaged as carriers for these forest products and then kidnapped as slaves at the coast. These details fit recorded history rather closely.

The hunters were from Bopolu, a town to the south-east of Liberian Gola (cf. Illustration 2.2, p. 44) In Bemba Gogbua's story the Bopolu hunters appear to be Gola-speakers, but elsewhere Bopolu is described as a 'Mandingo' town. The Liberian traveller Sims,[2] who visited Bopolu in 1858, describes a mixed community of Gola, Kissi, Vai and others, devoted to a rather piratical version of Free Trade. Judging by Sims' (1859–60) account, Bopolu was a clear example of nineteenth-century 'cultural creolization', where a community 'composed of Veys, Golahs, Kausaus, Pessahs, Bousas and several other tribes . . . [had] . . . composed a language for themselves, which is partly original, and some words from each of their respective tongues'. They had 'assumed the name of Condors . . .'. Sims judges them 'a set of roguish, kidnapping, knaves, robbing all the interior natives who attempt to come down and trade with us, and making slaves of all who resist. Memmoru Sowe, King of Condor, is nothing more nor less than a generalissimo of banditti. Nearly all of them are Mohammedans.' In twentieth-century Liberia and Sierra Leone the terms 'Mandingo' and 'Muslim long-distance trader' have become more or less interchangeable.

Seymour, a contemporary of Sims from Monrovia (their paths crossed while travelling up country), had that same year met a group of Vai and Gola traders at Passila on the St Paul's River. They were ferrying a small group of slaves to the coast. Outraged, Seymour intervened, and by a

---

[2] The accounts of Sims and Seymour have been made available to me by James Fairhead and Melissa Leach. I am grateful for their assistance. For further background on Bopolu see Holsoe (1966) and Schick (1977).

4.1   Trade gin bottles, Gola Forest

trick freed the slaves. He then noted in his journal that the traders were going to 'the French-man at Cape Mount'. 'Here is direct palpable proof', he writes, 'that the French slaver, Regina Coeli, Capt. Chevalier, at Cape Mount in 1858, was openly engaged in the slave trade and in defiance of the laws of Liberia, and the feelings of the people . . .' (Seymour 1860).

The young men of Sembehun, in Bemba Gogbua's story, invited to taste the high life on board the European ship, and then kidnapped into slavery, may have been sent to Cape Mount. Bemba insists the Europeans in the story were 'Spanish' (queried, he reiterates the infrequently-used Mende word *panyamɔ*, rather than the more usual *puumɔi*, 'white-person'). The Mende dictionary (Innes 1969) glosses *panyamɔ* as 'Spaniard', and Christopher Fyfe (personal communication) suggests the infamous Pedro Blanco, a trader in the Gallinas Estuary shipping slaves to Cuba as late as the mid-nineteenth century, may have been intended. But Fyfe points out a second interesting possibility, that *panyamɔ* in Mende might derive from 'panyar', a Portuguese term (lit. 'to seize') widely used in West Africa during the period of the slave trade to describe kidnappers.

The Gallinas is the south-eastern-most part of present Pujehun District, and therefore in Sierra Leone, on the western side of Gola. If the young carriers in the story went through Bopolu, as the story asserts, Cape Mount (in Liberia) was a more likely destination. Bemba Gogbua's insistence on involvement by the *panyams* might be a conflation with later events associated with the shipping of young men from Liberia as indentured labourers to the Spanish island colony of Fernando Po. This would explain the raised expectations of the parents in the story that their children had gone 'to London' and would one day remit riches back home.

The story ends in war, between the Bopolu settlers and the local chief. The point about cultivating cassava is an interesting detail. This South American crop has spread very widely in the African forest zone in recent centuries. It requires less field labour than rice, and, stored in the ground and harvested as needed, it is harder to loot than a granary filled with rice. Expanded cultivation of cassava may have an important role to play in 'smart relief' (cf. Conclusion).

Notwithstanding doubts about how some of the historical details of the story are to be resolved, it is a remarkably vivid testimony to the strong sense of blighted hopes and broken promises that hangs over the African end of the long trail leading to the respectable Victorian parlour with its ivory-keyed piano and mahogany sideboard. Enthusiasts for the notion that market principles are a universal force for civilization should pay more attention to these historical trails of violence, destruction and broken communities, and their cultural and cognitive consequences. As Charlie reminded us, many young people in Africa remain to be convinced that this particular leopard has changed its spots.

The RUF attacked Sembehun in early 1991. Accessible by bush path from RUF bases on the northern side of Gola North, the village was hit a second time, in 1992, when rebels heard that Red Cross relief supplies had been delivered there. Villagers also died in 1993, in a shoot-out over diamonds. I suspect Bemba Gogbua, if he has survived, might not be altogether surprised that forest history has repeated itself.

Bemba Gogbua's Story[3]

There was a hunter called Babu. He was a great shot, and killed all the elephants in Liberia. He and his brother Keba decided to venture north-west towards Gola Forest looking for elephants. They took their guns and crossed the Moro River into this forest.

They spent two nights in the forest without seeing anyone. But then they saw smoke from a cooking fire in a farm hut. They approached the woman and greeted her. She asked where they came from. They said Bopolu. She asked their mission. They said they were on the look-out for elephants. The women stated her husband's name. The two men asked to see him.

Then she offered them food. They noticed she cooked without salt, so they took salt from their bag and gave her some on a leaf and she added it to the food.

After they had eaten they all went to town and met the woman's husband.

[3] Translation of the text is by Esther Mokuwa and Paul Richards.

He asked about their mission and where they came from. When they told him they were from Bopolu and were hoping to hunt elephants the man exclaimed 'Elephants are very numerous in this forest'.

They lodged with the man, and he sent messages to people in the interior villages to come and meet the hunters. They assembled.

Keba was a hunter with magic powers – he could turn into a bird, and sitting in the branches would alert the other hunters to the position of the elephants. Following this advice they killed two elephants. At dawn they cut the tusks from the carcases.

Keba and Babu then said they should report to the chief who had sent them. So after resting they set off, but first they gave out salt, guns, cartridges, tobacco, rum and wine to the people. They took with them about 60 young men to carry their loads.

Later, after reporting to their principal, they returned to Gola Forest saying to the chief, Ome Dueh Koneh, that they also wanted other forest animal items in addition to elephant tusks – for example, skins of animals such as lions and zebra duiker. Chief Koneh gathered the people to hear the message.

The hunters from Bopolu then served the chief and elders generous helpings of rum. Pleased with the rum and in a mellow mood Ome Koneh asked one of his wives to sing [song in Gola]. The song was a warrior's song. Soon all the elders stood up to begin dancing briskly. The chief and bigmen then shared all the trade items from Bopolu, and in return handed over many animal products – tusks, skins of zebra duiker, pangolin skins, etc. They gathered everything together, and were told, while preparing to go, that there were many more animals and that they could collect them when they returned.

They then told Ome Koneh their own chief would like to come to meet him face to face; he would settle for some time if they gave him land to build his own town. Chief Koneh said the people should begin to prepare the place and houses right away – they called the site Layiwailu.

Once again the hunters from Bopolu asked for young men to help them with their loads. They said it would be good for the young men to accompany them to meet their brothers in Bopolu. The chief and parents were happy at this idea. They waited another two nights while boys came from far and wide to manage the loads. They tied many hampers and set off.

On reaching Bopolu the hunters were welcomed, and messages were sent to Spanish [Mende *panya*] trading partners on the coast to come and meet them in Bopolu. The Spanish arrived with a large consignment of guns, cartridges, tobacco, rum and wine. The chief then told the carriers that he wanted them to continue to the coast with the Spaniards to experience the world. The lads were happy at this, not knowing he had sold them into slavery overseas.

The hunters returned up-country to Gola Forest, to find the local people had killed and trapped even more animals than before. They exchanged these items for salt and tobacco.

In those days there was no salt and tobacco in Gola Forest. People used to make their own substitutes, e.g. from burning the rattan called *kavoi* [*Ancistrophyllum secundiflorum*] to ashes for a kind of salt called *pibi* [*libi*]. Salt was unknown in Gola Forest in those days. People also used to make a kind of tobacco from the pods of the tree called *hewei* [*Xylopia aethiopica*], which they smoked in pipes made from small bamboo sticks.

In those days all this area was forest, clear to Liberia and to Kenema in the west. There was no town, only villages.

Sharing out all the items to the chiefdom people, Ome Koneh said Babu and Keba should try and bring their chief on their next visit. He is a very great warrior, they replied.

Once again, a gang of young men was assembled to carry all the loads to Bopolu. Once again the chief in Bopolu told the young men that it would be fine if they went to the coast to see how the white people were living in their boat. To whet their appetite the chief plied the lads with tea and sugar and corned beef, and told them they would find an abundance of these items in the boat of the Spanish.

Enticed on board with food and drink the lads slept the night. In the early morning the ship sounded its alarm and set sail carrying them off into slavery. Meanwhile items such as sugar were passed back to Gola Forest, the people thinking these were items from their boys sailing to 'London'.

Ome Koneh was a great warrior and he had not yet ceased to think about war. Among the trade items were a large number of guns.

The chief from Bopolu set off for Gola. In those days there was much war, and no one travelled without making suitable preparations, taking with them guns and ammunition. On arrival he found the local people had prepared a large area for himself and his followers.

He sent to his new friend, Chief Ome Koneh, many alcoholic drinks (whisky, dry gin, Gordon's, rum). After this Ome Koneh paid a visit to the new town, accompanied by his young son. The people made a party with much food, and danced for a week.

The Bopolu people next year did a lot of farm work, and planted cassava.

Then one day after the two chiefs had taken a lot of rum, Ome Koneh turned to his visitors Babu and Keba, and said, 'I am the land owner here, you are doing me a lot of harm, go back to your own place'.

At daybreak they started to fight. The guns were so numerous that they could be heard all over the chiefdom. Koneh's people succeeded in driving their rivals back over the Moro River where they settled for another year doing farm work. But meanwhile they were collecting guns and ammunition in order to revenge themselves.

As soon as the rice had dried [November] they crossed the river westwards and resumed the fight, but were unable to prevail. This is why Ome Koneh, and his son, are the grandfathers of the present owners of the land in this area.

Dregman life: diamond mining and video shows on the border

Mining of alluvial diamonds in Sierra Leone requires little if any industrial equipment. Tributors dig gravel from swamps and stream beds during the dry season and then sieve the gravel before the rainy season flood overtakes makeshift workings. At times, a shovel, sieve and headpan will suffice, plus the equipment to camp in the bush. Licensed operators work the more accessible and better-serviced sites, sometimes using pumping and dredging gear, especially along the major axis of distribution of the Sierra Leone diamonds, the Sewa River basin. But diamonds are widely scattered throughout the region, and there are few swamps or streams that offer no prospects. Thus, a significant minority of unlicensed operators works very remote sites, off-limits in the forest boundary wildernesses of the border zone. Many of the miners within and round the Gola Forest operate a long way from roads and official scrutiny, using only the simplest and most readily transported equipment.

Normally the 'supporter' – the financial backer and licence-holder of a typical Sierra Leonean small-scale diamond mining operation – will be permanently resident in town (having a business to run, or official duties to discharge). The mining operation is left largely to the initiative of the tributors (site foreman, plus crew of young labourers). This is especially true on remote workings where conditions are arduous, and regular supervision by the supporter impracticable. Four Limba miners, encountered miles off the beaten track in the heart of the Gola North forest reserve, had been sponsored by a doctor in a government hospital in north-western Sierra Leone. His chances of making a site visit – two days by road and a day's trek across the forest – were zero.

In many cases the supporter supplies tributors with rice, tools, and sometimes, in addition, a shot-gun and cartridges to hunt for the pot. The digging crew generally split a two-fifths share of the local price for each season's haul of diamonds.

Much of the profit in diamonds is made exporting them to Europe and the Middle East. Members of digging crews are sometimes tempted to abscond with large diamonds. This is not as easy an option as it might appear. Most diggers lack the contacts, documentation and knowledge to risk selling directly on the international market. Collusion among crew members is threatened by whistle-blowers, always well-paid by supporters for information. The police also find themselves promptly rewarded for their vigorous pursuit of diamond cases. Not a few Lebanese supporters have their own guns and are at times prepared to take the law into their own hands. Finally, and perhaps most crucially, an absconding digger finds it hard to sell a stone without provenance at anything approaching its true value. The main dealers have good local intelligence networks, and offer suspect sellers the poorest prices. Many diggers consider it is hardly worth risking a long-term stable relationship with a supporter for such dubious returns. They prefer to save enough from regular work to acquire a licence of their own one day.

Meanwhile, ready cash is used to ease the hardship and tedium of life in the bush. The leisure-time activities of diggers are interesting, if at times somewhat basic. The occasional visit to town to stock up on supplies offers a chance to see the latest films in cinemas and video parlours. Not a few young miners have part-completed secondary (in

some cases university) education, and thirst for knowledge of contemporary political events. It is not uncommon to find them regular
listeners to BBC African Service programmes like *Focus on Africa* on
short-wave radios deep in the forest. During the Gulf War a Lebanese
diamond dealer in Bo did good business re-broadcasting each morning
in his cinema CNN footage of the Gulf War, taped from a domestic
satellite TV installation during the night. At dusk, one evening, a group
of 50 or so youths did a curious soft-shoe shuffle through the middle of
Bo town chanting anti-Saddam slogans, perhaps an obscure protest
aimed at the local Lebanese diamond dealers. In the bush, crews relax
with music, radio, drink, gambling and recreational drugs (mainly
cannabis, but 'crack' cocaine is increasingly available).

At weekends and holidays itinerant video shows touted around the
camps and villages of the mining areas are a greatly welcome diversion.

'Abdul' and 'Issa' are now in their mid-thirties. They were early
drop-outs from Koranic school; their father, a Mandingo merchant from
Guinea, forbade other forms of education on religious grounds. When
teenagers, they ran away to the diamond-mining areas, where they
picked up work as labourers on unlicensed diggings. Unmarried, and
still dreaming of making their fortunes in diamonds, the brothers today
scrape a living touring the remote mining localities of the border zone,
showing films on a borrowed video machine powered by a portable
generator. The video player and generator belong to a friendly Lebanese
supporter in Bo.

A token payment (perhaps some free tickets) to the village chief and
elders secures the use of the open-sided village court house – the *bari*.
Abdul borrows benches from the school. Issa is busy stringing up old
sheets and rush mats to block the sight lines of by-standers without
tickets. As darkness falls Abdul sells tickets, while Issa tinkers with the
generator. Soon the machine kicks into life, and the show begins.
Perhaps 50 or a hundred people (young men from the diamond
workings, but also village people) have each paid about 30–50 pence
sterling to see a Hong Kong Kung Fu film, or Hollywood's latest attempt
to live down the nightmare of the Vietnam war.

Abdul and Issa may exploit a pitch for a few days, and then move on
to the next largish village a few kilometres down the road. Some of their
takings are needed to buy fuel for the generator and pay other local
expenses and some is set aside to return to the owner of the set and
films. The balance (perhaps a third) is profit, to be saved for the day
when they will have enough to buy a licence and mine for diamonds on
their own account.

The brothers are skilled media critics of a post-modernist persuasion,
and happy to expound their ideas about audience tastes. Indian 'love'
films attract good audiences. Indian films, Issa explains, are about social
relationships. Abdul adds that 'people enjoy them because they help
you imagine how to build such long-term relationships for yourself'. For

this reason, young women, recognized as the makers of society *par excellence*, like them most of all.

But women are in a minority in diamond camps. Women are excluded from diggings for fear of spoiling the diggers' luck (*hajia*). The brothers explain that 'Action Films' (essentially a genre comprising Kung Fu and American war movies, but also embracing violent science fiction epics such as *Terminator*) have the greatest drawing potential among their best customers, the diamond tributors.

Issa continues, 'People like Action Films because they teach skills and attitudes needed to survive on your own in a hostile world.' Rambo is especially admired. Abdul joins in, enthusiastically re-telling the story of his hero's death-defying tricks in *First Blood*. John Rambo soon merges with Musa Wo, the youthful trickster figure whose wilful *Schadenfreude* is tolerated within the Mende moral universe as a harbinger of fruitful innovation (Cosentino 1989).

Rambo films, Issa insists, are a window on the world. But he quickly makes it plain he is no naive empiricist. He 'reads' *First Blood* as educational drama, not documentary. 'We Africans', he says, 'are slow to learn, but films help bring home quickly the skills you need to survive in a tricky world.'

The world seen through John Rambo's eyes provided him with a context within which to interpret the first news of the RUF invasion of eastern Sierra Leone in April 1991. 'We were looking for change', he says. The brothers had high hopes that the rebels would sweep away the corruption and inertia of the two decades in which the APC regime had presided over a collapsing economy and sharply diminished educational and employment prospects.

Abdul and Issa both wondered briefly about joining the rebels. Possessing little property themselves, they were undeterred by villagers' reports of extensive looting. They were more alarmed, however, by terroristic violence against civilians, and suspected that behind the insurgents there would be, as ever, a group of business backers little different from the class of supporters currently in the driving seat of the diamond economy. Their moment of infatuation with the idea of rebellion soon passed. Better the devil you know, was their argument. Both were now enthusiastic supporters of a youth-oriented NPRC military regime. Interviewed in September 1993, they were anxiously waiting for the insurgency to end.

Asked his views about the future, and the potential exhaustion of diamond reserves, Issa thought diamonds would always be there. New ones, he alleged, were always working their way upwards from deep in the ground. According to his own ideas, they carry within them their finder's names, if only the finder has the courage to keep on looking. But if the mining economy ever did collapse, he would go back to farming – cassava, probably. Abdul mocks his brother for lack of foresight; 'How will you ever make a farm with a slack body?', he cruelly observes.

Later that day, there was news that Tongo Field was reckoned secure again, after recent rebel attack. Abdul and Issa were soon heading for the Kenema motor park, their total possessions squeezed into a small box hardly larger than a woman's handbag. They planned to wash gravel until the dry season arrived. Then they would return to Bo for their equipment, and a new season's crop of films, to resume life on the road with their small dream machine.

Conclusion

In all three accounts there emerges a pointed and realistic analysis of the dilemmas of youth working and living in the rain forests of the Liberia–Sierra Leone border. Trade, violence and large-scale destruction of natural resources are old travelling companions in the African rain forests. All three accounts recognize that behind violence and destruction are 'big men', many of them foreigners, bent on rapid acquisition of forest resources at whatever cost. There is sharp irony apparent in Charlie's comments on the short-sighted cleverness of the chiefs who truckled with outsiders for a 'mess of pottage' (or, rather, a box of cigarettes) thinking to be shot of their 'strong-eared' youths – youths who have now returned as rebels to haunt them with a vengeance. There is continued acceptance of the reality of the patrimonial 'shadow' state, but still a desire for more transparent, accountable, predictable state institutions, and a Toffleresque sense that technological modernization might help straighten a few of the worst kinks. Abdul and Issa need peace and security to fix their generator, and a satellite link to run their business selling high-technology war as a fantasy of self-empowerment to unruly diamond diggers. Charlie's enthusiasm for ID cards and military discipline, enough to cause a civil libertarian to blench, goes hand-in-hand with his new-found prowess in mathematics. The modern state must be both disciplined and measured, or at least more so than the unruly growths flourishing in the dank bush that Charlie now finds so unsettling. Neither Charlie, nor Abdul and Issa, has much idea of the identity of the distant economic beneficiaries of the destabilization of their clandestine forested worlds, or how they might be brought to book (how the world might seek to deal with the European businesses, for example, that bought the logs 'creamed' by Charles Taylor's people from the forests of war-torn Liberia, cf. Block, 1992). But meanwhile, Abdul and Issa continue to develop their thoughtful, street-wise, post-modern deconstructions of the films they purvey. Here, at least, is a sign of hope that videos of violence may not be such a cause for alarm as some Western commentators choose to think.

5

Videos &
Violence

Youth Exposure
to Modern Media

Introduction

Television was well-developed in pre-war Monrovia. Influenced by American media, a 'rolling news' programme chased accidents, murders and ambulances up and down the town. When Samuel Doe overthrew President Tolbert he invited the TV cameras of the world to film the public execution of members of the Tolbert cabinet. Doe's own downfall also became a media event. When Prince Johnson seized Doe from the headquarters of the peace-keeping forces in Monrovia and tortured him to death, he didn't just kill him; he made a video as well (Davidson 1992). The video was circulated widely in West Africa, and (as noted) helped destroy Charles Taylor's chances of being seen as outright victor in the Liberian civil war.

It was once thought that TV would modernize a passive world. Now some commentators have had second thoughts, wondering whether electronic media in West Africa simply serve to facilitate the more powerful expression of an essential African 'barbarity'. The present chapter is a brief examination of the use and impact of modern media on young people in Sierra Leone. The idea that video rots the moral fabric of society and facilitates a return to the 'Dark Ages' is probably as wrong as the earlier idea that TV would automatically re-shape the consciousness of the modern world. The present chapter shows that young people in Sierra Leone use film and broadcasting as positive tools for the active construction of their own modernity.

The sample

The following analysis seeks to provide a framework for understanding media aspects of the war. The views of young Sierra Leoneans concerning the insurgency, environmental change and the future were surveyed in 1993–4. The interview schedule included a section on exposure to modern media, the results of which are summarized and discussed in the present chapter. More than 420 interviews were completed in three localities – the capital Freetown, Bo and surrounding rural areas (in the war zone), and Kambia (a rural town in north-west Sierra Leone only marginally affected by the war).

Freetown is an outward-looking city. If at times it appears somewhat cut-off, mentally, from the realities of provincial life, appearances can be deceptive. The city has long been a destination for young migrants from the provinces, seeking employment and social freedom (PEA 1989). Backed by the forests of the peninsula mountains Freetown is more easily penetrated by 'bush' issues than some other West African coastal capitals.

Bo is Sierra Leone's largest provincial town. Located in the forest zone in south-central Sierra Leone, it is a noted centre for diamond mining along the lower Sewa. The town is modern in origin, having grown around an overnight stopping point on the railway from Free-town to Pendembu. Subsequently the town developed as the most important provincial centre for secondary education, and attracts a large population of young people. Refugees from rural areas affected by the insurgency have added greatly to its population since 1991.

Kambia is a small town in the north-west of the country, on the boundary with Guinea. Kambia District has the highest rural population density in Sierra Leone. Within the forest–savanna transition, Kambia District experiences a number of environmental problems. In the local view at least, the hazard of dry-season bush fires is the most significant of these problems. Although remote from the main centres of the war, Kambia town was attacked, briefly, in January 1995 by a small insurgent group based on the Malal Hills. As a result of an attack that lasted no more than half a day, and involving perhaps a hundred lightly armed RUF fighters, an estimated 40,000 refugees from Kambia District crossed the international frontier into Guinea. A hundred or so young people from Kambia were captured for forcible induction into the RUF. A small group of Italian nuns was also taken hostage, but later released.

For the survey, a quota sampling methodology was employed. The aim was equal numbers of male and female interviewees divided into three main age-cohorts of roughly equal size (10–19, 20–29, and 30 plus) and three main groups by education (no formal education, primary and vocational, and secondary and post-secondary). Management of the survey was complicated by the security situation, especially around Bo, and intended quotas were not always fully made up. Males and females each account for half of the sample, but the 20–29 age-group (at 43 per cent) is somewhat over-represented, compared to the under-20 group (30 per cent) and the 30 plus age-group (27 per cent). The group with no formal education or only primary education comprises 51 per cent of the total sample.

Just under half (49 per cent) of all interviews were carried out in Bo and surrounding villages, an area of special interest since many inter-viewees had direct experience of the war. The balance of the sample was divided equally between Freetown and Kambia. Muslims accounted for 57 per cent of the sample and Christians 43 per cent (Muslims are in a majority nationally so this quota weighting is appropriate).

The material on attitudes to insurgency and environmental issues is analysed in Chapter Eight.

Exposure to film and video

Three-quarters of the sample claimed some exposure to films and video; 39 per cent saw films in cinema or on video 'occasionally' (once a month or less) but 57 per cent were regular watchers (once a week or more). Even in villages (around Bo) 55 per cent of the people interviewed claimed to watch videos – either the mobile shows described in Chapter Four, or when they visited relatives in town. The highest rate of exposure was in Bo Town (84 per cent). The slightly lower rate for Freetown (74 per cent) reflects the less reliable supply of electricity in the capital. From the late 1980s Bo had a 24-hour all-year-round supply based on a hydro-electric generating plant near Kenema supplemented by a heavy-fuel oil-fired station in Bo that supplies both Bo and Kenema during periods of low water. The hydro-electric supply was suspended due to rebel action in 1994.

There is some gender difference in exposure to films and video (61 per cent women and 92 per cent men) but young women, it should be noted, are substantial consumers of video entertainment. There is little variation in exposure rates according to religion (Muslims 77 per cent, Christians 73 per cent). A slightly more pronounced difference exists between exposure rates for the youngest age cohort (80 per cent) and the older age groups (73 per cent for those 20 years old and over). Those without any formal Western school education are least likely to report seeing film on video. This reflects low income and hence limited opportunity. But at 59 per cent (male 63 per cent, female 56 per cent) the figure is still much higher than might be imagined by outsiders unfamiliar with recent social trends in developing countries. Private video installations are often regarded as a facility for all the extended family, and friends and neighbours frequently drop in to view. The result is that there are now rather few younger Sierra Leoneans without at least some exposure to this form of home entertainment.

Preferences among film and video genres

Interviewees were asked to describe their favourite kinds of films and to say why they liked them. Illustrations 5.1 and 5.2 bear out Abdul and Issa's analysis of their clients' tastes, reported in Chapter Four.

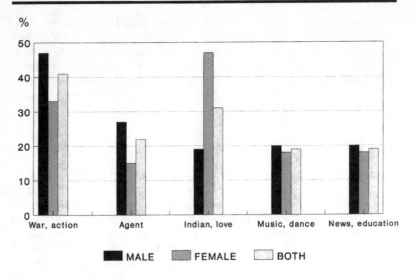

multi-preferences, column sums >100%

5.1 Video preferences of the young (Freetown, Kambia and Bo, 1993–4)

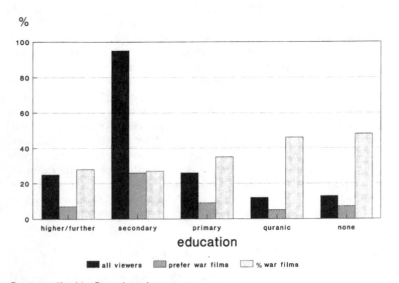

Freetown, Kambia, Bo and rural areas

5.2 Preference for war films among Sierra Leonean youth, by educational level

Indian (and love) films were cited as the single most popular kind of entertainment by just over 30 per cent of informants, but by 47 per cent of women. War films were close rivals in popularity (30 per cent, enjoyed equally by men and women). Many interviewees referred specifically to films such as *First Blood* and characters such as Rambo when identifying 'war films', but others within this category included newsreel and documentary film of war. Examples cited included Gulf War footage originally broadcast by the CNN satellite news channel and later dubbed on to video for wider local dissemination, the video of the killing of Doe, and a documentary film covering aspects of the insurgency in Sierra Leone made by a London-based Sierra Leonean broadcaster, Hilton Fyle (a presenter of *Network Africa*, the popular morning news magazine programme of the BBC Africa Service).

There was a more marked preference by men than women for Kung-Fu and Agent films ('Agent' is a categorization applied to James Bond features and the like). Interest in educational films, news (CNN), and music videos was shared equally between the genders. (Many inform-ants stated multiple preferences, so the columns in Illustration 5.1 add up to more than 100 per cent.) Preference for war films tended to be inversely correlated with educational level (Illustration 5.2).

Does video undermine social values?

Informants' rationalizations of their likes and dislikes provided clear refutation of the notion that international entertainment-industry media products have a damaging impact on African youth culture.

Many interviewees stressed that they liked these films because their production values coincided with local notions of a 'good night out'. Indian films are enjoyed because they have plenty of music, dancing and magic, and simple, sentimental story lines. In many cases, films of violence are considered attractive not because of the violence as such (though one 20-year-old female 'liked to see people killing themselves') but because the hero figures pit their wits against a wicked world and win (much as these young viewers see themselves battling against the odds for a better future), and because fights are arranged with balletic skill. A 13-year-old schoolgirl summed up this point of view when stating that she liked Rambo films because they were 'funny'.

Others had more serious points to make. The survey forms repeatedly record the viewpoint that young people in Sierra Leone find entertainment on video 'educative'. What they mean by this is that the films they see provide a stimulus to the imagination to tackle problems within their own world. As media sociologist Ien Ang (1985) has argued, in her study of the soap opera *Dallas*, the flights of imagination triggered by involvement in the plot of a film or soap opera are far from being exclusively 'relaxation', 'fantasy', and 'escape', but may have a direct bearing on the imaginative scope viewers bring to the construction of their own lives. Watching soap operas, in other words, is good for the sociological health and imagination.

Certainly, this seems to be the standpoint of many young people in Sierra Leone. Reflective respondents several times stressed that their generation lives in a more 'global' and 'multi-cultural' world. Films, for them, provide an important and valued 'window' through which, by sharing the experiences of rich Indian lovers or American veterans of Vietnam, they come to terms with global social and cultural variety. Indian films may not be anthropology textbooks, but young people in Sierra Leone view them as serving the same purpose for persons of their level of educational attainment.

A 28-year-old woman with secondary education considered Indian films important 'because of the world we are now living in'. A 23-year-old male student in teacher training college thought such films helped him 'to know my surroundings and the world beyond'. A 15-year-old boy with primary education watched Indian films 'to gain ideas about the world', and a 12-year-old primary school girl valued them because they 'showed how Indians made use of the gifts of God and Nature'. A teenage girl with some secondary education said 'Indian films teach us how to love, and maintain a household'. A 24-year-old with university education commented that Indian films 'shaped morals and perceptions'. A 13-year-old primary schoolboy thought they usefully 'revealed how some politicians could be wicked', and a 28-year-old woman with no formal education considered that they taught her 'how to play love'.

War films were repeatedly praised for introducing viewers to 'ideas about wars and skills for fighting' (an 18-year-old male with secondary education) and as a stimulus to 'develop skills to defend myself in times of attack' (26-year-old primary school teacher). Such films were also valued for providing a comparative perspective on current experiences within Sierra Leone.

A 31-year-old female said that it gave her a sense of confidence in relation to present troubles 'to compare war in different parts of the world', and a 13-year-old primary schoolgirl found war films helpful in 'showing how people fight and live in difficult situations'. Several informants stressed that a taste for war films helped their own psychological preparedness to deal with real-life war situations; 'to be aware and ready at any time' (female, 28, no formal education), 'to be prepared at any time since the country is not stable' (female, 28, no formal education), or 'how to manoeuvre in times of trouble' (male, 22, secondary school education). One 18-year-old with primary level education valued war films as a reminder that 'war is evil'; an older male, with no formal education, thought 'war films . . . show [how Foday] Sankoh [leader of the RUF] got experience on how to fight' (a percipient remark if it is indeed true that the rebels in Liberia and Sierra

Leone have used these kinds of films as recruitment and training aids).

The most poignant comment was that of a young displaced woman in Freetown who remarked that it was the thought of John Rambo coping in the forest without a friend in sight that had given her the courage to flee alone 'through the forest' to escape an RUF attack on her village in Kono. *First Blood* is not usually seen as a text of feminist empowerment.

These, then, are sophisticated, reflexively modern, 'readings' of the products of the global film industry. Far from being brainwashed by global media, young people in Sierra Leone use video features as a constructive resource for thinking out aspects of their own problem-beset lives. Nor is there any evidence here that Rambo and his kind serve as a stimulus to half-forgotten barbarism. The young people in the interviews, of all classes, are reaching out imaginatively to embrace a wider world of feeling and experience. If there is barbarity in that experience it is the modern barbarism of the Vietnam War and anti-authoritarian backwoods survivalism, not reversion to the values of a violent African past. Young video watchers in Sierra Leone are above all interested in comparing *modern* experiences across countries and environments; they look to a global, cross-cultural, future, not to a tribal past.

Radio news

The survey also assessed exposure to other media – radio, newspapers and international magazines. Eighty-three per cent of the sample listened to radio regularly, and 43 per cent had a radio of their own. Once again, there was a gender difference, but only slight (89 per cent of men and 77 per cent of women in the sample were regular listeners). Older female Muslims predominated among the small number of non-listeners to radio. Sixty-one per cent of radio listeners specified one or other of the recently-established FM radio stations in Sierra Leone (FM 94.9 in Freetown and FM 104.0 in Bo) as one of their main listening choices. The Sierra Leone Broadcasting Service's main AM trans-missions (carrying less music and more in the way of news, comment and social announcements) are a main choice of 51 per cent of the sample, but more commonly in Freetown (59 per cent) than Bo (44 per cent), where reception is sometimes poor; at times in APC days it was non-existent, and at best unreliable, presumably due to power-supply problems at the transmitter in Freetown.

BBC World Service/Africa Service is by far the most important international station; 48 per cent of the sample were regular listeners, but more in Bo (56 per cent) than in Freetown (41 per cent) and Kambia (37 per cent). This probably reflects the fact that Bo was from the early days of the insurgency directly in the path of the RUF advance, and its capture one of their known strategic ambitions. The BBC Africa Service (especially the morning and evening News Magazine programmes *Network Africa* and *Focus on Africa*) covered events in the wars in Liberia and Sierra Leone on a regular basis (with daily reports at times).

With one notable exception (an item on the evening of 24 April 1991 claiming the population of Bo had fled the town on a rumour that the insurgents would attack on 26 April) the reporting has been reliable, if sometimes rather under-specific. Details about the location of villages and small towns named as involved in the fighting have sometimes been very vague. This is an important consideration in a country where settlement names are frequently duplicated, and rebel tactics project power and spread panic by hitting sequences of obscure and underdefended villages, to imply more tangible military progress than is actually the case.

Survey results show interviewees using their radios as sources of both news and music, but the news comes first (Bo 82 per cent, Freetown 79 per cent). Music is mentioned as a use by only 56 per cent of listeners. Men stated that in 85 per cent of cases the main purpose of their radio was to listen to news. Although this figure is somewhat lower for women (65 per cent), it is, nevertheless, remarkable, given assumptions sometimes made about women's lesser involvement in 'public' events in Africa. On the other hand, listening to *BBC World Service* is a surprisingly gendered activity (males 73 per cent, females 27 per cent). Listening to BBC news broadcasts presupposes a good grasp of English. But the difference is larger than we might expect looking solely at differences of educational attainment between the two samples (a surrogate measure for competence in English) and requires further investigation. The philosopher Kant once suggested that reading newspapers made no sense without a good grasp of geography, to locate the items (Richards 1974). Maybe differences in the exact content of men's and women's education in Sierra Leone help explain why *world news* and *Africa-wide* items seem less meaningful to women than to men.

Interest in news broadcasting is constant across age groups (63 per cent of all radio listeners in the under-20 age group, and 64 per cent among those 20 and over). Those without formal education are, nevertheless, keen radio listeners (68 per cent, with 63 per cent listening regularly or mainly to news broadcasts). The group without formal education has much less English and necessarily listens mainly to national stations, broadcasting news in Krio or other local languages.

In rural areas around Bo the figures for news listening are, again, strikingly high; 70 per cent of the village sample were radio listeners and 69 per cent listened to news broadcasts. Education made no difference to the proportion of broadcast news consumers among village populations; 70 per cent of listeners without formal education listened to news. Although the rural sample is small, these figures suggest that the alleged isolation of village dwellers and the uneducated is only relative.

Newspapers and international magazines

Sierra Leone newspapers are lively broadsheets, at times containing more political opinion than factually based news, with low circulations and produced in difficult circumstances, to a low technical standard. Most are produced in Freetown, on a weekly or intermittent rather than daily basis, and in any case take a day or two to reach the provinces. Successive governments have attempted to control their at times unruly political spirit. In the last, reformist, days of the Momoh regime restraints on press freedoms were lifted, but the press's relationships with Siaka Stevens, and, after Momoh, with the NPRC government, have been far from smooth.

The main international news magazines circulating in Sierra Leone are the American *Newsweek*, the London-based but Nigerian-owned *West Africa* magazine, and Nigerian *Concord*. These are all expensive items, beyond the pockets of most ordinary Sierra Leoneans on a regular basis. However, a single copy will pass through many hands. Also the local newspaper sellers are alert and resourceful, and items of particular relevance to Sierra Leone sometimes pass down the street to the local copy shop, and xerox 'reprints' appear for sale at more affordable prices. This happened in May 1994 with an article published in *West Africa*, highly critical of the NPRC regime. Most regular copies of the magazine disappeared overnight (allegedly because someone in the government made a bulk purchase to try and dull the article's impact) but xerox copies of the item were soon available for sale all over town.

The 27 per cent of interviewees totally without formal education cannot be expected to be readers of newspapers and magazines. But among the remainder (the 73 per cent of the sample with formal schooling to primary level at least) readership of newspapers and magazines is high; 78 per cent (57 per cent of the total sample) said they read newspapers, at least from time to time, and 57 per cent (42 per cent of the total sample) were readers of international magazines. Because of the high cost (even local newspapers are significant items of expenditure for the poor) only 22 per cent of newspaper readers took newspapers on a weekly basis, and among magazine readers only 14 per cent described themselves as 'regular readers'. *Newsweek* and *Concord* are the main items for this group: 41 per cent of magazine readers saw *Newsweek*, and 38 per cent saw *Concord*, at least 'sometimes'. *West Africa* is Nigerian-owned, and not surprisingly Nigeria-centric in its news coverage. Coverage of the conflicts in Liberia and Sierra Leone has, at times, been disappointingly thin. But the magazine tries to deal with this recognized deficiency by producing occasional country-special issues, and those devoted to Sierra Leone achieve, locally, very high levels of readership.

Conclusion

If West African urban youth are 'loose molecules' they are surprisingly well-informed about events in the modern world, via radio news and journalism. In fact, they are probably better informed about international trends than many of their young American or British contemporaries. Additionally, social survey results confirm something first apparent in the account of Abdul and Issa's video machine in Chapter Four. This is that young Sierra Leoneans appropriate the products of the global media industry in a sceptical but constructive way, re-interpreting the imaginative content of video and film to match their own social needs. Video and film are invitations to the sociological imagination and a stimulus to the power of positive thinking. We should think twice before too hastily concluding that rebels feed Rambo films to their young conscripts as an incitement to mindless violence. It seems more likely that such films are intended to support a political analysis about the wider society's neglect of the creative potential of the young. Far from supporting a thesis of New Barbarism, the cultural inventiveness triggered by exposure to film provides grounds for optimism that Africa's rising generation may have an underestimated capacity to devise its own imaginative solutions to the challenges posed by the global epidemic of drugs and violence.

6

**Environment
& Violence**

Is Population Pressure
a Likely Cause
of War?

Introduction

At the heart of New Barbarism is the idea that young people in Africa
are driven to violence by population pressure and ecological collapse.
According to the demographic theory of Malthus, war is one of the
'positive constraints' through which people and resources are brought
back into balance after a period of population growth. What is the
evidence that wars in Liberia and Sierra Leone are influenced by
Malthusian pressures? Liberia and Sierra Leone both have high rates of
deforestation. Much of the fighting has been done in forested terrain.
But to make the Malthusian argument stick we need more precise
evidence that insurgent 'loose molecules' are direct victims of land
shortage and environmental degradation.

This chapter discusses deforestation and demographic trends in
Sierra Leone (with some parallel assessment of Liberian evidence),
leading to a closer examination (in Chapter Seven) of the character of
forest-edge communities over-run by the RUF rebellion. Chapter Eight
looks more broadly at the knowledge and attitudes of young people in
both rural and urban areas of Sierra Leone to deforestation and
processes of environmental change.

No direct connection between deforestation and war is found. More
advanced in Sierra Leone than Liberia, deforestation (as noted in
Chapter Three) is a long-term process, with several distinct phases,
none of which has yet produced 'environmental refugees'. As already
suggested, the typical Sierra Leonean insurgent is likely to be a
youthful, diamond-digging victim of state recession. The forest is, from
the standpoint of the RUF leadership, a practical theatre for educational
revival, in which the young captives learn bush-craft skills and develop
Rambo-like self-belief.

Both countries face environmental problems but *not* environmental
crises. Historically, local communities have long shown that they

understand, and are competent managers of, the ecological consequences of forest clearance. There seems little reason to suppose that
this capacity is about to desert them. Further broadly stable adaptive
changes might be expected, consistent with evidence from other parts of
Africa that 'more people' means 'more care for the environment' (Tiffen,
Mortimore and Gichuki 1994). The survey of young people's attitudes
supports this broadly optimistic assessment of prospects for managed
ecological change (Chapter Eight). Young people in Sierra Leone, of all
social backgrounds, living in both cities and rural areas, are
demonstrably rational, but far from complacent, about the ecological
changes they detect in their own environment. Even 'loose molecules'
have realistic and constructive ideas about how to deal with the
challenges of resource conservation in Africa today.

Deforestation in Liberia and Sierra Leone

The war in Sierra Leone grew out of the prior civil war in Liberia. It
makes little sense to pursue an argument linking land shortage,
environmental collapse, and the spread of violence, in Liberia, since it
is the least densely populated, and most thickly forested, country in the
region.

A ground survey of forests showed that in 1951 58 per cent of Liberia
was covered in closed-canopy rain forest, of which two-thirds was
unlogged (Parren and van der Graaf 1995). That figure has been eaten
into since, both by farming and lumbering, but even as recently as 1968
it was estimated that 25 per cent of the national territory was covered in
closed-canopy rain forest. So impenetrable were parts of the Liberian
forest that as late as the 1980s zoologists discovered a mammal species,
the Liberian mongoose (*Liberiictis kuhni*), hitherto unknown to science
except from skeletal remains. During the 1950s up-country communications and lumbering activities were so poorly developed that the
country *imported* its timber.

President Tubman opened the door to logging concessionaires at the
end of the 1950s, and transnational corporations were given a free hand
(Parren and van der Graaf 1995). Timber exploitation peaked in 1978/9
but steps were then taken to reserve forest land and develop more
sustainable methods of timber exploitation.

German forestry teams carried out many important scientific surveys
to establish a basis for conservation and rational forest management from
the 1960s onwards. A government forestry department was established
in the 1950s (half a century later than in neighbouring countries) and
was active, after the timber 'boom' of the 1970s peaked, in trying to
regulate the activities of concessionaires and implement scientific
management principles. On the eve of the civil war about 15 per cent of
the country remained in extraction reserves (National Forests).

The war has had serious consequences for rational management and conservation. The work of the forestry department was brought to a halt by the NPFL rebellion, and several forestry personnel killed. By 1993 there were two such departments, one in Monrovia and another in so-called 'Greater Liberia' (NPFL territory). Key scientific reports and data bases have been lost for ever. Parren and de Graaf (1995) were unable to trace some important records of the German-Liberian forestry research programme, even in Germany. According to Block (1992) France, Germany, UK, Italy, the Netherlands, Spain and Greece imported timber from NPFL territory. France is the destination for two-thirds of all Liberian timber exports, and Parren and van der Graaf (1995) note 'these operations fuel the . . . war and allow . . . uncontrolled creaming of [reserves]'.

Sierra Leone is two to three times more densely populated than Liberia, and the process of deforestation is much more complete. Kaplan (1994) believes there is here a clear link between population pressure and violence. But in making his point he relies upon two recurrent but erroneous statistical claims.

The first of these is the myth that 60 per cent of Sierra Leone was closed-canopy rain forest until recently. Variously the base-line is stated to be 'about the time of Second World War' or 'around Independence' (1961).

If Liberia was the last country in West Africa to become involved in international export of tropical timber, Sierra Leone was one of the first. British demand for mahogany (tropical red wood) dates to Elizabethan times, but over-exploitation of New World species caused importers to look to other regions (Parren and de Graaf 1995). The first trunks of West African mahogany (*Khaya* and *Entandrophragma* spp.) appeared on the British market in 1833. A substantial trade in *Khaya senegalensis* then developed from the Gambia, Senegal and Sierra Leone. This peaked during the 1850s and 1860s and 'then almost came to a standstill due to overexploitation' (Maloney 1887, cited in Parren and de Graaf 1995).

In 1908 the colonial government of Sierra Leone commissioned A. H. Unwin, Assistant Conservator of Forests from Southern Nigeria, to tour Sierra Leone and report on the forest estate and plans to set up a forestry department. Unwin (1909) reported that little if any closed forest remained along the line of rail from Freetown to Kenema. But east of Kenema, travelling down to the Liberia border, he was surprised to discover that in the vicinity of Faama (Nomo Chiefdom) there was a considerable area of true forest *west* of the Moro-Mano River (the boundary with Liberia).

He had expected the 'Gola Forest' to be entirely within Liberian territory. The unanticipated westward extension of the Gola Forest in Sierra Leone bore marks of old secondary forest (forest recovering from an earlier farming cycle). Local enquiries ascertained that this area had been earlier inhabited, but was depopulated as a result of struggles between Mende and Gola war-lords in the nineteenth century. Unwin recommended this area for reservation. Eventually (in the mid-1920s) three Gola reserves, today the major area of closed rainforest remaining in Sierra Leone, were delimited.

Commenting on the establishment of Gola East and West D. G. Thomas, Assistant Conservator of Forests, noted (in the 1923 *Annual Report*, Sierra Leone 1924) that no more than an estimated 3.5 per cent of the original forest cover of Sierra Leone remained intact. Effectively, the historical work of opening up forest land to new agricultural settlement in Sierra Leone had been completed by the beginning of the colonial period. Sierra Leone agriculture has been going through a period of consolidation and modest intensification of forest land use ever since (Richards 1985).

The second statistical 'myth' is that fallow periods for rotational bush fallowing in Sierra Leone have suffered a catastrophic reduction in recent years, and that this reduction signals a fast-approaching population/land-resource crisis. It is sometimes stated that fallow periods were anything from 30 to 100 years in the past, but that this interval has now been reduced to an average of about seven years (cf. LRD 1980).

Yet older descriptions of rotational fallowing rice farming systems in Sierra Leone and adjacent areas report even shorter fallow intervals, of three to four years (Cape Mount, c. 1640s [Dapper, 1668]) and four to seven years (Freetown peninsula, 1790s [Winterbottom 1803]). Douglas Scotland, the agriculturalist who first laid out a government experimental farm at Njala in 1912, planted his first rice trials on land that had been fallowed six to seven years, because this (he noted) was the local norm. The same norm prevailed in the Njala region 70 years later (Richards 1986).

Commentators pushing ecological-breakdown scenarios have failed to distinguish two distinct systems of utilization of farm land within the forest zone (Davies and Richards 1991). Pioneer shifting cultivation is a system for opening up high forest, undertaken every once in a while, when communities expanded or needed to relocate, perhaps for security reasons. It requires truly enormous efforts to fell the large trees. Thereafter the land is used in a rather intensive cycle for perhaps ten years. The very fertile forest soils can be farmed two years in succession. Farmers report that rice yields are better in the second year than in the first. Local rice varieties frequently lodge (over-extend the stalk and fall over) where soils are rich in nitrogen. The land newly released from forest may be left for three to five years and is then farmed for a third time, this time generally just for one year. Thereafter the land is either incorporated into a regular short-fallow cycle sequence, and used every six to ten years (depending on soil type), or it is allowed to revert to secondary forest until required (perhaps in the next generation).

Throughout periods of extensive forest conversion communities alternated between short expansive periods of pioneer long-fallow agriculture, to establish or relocate settlements and open up new farm land, and longer periods of more routine short-fallow agriculture. Farmers prefer short-fallow sites for regular use since these are easier to clear, and produce an abundance of poles suitable for house frames, farm huts and granaries. Older farmers, recalling some of the once-in-a-lifetime forest clearances of their youth, correctly report long-fallow intervals of '30 to 100 years'. But the evidence cited above shows that there must also have been plenty of short-fallow land around. The two systems co-existed, and it is wrong to project a trend from conflation of the two sets of figures.

The first rice farmers in the forest may have found it easier to manage somewhat open swampy sites rather than tackle the felling of the main upland forest (Chapter Three). Mende farmers call lowland sites of this kind *bului*. This is seemingly a loan-word from Sherbro, where the root means 'low' or 'bottom' (as in the ethnonym Bullom – 'the people of the coast' – or *boli*, a name applied in northern Sierra Leone to seasonally flooded grassy depressions with no drainage). Dutch traders, based at Cape Mount in the early seventeenth century, supplied Olfert Dapper with a good description of *bului* rice farming (Richards 1996b), and diamond diggers at Pandebu (a place too remote to headload white rice from town) were growing their own rice supplies in a classic *bului* at Vaama on the Moro River in 1989 (photograph in Richards 1996d). The boggy basin they farmed was sufficiently fertile to supply crops on a continuous five to six year cycle, with plots rotated around the basin without need for clearing the adjacent heavily forested uplands (this area of the Moro floodplain is closed-canopy forest, but outside the forest reserve).

As populations became more dense *bului* sites often proved insufficient, thus requiring upland rain forest clearance, and leading to the establishment of regular upland short-fallow cycles, with the occasional inter-generational 'gear change', as described above. Once forest conversion was complete (sometime during the nineteenth century) new processes – *in situ* intensification – began to play a more important part. In southern and eastern Sierra Leone (in the forest zone proper) this intensification also involved crop diversification, with farmers drawing upon New World root crops (cassava and sweet potatoes) and planting small areas of cash tree crops (especially coffee and cocoa). On many *bului* sites in the border region rice has now been replaced by cocoa.

Towards the margins of the forest in northern and north-western Sierra Leone intensification of farming systems was achieved by emphasis on groundnuts, planted, often by women, as a 'second season' crop following rice (Nyerges 1996), and by a steady move to greater rice cultivation in swamps (Richards 1985). Wetland rice cultivation is unattractive because of heavy initial labour requirements and health problems, but becomes an important option when rice yields begin to fall due to over-cultivation of uplands.

In the forest-transition zone fertility reduction sometimes leads to the interpolation of a fire-maintained grassy phase between cultivation and the return of bush fallow. Nyerges (1989, 1996) demonstrates, for a Guinea Savanna environment, that a second season of groundnut inhibits bush recovery by limiting the coppicing potential of tree stumps in upland farm sites. Waldock, Capstick and Browning (1951), noting the correlation between increased cultivation of groundnuts and the reduced potential of the bush to recover during fallow cycles, considered expansion of savanna to be one of the most serious ecological problems facing Sierra Leone. Although spreading at a much less rapid rate than they predicted, grassland invasion is a problem to some farmers within the forest-savanna transition, and accelerates their move into swamp cultivation. Leach and Fairhead (1994) show that, on the other hand, for at least some parts of the Upper Guinean forest-savanna transition (around Kissidougou in the Republic of Guinea), farming and local community management of environmental resources causes forest islands to *expand* at the expense of grassland (cf. Fairhead and Leach 1996). This innovative study provides strong confirmation that local farming communities understand the dynamics of vegetation change and are capable of ameliorating undesirable effects.

A similar point can be made in regard to intensification of rice agriculture through greater use of wetland. The trend to greater use of wetlands for rice cultivation in Sierra Leone can be traced to the late nineteenth century, and was well-established by the 1930s when Glanville (1938) wrote a report suggesting that local methods of development were often well-adapted to swamps with difficult water regimes, where dry season cultivation of groundnuts and sweet potatoes tended to be sustainably diverse, and an effective use of scarce labour. Studies since have confirmed the effectiveness of local wetland management systems (cf. Johnny, Karimu and Richards 1981).

Development agencies, inspired by Asian experience, and impatient (where they bother to look at all) at the slow rate of progress in agricultural intensification in Sierra Leone, have since anxiously tried to stimulate a major shift of emphasis from upland to wetland cultivation. These interventions have often backfired. As a result, many swamps now suffer desiccation or iron toxicity. Farmers demonstrate a willingness to *combine* wetland and upland production systems, but not to replace the latter with the former (Richards 1986). Glanville's stance, probably still sound as a basis for policy today, was to support local agronomic initiative and provide incentives for the greater use of indigenous discoveries in wetland management.

The three main points that emerge from this brief consideration of environmental changes associated with forest conversion in Sierra Leone are that:

- the process has taken place over many centuries, involving a number of distinct phases
- each phase has positive and negative features, well-understood by local land-users, who respond in sensible ways
- there is no evidence that environmental degradation has spiralled out of control in recent years.

Demographic change

On a world scale population densities over much of Africa are still low, but African growth rates are among the highest in the world. There is much argument and uncertainty about the historical context for these present high rates of increase. Is Africa, starting from a low base, the result of several centuries of slave raiding, infertility, and disease (the price of its contact with the global economy), 'catching up' the rest of the world? Or do present rates of rapid population growth represent the poor cashing in on one of the only assets open to them, the capacity to reproduce?

With little apparent confidence in the humanity, sense and collective commitment of the poor to the common good, neo-Malthusians tend to believe that ordinary Africans will 'sink their ship' by over-reproduction, unless checked by famine, war and disease. War is a process through which the poor in Africa will learn their limits.

Others, however, see evidence that a demographic transition to lower fertility is already under way. A key area is the behaviour and attitudes of young women. A general finding in developing countries is that when young women gain more access to schooling and employment they have fewer children. Clear evidence for this is apparent in African countries (Bledsoe and Cohen 1993).

Sierra Leone was, at Independence, the sixth most densely populated country in Africa (30 persons/km² in 1963). This figure should be qualified by mentioning that one of the countries ahead of Sierra Leone in the list was Nigeria, Africa's most populous country, containing perhaps one-fifth to one-quarter of the total population of sub-Saharan Africa at the time. Since then the population of Sierra Leone has grown at between 2.0 and 2.5 per cent/per annum. The final corrected figure for the 1985 census was a total population of 3.22 million (45 persons/km²), 150 per cent of the 1963 figure. The population, mid-1990s, is likely to be around or slightly more than 4 million.

In 1963, at district level, the highest population densities were found in the north-west (in Kambia and Port Loko Districts, 44 and 43 persons/km²) and the lowest in the savanna north (Koinadugu

District, 11 persons/km^2). By 1974, with the continued strong growth of alluvial diamond mining in the east, the pattern had changed, and Kono District was now the most densely populated district (58 persons/km^2). By 1985 population densities varied between 15 persons/km^2 in the savanna north of the country (Koinadugu District), through 27 persons/km^2 in Pujehun (the lowest density for any district in the forest zone) to high figures for Kambia and Port Loko (58 and 57 persons/km^2) and for the three main mining districts in the south and east (Bo, 51 persons/km^2; Kenema, 55 persons/km^2; and Kono, 58 persons/km^2). It is interesting to note, however, that Kailahun District, with a mixed economy based on cash crops, diamonds and trade (much of it smuggled) had become the most populous district in the whole of Sierra Leone (61 persons/km^2).

At chiefdom level census figures reveal a varied pattern of population densities. The two main areas of high population density are confirmed as being an area of old commercial and agricultural development associated with the navigable stretches of the rivers between Freetown and the Guinea border in the north-west (i.e. around Kambia and Port Loko), and chiefdoms in the east and south of the country along the axis of the Sewa River from Kono to Bo and beyond, to which young men have been migrating from all over Sierra Leone since the first days of the diamond 'boom' (1953–56). These 'diamond chiefdoms' are character-ized by a strong excess of males over females in the population.

In some areas, by contrast, rural population densities are low and declining. In the still heavily forested country north of Bo the largest local chiefdom, Valunia, experienced absolute population decline between 1963 and 1985 (in common with about 20 per cent of all chiefdoms in the country). Throughout Sierra Leone local land-tenure systems are flexible. In-migrants ('strangers') are nearly always welcomed, and encouraged to stay by being given land on which to farm annual crops without rent (a token payment is made to acknowledge the rights of the land-owning lineage). The existence of areas such as Valunia Chiefdom, with good agricultural land going begging, shows that there is little 'land hunger' in Sierra Leone as such. This is confirmed by research in and around the Gola Forest reserve in 1989 (Davies and Richards 1991).

Adjacent to the most densely populated rural region in Sierra Leone the Gola reserves, it might be expected, would be subject to considerable encroachment by landless farmers. In detailed studies in three villages on the edge of Gola North we came across only four cases of agricultural encroachment on the forest reserve, all by local farmers with abundant land elsewhere, but still regarding land acquired by government in 1926 as belonging to their lineage. In other words, they had moved into the forest not because they were driven by land shortage but because they wished to make a political point.

One reason why there is still under-utilized agricultural land in

Sierra Leone, despite quite high population densities and little constraint on internal migration, is that government has subsidized urban and mining populations with cheap food from overseas. Agricultural advance in other parts of the world, including the Green Revolution countries of South-East Asia, has made rice cheaper relative to other commodities. The bag of imported white rice is, *par excellence*, both the symbol of political patronage (a sign that the government 'cares' for its employees and populace at large) and also the means by which sponsors in the diamond mining business supply their diggers in the forest. As noted, many diamond sponsors are busy entrepreneurs or government employees, and few have time to buy and bag husk rice in the villages. They prefer to send a truck to the dockside and then send on the bags of rice to the 'boys in the bush' with minimum fuss. The APC government, using its control over the Central Bank, money supply, and foreign exchange reserves, and access to overseas credit, bought in cheap rice whenever prices to farmers looked set to rise. Private entrepreneurs used their own foreign exchange from smuggled diamonds or parallel market sources for the same purpose.

A second reason for under-utilization of agricultural land in Sierra Leone is that government, through a monopoly marketing board, maintained price controls for the purchase of the main cash export crops, coffee and cocoa. This, in effect, taxed farmers on their output, unless they were in a position to smuggle to Liberia. Many did, thus weakening government political control over border districts. Elsewhere farmers paid up, grumbled, and (in some cases) returned to subsistence agriculture. If they were young enough they thought about spending time as a diamond digger.

Marketing board taxes were used by government to strengthen its patronage over the political system as a whole, paying (among other things) for more imports of white rice. As noted earlier, the political economy of Sierra Leone was one in which the political classes and their business allies made their money from mining – principally diamonds – and used their political power further to extend this interest at the expense of agriculture. Despite the many schemes devoted to the development of rice farming in Sierra Leone, government was never interested in rice, only in *cheap* rice. In fact this rice had to be increasingly cheap, since it was needed to support large numbers of young men combing the less rich gravel deposits, as diamond mining fanned out to the limits of potential production along the border.

Conclusion

If there is a demographic crisis in Sierra Leone it is not in farming, but in what is happening to armies of young tributors as they reach the limits of the present mineral economy. Here they are faced with

Hobson's Choice – continuing to hustle for a living under increasingly adverse conditions or returning to an agricultural sector long sucked dry by the macroeconomic needs of diamonds. As the slogan on the front of a shiny new truck plying the Bo-Freetown highway on the first day of the APC 'economic emergency' in October 1987 put it, 'The Party's Over'. The party in question was not a neo-Malthusian binge, but more specifically the APC one-party regime, and the patrimonial shadow state over which it presided. As in Liberia, war is a consequence of political collapse and state recession, not environmental pressure. In both countries violence has been incubated in forest fastnesses. From a strategic perspective, the problem in Liberia and Sierra Leone is too much forest, not too little.

7

On the Edge State Recession
& Social Exclusion

Introduction

If there are (in Kaplan's phrase) 'loose molecules' in Sierra Leonean
society (young people detached from the wider social fabric) who are
they, and where are they to be found? Kaplan looks for them among the
urban unemployed. The present chapter looks beyond the recession-
shrunk edges of the state. Here we find not impoverished criminals but
entrepreneurial types lured by diamonds. Stranded by state recession,
these 'young people' seek not revolution but re-attachment to a
functioning state system.

Agricultural flux and urban unemployment

According to the 1985 census most rural Sierra Leoneans (on average
85–90 per cent) were enumerated in the district in which they were
born (with the percentage for women generally being two or three points
higher than for men). But there is some social flux in the countryside.

There was a 35 per cent turnover in heads of farm enterprises within
five years, in a Mende farming community, Mogbuama, studied in 1983
and again 1987 (Richards 1986, 1995b). Some of this turnover was
accounted for by young men leaving to try their hand as tributors in the
diamond mining areas, but the balance was accounted for by moves in
the other direction (young people returning home after a period,
sometimes successful, sometimes not, as migrants to city or mine). The
home community acts as a safety net for the young, and contacts tend to
be carefully nourished. The rural social flux tends to be conservative (cf.
Burnham 1980).

There were, however, two areas where substantial numbers of people
were enumerated outside the district of their birth – Freetown, and the
diamond mining districts (Bo, Kenema and Kono). Migrants amounted
to more than a third of the total population in both Freetown and Kono.

To what extent are migrants excluded from society by unemployment? A 1989 labour force survey reveals basically low rates of unemployment in Sierra Leone (Central Statistics Office, 1991). Once a methodologically satisfactory definition of 'work' is employed there is very little, if any, unemployment in the countryside. People are too busy surviving, or washing gravel.

Unemployment in Sierra Leone is an urban phenomenon (Illustration 7.1). But perhaps surprisingly, it is for males mainly a problem for the educated classes (Illustration 7.2). The highest rate is found among those who have completed secondary school without achieving qualifications. Members of this group will tend to report themselves 'unemployed' because they have left school, but perhaps for several years they repeat examinations in the hope of better results. If these are Kaplan's 'loose molecules' then the chances are they could flourish a well-thumbed copy of *Newsweek* and quote liberally from Macbeth.

Pandebu, 1989[1]

Let us take a different path, and cross the Gola Forest to the Liberian border. Here, state influence (from either Liberia or Sierra Leone) is at its weakest. Insurgency has been the norm since 1990, in territory variously contested and controlled by RUF, NPFL, ULIMO, ECOMOG, and Sierra Leone government forces.

Pandebu is the last village in Sierra Leone (Illustration 2.3). There are paths to Pandebu from Faama, the roadhead and headquarters of Nomo Chiefdom, and from Lalehun, an old logging camp on the western edge of the Gola North Reserve. In each case the journey is a full day's trek.

The track from Lalehun crosses the full extent of Gola North from west to east. The first section is an old and overgrown timber road abandoned when logging of the Gola North reserve proved too difficult and expensive in the 1970s. The track then turns into a rocky footpath through unlogged forest, finally climbing to the low but rugged summit of the Gendema Hills, before dropping sharply into the valley trench of the Moro River, the international border between Sierra Leone and Liberia. Our party, from the Gola Forest Project, was on its way (in July 1989) to Pandebu hoping to carry out a census, one in a series covering villages in the immediate vicinity of the Forest Reserve. The outskirts of Pandebu were reached towards dusk.

The first (and surprising) sign of human habitation was a lean-to mud out-building with a large oven. This proved to be the village bakery. Here, in one of Sierra Leone's least accessible villages, a Fula migrant from the Republic of Guinea supplied his rural clientele's sophisticated taste for the fresh *baguette*. Diamond diggers do not deprive themselves of life's little luxuries.

[1] This passage draws on material to be published in Richards (1996a) and (1996b).

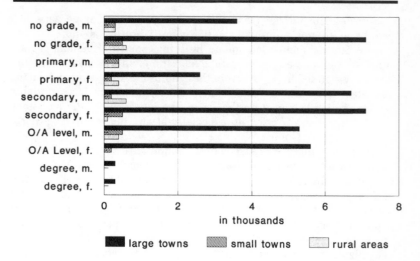

7.1   Unemployment in Sierra Leone, 1988–9, by gender, location and
      educational level

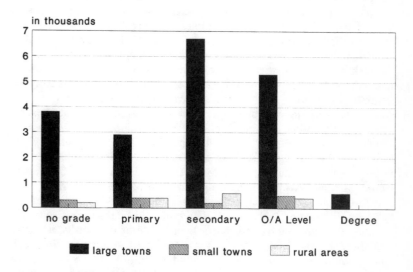

7.2   Male unemployment in Sierra Leone, 1988–9, by location and educational
      level

Entering the village we discovered a settlement of perhaps 350 people, with numerous substantially built houses, a mosque, and several *semei* (open-sided square buildings in which hammocks are slung for their owners' evening-time relaxation and conversation around a rainy-season log fire). Several of these buildings were already relaying the latest news on the BBC's *Focus on Africa*, from large portable cassette-radios balanced on the *kakei* (the low walls of the hammock houses). Ears would prick up especially at any items covering Sierra Leone, Liberia or Guinea.

Tired and hungry, we caused consternation on arrival. If our visit was unannounced it was not for want of trying. Several times we attempted to complete the formal procedures for a survey visit to Pandebu, as part of a reconnaissance of forest resources on the eastern side of the Gola reserve. A letter prepared by the Senior District Officer in Kenema requested the Paramount Chief to offer every assistance in our work. But the elegant official missive proved hard to deliver. The chief was unavailable to us on several visits to his headquarters at Faama, called away at short notice from meetings booked days in advance, or indisposed. Finally, a research assistant decided to short-cut the problem by carrying the letter directly to the town chief of Pandebu. As a teacher in the nearest school to Pandebu (30 km away) he was well-known to parents of Pandebu children lodged in Lalehun to attend his class. But despite protracted negotiations the village authorities in Pandebu decided they would still need to consult higher authority. Again we waited. No reply came. Survey plans were falling seriously behind schedule, so it was decided to chance a casual visit, hoping local standards of hospitality might prevail over political diffidence. After considerable initial awkwardness places were found for us to sleep.

Walking down to the Moro River we encountered, on the Sierra Leonean side, a group of Liberians mining diamonds. Hearing us approach, a Liberian ferry-man was already half-way across the river to collect us, assuming we were diggers intending to cross back into Liberia. There must be other unsupervised border crossing points, 'unknown' to the authorities of either country, behind the leafy curtain of the Gola Reserves. The unlogged forest is penetrated by several tracks, and the upper portions of the Moro and Mano rivers pose no great obstacles to canoe passage, except when in spate at the height of the rains. The splendid rapids at Vanjema on the Moro some seven kilometres north of Pandebu (Illustration 7.3) can even be forded during the dry season.

Liberian influence on the Sierra Leone side of the border is easily explained by the basic facts of local transport geography. To reach Faama, the headquarters of Nomo Chiefdom, from Pandebu requires an eight to ten hour trek on a rough track skirting the river. A rickety vehicle might or might not be available the next morning for the expensive and unreliable trip over 60 km of very poorly maintained dirt roads to Kenema. Onward travel to Freetown takes a third day. After the canoe

7.3   Vanjema rapids, Moro river: the Sierra Leone–Liberia border

trip across the Moro, Pandebu people reach the Liberian roadhead in
three hours, and expected to be in Monrovia that same evening. It was
from Monrovia that the Fula baker obtained his flour, and Pandebu
householders their cement, corrugated roofing sheets and all other
heavy building supplies. Monrovia was also the place where diamonds
mined in Pandebu would be sold. Some of the Pandebu miners had
Liberian family connections, and Monrovia-based supporters. Prudently,
most Pandebu residents seemed to have identity cards for both
countries. In effect they were citizens of two states, or perhaps (in their
hearts) of neither.

'Loose molecules' in context

A few facts will serve to place Pandebu in broader geographical and
sociological context. The 1989 Gola survey (Davies and Richards, 1991)
studied 12 villages at various distances from the Gola North reserve.
Data were collected on demographics, household organization, kinship,
and occupations. Detailed studies were then undertaken of farming and
forest activities in three settlements (Richards 1992a). Data were
aggregated for two distinct groups of settlements – those located
immediately on the forest edge and larger, established villages, farther
from the forest, where forest conversion was a more distant memory.

One of the issues the study sought to clarify was whether there were
major differences between forest-edge and non-forest villages in terms of
occupations, social structure, and political stability.

Due to past low population densities and the heavy labour demands of high-forest agriculture, Mende communities along the border, in common with rural communities throughout much of the forest zone in Liberia and Sierra Leone, have long had an open and welcoming attitude to 'strangers' (*hota*). Valued and high-status strangers, such as Mandingo traders, are encouraged to settle, and merge their interests with those of the local political elite, through marriage to the daughter of a chief. Lower-status strangers will at first seek the protection of a village landlord (*hotakɛɛ*), working for the landlord for a number of years as farm labourers. A valued worker may then be granted land, marry locally, and become a settled stranger, fully subject, as an independent citizen, to community norms and laws. Prior to this point a stranger is not expected to be fully cognizant of community laws, and will be represented in any legal matter by his *hotakɛɛ*.

Murphy and Bledsoe (1987) show that these two processes for the incorporation of strangers are the historical basis for the emergence of characteristically heterogeneous Kpelle communities in north-west Liberia (cf. Currens 1972; Leopold 1991). Over time Kpelle history has been 're-written' so that the descendants of loyal and successful strangers are presented as members of the foundational elite. Similar points could be made for the historically diverse Mende-speaking communities of the Gola forest and its environs.

Modern conditions have significantly reduced the effectiveness of these processes of social incorporation and local institution building. By how much is a matter for debate (cf. Hardin 1992). Not all strangers have plans to settle, even if offered the chance. This is especially true of tributors, because diamond sites are easily exhausted, and new finds, or rumours of finds, brightly beckon elsewhere.

At one point in the late 1980s a group of perhaps several hundred tributors was camped in the catchment of the Mobai stream in the heart of unlogged forest in Gola North. Many left in a matter of weeks when new and more profitable sites were discovered elsewhere. In August 1989 diamonds were discovered in river terrace deposits close to the village of Mendekelema. Within a few days the population of the settlement had almost doubled with the influx of diggers and camp followers (Illustration 7.4).

Among the camp followers are the traders in second-hand clothing; frequent bright displays of hand-me-down fashions – *jɔnks* (junk) in Krio – hanging from the rafters of village mud house verandas, are a sure-fire indicator of a diamond village in eastern Sierra Leone. The coffee plantation in which the diamonds were first discovered was transformed into a series of excavations resembling the foundations of a new housing estate almost overnight (Illustration 7.5), to the chagrin of land owners anxious about compensation for their trees. Village political authorities often have great difficulty in establishing control when a diamond rush breaks. The difficulty is compounded by the fact

7.4 *Diamond diggers, Gola Forest, 1989*

7.5   *Diamond workings, Gola Forest, 1989*

that a significant proportion of the diggers and the traders in their wake are long-distance migrants sometimes with little knowledge or respect for the spiritual sanctions on which village political institutions still depend for their effectiveness.

Forest-edge villages around Gola in 1989 did indeed contain a much higher proportion of strangers than the non-forest villages; 76 per cent of all stranger-headed households, 65 per cent of 15-plus stranger males, and 55 per cent of all 15-plus stranger females, were to be found in forest-edge settlements, whereas forest-edge villages accounted for only 47 per cent of the total population of the 12 sample villages (Table 7.1). In fact, in forest-edge villages the stranger element constitutes a majority – 59 per cent of the total population and 53 per cent of all heads of household, though this latter figure is reduced to 36 per cent if the old logging camp at Lalehun, dominated by strangers, is removed from the sample (Table 7.2).

How many of these strangers were incorporated through the established social institutions? It is not easy to tell from social surveys and censuses since true squatters do not readily reveal themselves to an interviewer. I recall several times arriving in one of the smaller and more dubious diamond villages on the Gola border to meet cooking pots on the go, a faint cloud of *jamba* (marijuana) wafting on the breeze, even a tape player singing to itself, and not a single inhabitant in sight. But data on geographical origins and marriage patterns among strangers painstakingly compiled by our diamond-digging, street-credible, Gola Forest research assistants provide some clues (Table 7.3).

The single largest category of strangers comprises men and women who have moved from a neighbouring village within the same chiefdom, or from a chiefdom elsewhere in Kenema District (53 per cent); migrants from elsewhere in Mende country comprise 36 per cent, migrants from elsewhere in Sierra Leone account for 6 per cent, and foreigners (mainly from Guinea and Liberia) the remaining 5 per cent. The numbers of long-distance migrants are not large, though some may have taken pains to evade the census. What is important about Table 7.3, however, is that it shows that in every case the more distant the category of origin the lower the percentage of strangers in this category residing in non-forest villages. In other words, long-distance migrants, least likely to be familiar with and to show respect for local cultural and political norms, are concentrated in forest-edge villages; 62 per cent of foreigners and 70 per cent of non-Mende strangers in the sample were found in the villages closest to the forest reserves on the Liberian border.

A detail worth noting is that the figure for the small but important group of Guinean foreigners is somewhat out of line with the general trend (just over half of all Guineans are found in non-forest villages in the sample). This is because, as traders and Islamic teachers, the Fula and Mandingo tend to be attracted to longer-established villages with transport connections, than to pioneer communities along the forest edge. The converse is true of Liberians (over three-quarters of all Liberians in the sample are found in forest-edge villages). This is due to the proximity of the forest reserves to the Liberian border, and to the fact that many Liberians are involved in hunting or cross-border trade.

Data on marriage patterns also reveal important contrasts between forest-edge and non-forest villages. Women strangers account for 54 per cent of all strangers in the 12 villages. Most (77 per cent) have come as spouses, their geographical origins similar to male strangers. The size of this group in any village is a measure of the relative lack of incorporation of strangers into the local fabric of society through marriage alliances with land-owning elites, and of the 'pioneer' opportunities that call migrants to the forest edge (Table 7.4). The numbers of such marriages range from a mere 7 per cent of all spouse-pairs in Sandaru, the village farthest from the forest margin, to 75 per cent in Lalehun Barracks, the former lumbering camp on the forest boundary. Lalehun (because of its history) has an especially large number of marriages in this category, but other forest-edge villages tend to have more stranger pairs than the non-forest villages.

Turning to marriages between citizen-wives and stranger-husbands (the marriage pattern that promotes 'neo-traditional' stability) the picture is less clear-cut (Table 7.5). We might expect that villages open to migration but expanding in an orderly 'neo-traditional' way, with local political institutions intact, will show significantly higher propor-tions of citizen-wife/stranger-husband alliances as a proportion of all marriages involving citizen-wives.

This is indeed the case in the smaller 'neo-traditional' settlements close to the forest edge, with a recent history of largely agrarian 'pioneer' expansion. For example, stranger-husband/citizen-wife marriages account for between a third and a half of all marriages involving citizen-wives in Lalehun Tawovehun, Waiyehun, Jagbema and a series of forest hamlets on the western side of Gola.

But in Sandaru, Sembehun and Pandebu this form of marriage accounts for only 10, 25 and 24 per cent of marriages involving citizen-wives (Table 7.5). What links these three settlements, despite the different points they occupy on the forest-conversion continuum? Sandaru is the most strongly 'non-forest' village in the sample, and as a large, established settlement, has the human resources to 'fund' intensification (e.g. the move to cash tree crops) from within, without needing to attract many in-marrying migrants. Sembehun and Pandebu are also large villages. But they are also the most strongly oriented towards diamond mining. Both have more than 50 adult males declaring diamond mining as one of their occupations (61 per cent of the male labour force in Pandebu and 35 per cent in Sembehun). In the other large villages in the sample (Lalehun, Jagbema and Sandaru) diamonds accounted for less than 5 per cent of male employment (Illustration 7.6). The point has already been made. The tributors by virtue of their

Table 7.1   Social and age categories, forest-edge and non-forest villages compared, Gola Forest, 1989

	Forest-edge villages	Non-forest-edge villages	All villages
heads of household	244 (47.7%)	267 (52.3%)	511 (100%)
stranger heads	128 (76.0%)	41 (24.0%)	169 (100%)
female heads	4 (44.4%)	5 (55.5%)	9 (100%)
females 15-plus	460 (44.7%)	568 (55.3%)	1,028 (100%)
males 15-plus	478 (49.2%)	494 (50.8%)	972 (100%)
female strangers 15-plus	302 (54.9%)	248 (45.1%)	550 (100%)
male strangers 15-plus	247 (64.7%)	135 (35.3%)	382 (100%)
all persons 15-plus	938 (46.9%)	1,062 (53.1%)	2,000 (100%)
all strangers 15-plus	549 (58.9%)	383 (41.1%)	932 (100%)
all strangers	648 (57.9%)	472 (42.1%)	1,120 (100%)
all female strangers	341 (56.0%)	268 (44.0%)	609 (100%)
all male strangers	307 (60.1%)	204 (39.9%)	51 (100%)
Total Population	1,487 (46.4%)	1,719 (53.6%)	3,206 (100%)

Source: Davies and Richards 1991

Table 7.2   The importance of strangers and stranger-headed households within villages, Gola North Forest Reserve, 1989

	Stranger heads/ All heads	Adult strangers/ All adults
Forest-edge villages	128/244 52.5%	549/938 58.5%
Forest edge (excluding Lalehun Barracks)	62/172 36.0%	395/673 58.7%
Non-forest-edge villages	41/267 15.4%	343/1,062 32.3%

Source: Davies and Richards 1991

Table 7.3   Geographical origins of strangers in survey villages

Place of origin	A. Total number of strangers		B. Strangers in non-forest settlements		
Kenema District	560	52.8%	236	B/A	42.0%
Gaura	227				
Tunkia	87				
Nomo	74				
Other Chiefdoms	172				
Other Mende- speaking districts	384	36.2%	154	B/A	40.1%
Bo	76		28		
Bonthe	19		10		
Kailahun	188		89		
Moyamba	50		13		
Pujehun	51		14		
Non-Mende districts	67	6.3%	18	B/A	26.9%
Bombali	18		6		
Kambia	0		0		
Koinadugu	10		2		
Kono	13		3		
Port Loko	11		1		
Tonkolili	12		5		
Western Area	3		1		
Foreign countries	50	4.7%	19	B/A	38.0%
Guinea	27		14		
Liberia	22		5		
Nigeria	1		0		
Total	1,061	100.0%	427	B/A	40.2%

Table 7.4 Marriage patterns in border-zone villages

Village	Stranger-husband/ Citizen-wife	Citizen-husband/ Stranger-wife	Stranger-husband/ Stranger-wife	Citizen-husband/ Citizen-wife
Sembehun (n=173)	20 12%	76 44%	19 11%	57 33%
Sandaru (n=199)	13 7%	64 32%	12 6%	108 55%
Jagbema (n=91)	16 18%	29 32%	21 23%	25 27%
Lalehun Barracks (n=71)	53 75%	7 10%	9 13%	1 1%
Lalehun Tawovehun (n=40)	8 28%	19 45%	7 18%	6 15%
Forest hamlets (n=101)	35 34%	39 38%	12 12%	14 124%
Pandebu (n=72)	9 13%	34 47%	7 10%	22 31%
Waiyehun (n=48)	11 23%	23 48%	6 13%	8 17%

Source: Davies and Richards 1991

Table 7.5 Social incorporation by marriage, border villages

Village	A. Citizen-wives	B. Citizen-wives with stranger-husbands	Percentage B/A
Sembehun	76	19	25
Sandaru	120	12	10
Jagbema	46	21	46
Lalehun Barracks	10	9	90
Lalehun Tawovehun	13	7	54
Forest hamlets	26	12	46
Pandebu	29	7	24
Waiyehun	14	6	43

Source: Davies and Richards 1991

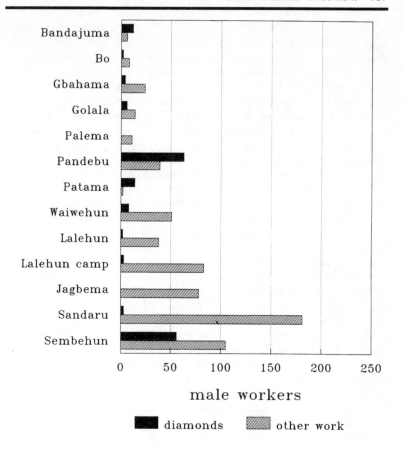

male workers

■ diamonds   ▨ other work

Source: fieldwork

7.6   Patterns of male employment, Gola Forest villages, 1989

work tend to be less well bound into local civil society. This makes it doubly important that they should have a clear sense of national identity. Schools and roads would have helped. But denied these facilities, the diamond tributors of Pandebu floated in political limbo. The RUF stepped smartly into the breach. Perhaps, in the rural diamond-mining slums of Sierra Leone we have met our 'loose molecules' at last?

Conclusion

The tributors of Pandebu had an intuition of the disaster ahead. It transpired that keeping the village off-limits was convenient only to the external sponsors of diamond mining, not to the tributors themselves. Radios and baguettes for breakfast were no compensation for the disadvantages of social detachment. If it was up to them, tributors would prefer to be recognized as citizens of a real state and the modern world. Well-coached by international news broadcasts, they were convinced of the importance of education as a passport to modernity. Several young diamond diggers had part-completed their secondary education. Some had come to Pandebu as school drop-outs seeking a more exciting life during the heady days of the 1960s and 1970s diamond boom. But others – the greater number – had been forced into digging and washing gravel by lack of funds to complete their schooling.

Now half a generation later they were raising children of their own, and preoccupied with the problem of education. Lalehun, a day's march away, had a small primary school in a half-rotten building with two teachers unpaid for months on end. Pandebu had no school at all. Parents in Pandebu were struck by the fact that national political leaders sometimes sent their own children to expensive schools overseas, drawing on diamond wealth from Pandebu and villages like it. Overseas schooling might cost ten times per child what it would take to run an entire village primary school for a year. Their first priority, then, was to establish a primary school. But this would depend on having a road. 'What school teacher would ever stay in a place like Pandebu when it is so hard to enter and leave?', they asked. Initial suspicion of our census gave way to enthusiasm. They reasoned the census would support their case for demanding these two key facilities; the figures would reveal to the world exactly how many children in these 'stateless' backwoods had no chance of any schooling at all.

The adviser to President Momoh heard the case for the road without comment, and politely but promptly changed the topic of conversation. The same argument drew a more animated response from professional colleagues in conservation. Keen to maintain the isolation of communities like Pandebu to protect Africa's remaining forest wildernesses, they were quick to distance themselves from any suggestion of road building as an element in an integrated plan for the Gola reserves (cf. Adams and McShane 1992). Liberian and Sierra Leonean Gola should not be divided by a road for the sake of the elephants. But the Pandebu people had correctly divined, what might happen to the region's human population, without road and school. In the end it was not population pressure, but the remoteness of the state, the weakness of its infrastructure, and the lack of political imagination of its leaders, that served to draw insurgency into this border region. War, feeding upon the frustrations of exiles, not only destroyed villages like Pandebu but threatened the survival of the state, and with it the forest itself.

8

War, Resources & the Future

Youth Attitudes to Forest Insurgency

Introduction

New Barbarism considers the young in Africa to be an anarchic element. Is this how young people see themselves? This chapter asks young Sierra Leoneans to explain their own ideas about war, resources and the future. The material comes from a sample survey of knowledge and attitudes of young people in three areas of Sierra Leone. As described in Chapter Five, a quota sampling methodology secured approximately equal representation of males and females, three age classes, and three educational groupings. Young people with incomplete secondary education, the group with the highest unemployment rate in Sierra Leone (see Chapter Seven), are particularly strongly represented in the sample. If the fabric of society has been stretched thin this is where problems might be expected to be most apparent.

Forest products and youth subsistence

Forests were once seen by economists largely as sources of timber. More recently, various studies have established that a wide range of forest products is of importance in the lives and survival strategies of the rural poor in tropical rain forest countries. A review by Falconer (1990) brings out the importance of a range of non-timber forest products (NTFPs), including medicinal plants, food items and 'bush meat', throughout West Africa. Foraging provides many of these items (Richards 1992a). Other items are in such high demand that they are regularly traded (Henkemans 1995).

Our survey attempted to gain some impression of whether young people in Freetown, Kambia and Bo remain in any way dependent on items of forest produce, and what that pattern of dependence might be, as a prelude to asking questions about attitudes to the forest and forest conservation. The interview schedule included questions about items of forest produce used in the household at large, and then personally by the interviewee (it was anticipated that the youngest age group in the sample would not have their own items of kitchen equipment, for example). The data reported here cover only the items of forest produce young people depend on for personal use. Interviewees were then asked whether it was becoming more difficult to obtain these items, and why, and how they were acquired (by collection or purchase).

In all, 421 interviews in Freetown, Kambia and Bo yielded information on a total of 1,756 items. The single largest category of items (21 per cent) was kitchen implements (mainly mortars, pestles, grinding boards, and cooking spoons). Food items accounted for a further 21 per cent (vegetable products 10 per cent, fruits 6 per cent and bush meat 5 per cent). The last figure confirms that bush meat is of smaller importance in Sierra Leone, where fish is the main animal protein, than in Ghana and Nigeria (cf. Falconer 1990). The other items were fuel (mainly firewood, 14 per cent), building materials (12 per cent), medical and hygiene requisites (9 per cent) and household goods (furniture, mats, bedding) (9 per cent).

The majority of items (62 per cent) were bought, but the importance of purchasing varied according to locale (Table 8.1). In Kambia (the smallest urban centre) 62 per cent of items were gathered; in the capital Freetown this figure drops to 10 per cent. The relative importance of purchase and collection varies by category of item. Building materials, food items and medical supplies are 63 per cent, 54 per cent and 53 per cent gathered, but 88 per cent and 93 per cent of kitchen and household items are purchased. This translates into a gender difference. Except perhaps in Freetown, young men hunt and often do quite a lot of construction and repair work on their dwellings. Women's kitchen and household items, by contrast, are mainly purchased from a craft specialist. Women accounted for 57 per cent of all bought items, but men accounted for 57 per cent of all collected items (Table 8.2). This, it seems, tallies with a later finding that young men tend to propose draconian 'protective' legislation to halt the decline in supplies of forest products, whereas young women favour technological options for increased output of essential supplies, when asked how to halt the damage caused by deforestation.

Overall, it was reported that for 56 per cent of items procurement had become more difficult over time, whereas in 44 per cent of cases there was said to be no difference, or items had become more readily available. Price escalation was given as the major cause of difficulty in 14 per cent of cases, and deforestation was directly cited in another 9 per cent of cases. Uncontrolled bush fires were cited by 76 interviewees, nearly all (91 per cent) in the Kambia sample. The problem of annual grass fires in the forest–savanna transition zone has already been noted. Thirteen interviewees (six in Bo and seven in Freetown) specifically

Table 8.1   Young Sierra Leoneans' access to forest products

	Bought	Collected
Freetown	356 (90%)	38 (10%)
Kambia	153 (38%)	255 (62%)
Bo	513 (65%)	278 (35%)

Source: 1993–4 survey

Table 8.2   Source of forest products by gender

	Male	Female
Bought	467 (43%)	618 (57%)
Collected	355 (57%)	266 (43%)

mentioned the rebel incursion as a cause of supply difficulties, because people were too afraid to venture far into the bush without military protection. But overall, fewer interviewees complained that bush products were harder to acquire in Freetown (43 per cent) than in Bo (57 per cent) and Kambia (69 per cent). This seems to be directly related to the fact that 90 per cent of NTFPs in Freetown are acquired through market channels. Although some informants were worried about price trends, in a period of steep inflation and falling real incomes, others detected the impact of improved fuel supply and transportation following the NPRC coup in 1992.

Experience of the forest

What direct knowledge of forests do young Sierra Leoneans possess? How well-based in experience are their ideas about deforestation and its social significance?

Over two-thirds of the sample (68 per cent) claimed to have visited a forest, and were able to provide a date and location. Women (50 per cent of the sample overall) were not far behind the men in accounting for 48 per cent of all such visits. Over three-quarters of all interviewees in Kambia had visited a forest, but the figure was high (66 per cent) for Freetown interviewees as well. Bo slightly lags behind the other two centres, with only 64 per cent of interviewees having visited a forest. This is slightly surprising in a place where forest-capped hill tops can still be glimpsed from within the town. Age made some difference, with the under-20 age group (as might be expected) somewhat less likely to have visited a forest (60 per cent of all under-20s) than older interviewees. The small group (33 persons) of city-born interviewees in the Freetown sample was least likely to have direct knowledge of a forest (45 per cent). Even so, this figure is quite high, and reflects the fact that the protected forests of the Peninsula mountains are within easy reach of the city.

The more highly educated are the *most likely* to have direct experience of forests (74 per cent of all interviewees with secondary or higher education). But a surprisingly large proportion of the sample overall (25 per cent) had made such a visit for the sake of seeing the forest, and without having any direct practical motive; two-thirds of this group had secondary or higher education. Some had made their visit on an organized field trip from school, but others were responding to a whim or private intellectual enthusiasm. Some were drawn by the hope of seeing wild animals. Others wanted to know the different kinds of forest trees. One interviewee claimed his visit was made 'to see how life began'. There is no clear evidence, here, that modernity cuts off young Sierra Leoneans from their forest roots. Forests remain an important part of the heritage of the young in Sierra Leone.

Many interviewees, of course, had more directly practical reasons for visiting forests. Eleven per cent had entered forests in the course of hunting expeditions (including six women). Society initiation or forest burial were cited in another seven per cent of cases. But experience of forest when gathering firewood accounted for 21 per cent of visits. Women gave this as their single most important reason for visiting forests (61 per cent of all firewood collection visits).

Seven interviewees had experienced life in a real rain forest for the first time as a result of the insurgency; as one interviewee put it, forced to flee through the forest 'to escape rebel bondage'.

In all, 334 interviewees thought there were clear differences between 'forest' and 'bush', and proceeded to describe these differences with considerable accuracy. Most interviewees noted obvious features such as the size and type of trees, and other vegetation features distinguishing a true rain forest from 'farm bush'. Several noted that elephant grass and 'bush razor' (*Scleria barteri*) are signs of secondary disturbance. Some remarked that wild fruits and palm trees are much more numerous in bush than in forest. Many saw 'wild', 'large', 'strange', 'bad' and 'tricky' animals as a distinguishing feature of forest, and correctly associated small animals such as 'cutting grass' (the cane rat, *Thrynonomys swinderianus*) with bush (the cane rat depends on grassy wetland areas for dry-season survival, so its numbers may sharply increase when swamp forest is cleared for farming). Someone correctly noted that snakes were more common in bush than high forest. Interviewees frequently remarked that high forest was relatively clear at ground level, and visibility was good, whereas bush was impenetrable thicket; the point was often made that 'you can run through forest, but not through bush'. Forest was frequently characterized as 'cool', 'moist', and 'dark' whereas bush was more open to sunlight, hotter and drier. Bush soils were 'drier than forest soils', and one School Certificate candidate, perhaps reflecting a well-taught geography lesson, remarked that the canopy leaves held moisture, but that in bush 'rain runs on the ground'.

A number of interviewees, all in Kambia and Bo, were impressed by the forest as a lonely and dangerous place, containing grave sites, evil spirits, and many large trees behind which wicked persons might lurk. Bush, by contrast, was open and friendly, with frequent marks of human occupance. One young woman in Freetown observed that middens were one of these marks.

To assess informants' understanding of some of the biological changes associated with deforestation we then asked what plants and animals could only be found in high forest. In all, 336 respondents made a total of 1,517 suggestions.

The elephant dominated the list (55 per cent of all respondents), but chimpanzee, leopard and various species of monkeys were each cited by a quarter of the sample. Harnessed antelope, bush hog and buffalo were also mentioned frequently. Specific reptiles, snakes and birds mentioned included tortoise, pangolin, monitor lizard, python, Gaboon viper, and various birds of prey. Where plants were cited, they tended to be useful species associated with secondary forest rather than closed-canopy rain forest, e.g. the silk cotton tree mentioned by 15 per cent of respondents. Fruit trees and others items which the young frequently forage in the bush were frequently cited (e.g. bush yams and *Dialium guineensis* (*blak tombla* in Krio)).

About 20 per cent of responses might be considered dubious. These mainly concerned large animals (lions, tigers, bears, foxes, zebras, horses, and even a kangaroo or two). Despite the country's name (literally 'Lion Mountain'), the lion is no forest creature, though lions may have once been present in the northern, savanna, part of the country. Lion skin does turn up from time to time in ritual objects in rural areas of Sierra Leone; in the Gola Forest I was once shown a warrior's jacket from pre-colonial days, made of strips of red cloth alternating with leopard and lion skin.

Whether all 'dubious' responses were correctly classified as such is itself open to doubt, due to variations in the terms in common use for animals in Sierra Leone and Liberia. Americo-Liberians re-applied a number of North American names to animals found locally (most notably 'alligator' for Nile crocodile, as in 'Alligator Society'), and these usages have spread into parts of eastern and southern Sierra Leone. The informant who noted that 'elk' was only found in high forest was quite correct, since he meant the large antelope *Boocerus* (this animal has no common name in English – reference books call it 'bongo'). Similar problems occur with 'tiger' (*taiga* in Krio) since this word is quite widely used in West African English-oriented pidgins and creoles to refer to any large cat (including leopard, specifically *lɛpɛt* in Krio).

Attention was paid to whether or not any specific social patterns could be detected in these dubious responses.

The dubious plants were mainly the work of the 27 informants who thought oil palms and *yemani* (*Gmelina arborea*) were high forest species. Oil palm is a light-dependent species common only in secondary bush, and *yemani* is an introduced quick-growing timber and fuel-wood tree, common in roadside plantations laid down in the colonial period. It was mainly women who made the mistake about palms, and men who were confused about *yemani* (but total numbers were very small in both cases). Over two-thirds of dubious responses concerning these two plants came from people with secondary or higher education.

Turning to the much larger category of dubious forest animals (92 per cent of all such responses), there were no distributional differences according to gender, level of schooling, religion and location. Nor is this conclusion changed by removing 'lions' and 'tigers'. (These responses account for 75 per cent of all animals in the dubious category, and, as noted above, may not be 'dubious' at all.) The result is surprising, since we might (for example) have expected 'bookish' responses (kangaroos and zebras) to be more concentrated among those with higher levels of formal education.

From the evidence, it would appear that most young Sierra Leoneans have realistic, and accurate, knowledge of forest environments, and some of the biological changes taking place within these environments, based largely on direct experience. The type of experience varies with schooling and gender, and changes in character as patterns of urban-rural interaction also change. Incidental contact with the forest (helping parents on the farm, for example) will continue to decline with schooling and urbanization, but there is evidence that young people now organize deliberate visits to compensate for lost informal opportunities. This suggests that young people in Sierra Leone view environmental knowledge as an important component in their modernity and not a 'relic' knowledge belonging to the rural past.

Forests and the future

Despite insurgency from 1991, a coup in 1992, and grave economic difficulties over the preceding 15–20 years, the majority of the young people, interviewed mid-1993 to mid-1994, were remarkably optimistic about the future. Asked to say whether, and why, they thought their own lives would be different (better or worse) in 10 years time, 91 per cent of the sample had definite views. Of this group, 86 per cent were confident things would be better. This confidence was evenly distributed across the genders and age groups. Of the 14 per cent predicting no change or a worsening of personal circumstances three-quarters of responses came from those with only primary education or no formal education at all.

The reasons for confidence related, not unexpectedly, mainly to plans being made or already undertaken, concerning, for example, specific educational activities or commercial ventures. The single largest ground for hope (20 per cent of responses) was the age-related expectation of achieving financial independence (to have an income, to be in charge of one's destiny, to have come out from 'behind' a parent or sponsor). Some informants (12 per cent of responses) believed life would be better because of self-confidence in their ability to survive and prosper come what may. Others (9 per cent of responses) couched their optimism in religious terms (they would succeed through prayer, ancestral blessing, the power of God, etc).

But quite a number of responses were quite specific about the route to self-improvement, and outlined definite career plans or business undertakings. Independent business activity was the single largest category of projected activity (18 per cent of responses, but with females outnumbering males two to one). Men were to the fore in claiming agriculture as their route to success, or in believing that the country's political prospects were brighter, despite the war, without the APC.

Interviewees were then asked about specific career plans. The professions (31 per cent) and business (29 per cent) were the most popular choices. There was a 50:50 gender split among those aiming for professional employment (though with girls tending to aim lower than boys, with the latter typically hoping to become doctors and lawyers, where girls had in mind nursing or teaching). Females (67 per cent) were to the fore in the group with business ambitions (these varied from petty trade to international commodity dealing). Agriculture, especially plantation work and market gardening, accounted for 20 per cent of responses. Less than a third of the agricultural responses came from women. Artisanal activities featured relatively rarely (only 7 per cent of responses). The single most notable feature of the entire set of responses was the lack of interest in diamond mining. Only two respondents (one female) *intended* to make mining their choice of employment. In practice, many young men are sucked into diamond mining, but, seemingly, few young Sierra Leoneans see it as a long-term stable future.

The survey then enquired whether interviewees thought that forests in Sierra Leone were increasing, decreasing or remained stable, and whether this would have any direct impact on the interviewee's own future. Definite views were entertained by 90 per cent of the sample; of this fraction of the sample 80 per cent thought forests were decreasing, 8 per cent that there was no significant change, and 12 per cent that they were increasing. This last group tended to argue that young people had left farming for the city, and that the insurgency had further depleted the populations of forested districts, so it was to be expected (given the strong recuperative powers of the bush) that there would be much more forest in future. This response was somewhat commoner among older age groups (20–29 year olds), and less common among the teenagers. A 'holiday' for the land may indeed be one of the unintended practical benefits of the insurgency.

Altogether 308 informants gave a total of 515 explanations for decrease in forest cover. Farming was thought to be the single most important factor (28 per cent of responses). The second largest set of responses, somewhat surprisingly, cited construction, the expansion of settlements and road building (21 per cent). Uncontrolled logging and mining accounted for a further 10 per cent and 7 per cent of responses. Of those citing mining as a factor in deforestation 70 per cent were males. Several respondents gave graphic, and presumably first-hand, descriptions of the kinds of damage caused by uncontrolled diamond mining in forest reserves. Others had been more impressed by a BBC TV film widely available on video copies in Sierra Leone documenting the environmental damage caused by international bauxite and rutile mining operations in southern Sierra Leone. Informants were often very well informed about, and gave chapter and verse for, specific abuses by loggers and miners. This aspect of youth culture in Sierra Leone (the idea that young people are watching the activities of the older generation and keeping score) is well summed up by the chorus of an anti-APC song composed by the band Blind Musical Flames and released shortly after the NPRC coup – *lɛ dɛm lɛf wi noo, dɛm fil sɛ wi nɔ no* ('let them clear off, they think we don't know [what's being going on]').

Of those thinking the forest to be decreasing 85 per cent believed it would affect them directly, and gave 515 examples of reasons for preserving tropical rain forest. The great majority were directly practical – loss of non-timber forest products (9 per cent), shortage of timber (7 per cent), reduced agricultural productivity (19 per cent), lack of further opportunities for opening up new farms (4 per cent), shortage of firewood (6 per cent), shortage of medicinal herbs (3 per cent). But there was also concern for the environment in general, and a particular focus on climatic factors.

In all, 25 per cent of responses (the single largest group) linked deforestation and climatic change, and expressed fears that the country would be afflicted by drought, that temperatures would rise, that bush fires would become more prevalent, that Sierra Leone would become as hot and unpleasant as Guinea in the dry season. About 10 per cent of responses concerned animals; some interviewees were specifically worried by loss of access to bush meat, but others regretted that they might never now have the chance to see rare animals, like elephants, for themselves. Three people mentioned extinction as a bad thing in itself.

A small number of interviewees were concerned by the macroeconomic consequences of forest loss (citing reduced government revenues and extra pressure on foreign exchange reserves for substitute imports). Seven respondents specifically regretted that the next generation would no longer enjoy forest benefits. Four interviewees mentioned the potential threat posed by forest loss to the confidentiality of secret societies. Nine informants (eight in Bo) were concerned that depletion of forests would reduce the number of potential refuges in which villagers 'might hide from evil people like rebels'.

Deforestation and war

The early stages of the war were fought in some of the most heavily forested parts of eastern Sierra Leone, and after the failure of its initial advance, the RUF took to the forests. As noted, bush survival skills were emphasized in the training of RUF conscripts/recruits. Displaced populations from the war zone also had an intense experience of the forest, escaping through secluded forest byways, or hiding for long periods from both insurgents and government troops. Some villagers were required by government forces to clear plantations, 'society bushes' close to settlements, and roadside forests (many left as shade for travellers from the nineteenth century) in order to create free-fire zones and reduce risks of ambush. The war, then, has heightened fears of dangers in the forest (both mystical and practical) and accelerated the process of local deforestation.

Respondents were asked to comment on the proposition 'rebels hid in forests, so the government should clear all remaining forests to make the area safe'. Asked to rank responses on a five-point scale from 'strongly agree' to 'strongly disagree', some interviewees took time to clarify their choice in additional, often quite lengthy, comments.

There was a 90 per cent response rate to this item, and the results are symmetrically distributed (31 per cent of respondents opting to 'strongly agree' and 31 per cent to 'strongly disagree'). Only 3 per cent of interviewees opted for the neutral middle point (a testimony to the vividness of their experience), with 25 per cent favouring the 'agree somewhat' option and 10 per cent favouring 'disagree somewhat'. Strong support for the idea of accelerated deforestation to make the countryside safe was more marked among women than among men (39 per cent of all women's responses, but only 22 per cent of men's responses). Age made only a slight difference, with the youngest age group (perhaps less fully aware of the longer-term economic implications than their elders) slightly more bullish about clean-felling the war zone to help bring the war to an end.

Education was the single biggest factor in determining the pattern of responses. Those with no formal education or only primary education

Table 8.3   War-influenced attitudes to forest conservation of young Sierra Leoneans
with no formal education

'Forest should be cleared to prevent rebels hiding.'
(Respondents with no formal education).

	Strongly agree	Other responses	Strongly disagree	
Freetown	28%	32%	40%	(n=40)
Kambia	41%	45%	14%	(n=37)
Bo	50%	42%	8%	(n=100)

(1993–4 survey results)

were twice as likely to 'strongly agree' with the proposition as
interviewees with post-primary education. The firmness with which the
less educated supported the clearance option increased as one left
Freetown and moved towards Bo, the most war-affected area (Table 8.3).
This result, taken in conjunction with the gender difference noted
above, stands in marked contrast to earlier evidence suggesting little
variation in knowledge and experience concerning the forest by gender,
religion or educational background. Nothing has served more to
differentiate the experience of deforestation among Sierra Leoneans
than the RUF rebellion.

Two points can be made. The first is that insurgency mainly affected
rural areas, and, as in any such war, it is the rural poor (many displaced
in towns like Bo, Kambia and Freetown) who have suffered the most.
They have suffered not only loss of family and property, but also social
amity. Embroiling young conscripts in violence against their own
families, or burning houses by religion, were techniques of war
calculated to destroy social cohesion, and allow insurgents later easy
access to chronically divided communities. Small wonder, then, that in
conditions of heightened tension and incipient social collapse, the rural
poor and women (perhaps more fully aware of what it takes to sustain
amity) are so keen to let in as much light as possible on the scene, and
to see who their enemies are, and where they are coming from. A desire
for forest clearance is a wholly understandable response of those whose
priority is the protection of the social fabric of rural society.[1]

The more highly educated, and males more intensely engaged with
the cash economy, by contrast, see with clarity that forests offer future
income, and that their own economic wellbeing is tied up with this
reserve source of economic strength. Cutting down forest as a short-term

[1]Conversely, the RUF claims to have developed a conservation ethic as a result of its
dependence on the forest: 'We have come to know our country better and understand the
potential of its pristine flora and fauna . . . The developing consciousness is all embracing
and enriching' (RUF/SL: 1995: 14).

security measure offers few attractions to this group. Many comments stressed that deforestation was strategically short-sighted. Where women, the less educated, and those most in touch with the needs of rural society, prioritized the need 'to make people safe', 'to protect lives', 'to ensure that these evil thugs have nowhere to hide', men, and the more highly educated, tended to make points like 'rebels don't just hide in forests, they are present in the towns as well', 'the war will be over one day, but we will still need forests for income', and 'cutting down forests for security will lead to environmental insecurity'. One man even brought in Star Wars technology in support of his case, arguing that American spy satellites had already solved the problem of working out where, and who, the insurgents were, and on whose behalf they were operating.

What is to be done?

Two-thirds of interviewees believed that forests in Sierra Leone are diminishing and had concrete ideas about what to do to reverse the trend. They provided 614 suggestions (39 per cent from women). The majority involved either regulation (41 per cent) (toughening up and implementing the law on forest exploitation, delimiting forest reserves, fining those who abused resources and caused environmental damage) or technical solutions (42 per cent) (scientific management of reserves, development of sustainable agriculture through research into better crops and farming systems and use of fertilizer, and, above all, through re-afforestation (26 per cent of all suggestions)). Parren and de Graaf (1995), dampening enthusiasm for 'tree planting schemes' so strongly espoused in development circles (and especially among NGOs), argue strongly in favour of 'scientific management' of natural rain forest as generally being a superior option to tree plantation in West Africa. But Sierra Leone has little natural forest left to manage, and local perception may, in this case, be pretty much on target.

Tree planting is a 'common-sense' solution, and fits well with local experience of not clearing forest but modifying and enriching it with 'plantation crops' (cf. Fairhead and Leach 1996). A small-scale farmer around Gola, with forest to convert, rarely considers clear-felling the forest for a cocoa or coffee plantation, but prefers to open up and thin the canopy with selective felling, before introducing a scatter of seedlings to see how they fare (Davies and Richards 1991). In a couple of years the farmer returns to assess progress, and then decides whether it is worth investing more labour to fell some of the smaller trees likely to compete with the coffee or cocoa seedlings. Large trees will be left, especially economic trees such as kola and timber species, to provide shade, and a source of additional income (the timber will be ear-marked for felling in 15–20 years time when the plantation has passed its peak).

Once derided by development experts, who wanted to encourage high-productivity plantations with trees correctly spaced and established in straight lines, this type of low-intensity, slow, step-by-step, modification of the forest environment has a number of clear environmental advantages, as well as providing steady, if modest, returns to the farm household. Although it falls between two stools (admired as little by conservationists as by developers), this 'hybrid' between 'proper' plantation and natural secondary vegetation may prove to be a useful basis for further technological elaboration.

Women, it is interesting to note, tended to favour *technical* solutions (and the tree-planting option in particular) more than men. Men proposed 59 per cent of all regulatory and control options and women 57 per cent of all technical solutions. Since women provided fewer suggestions overall (39 per cent) than men (although they are as numerous in the sample) the difference is even more marked than these percentages at first indicate. There is also a rather interesting regional 'slant' to the figures; technical solutions tended to be favoured, among all informants, more in Bo (48 per cent of all suggestions from Bo) than in Kambia (37 per cent of suggestions from Kambia) and Freetown (35 per cent of all suggestion from Freetown), the pattern then reversing for regulatory options (Freetown 48 per cent, Kambia 44 per cent and Bo 34 per cent). Perhaps there is greater confidence in Freetown than in the provinces in the capacity of a reformed state to enact and implement the draconian measures these young informants often had in mind.

Education and persuasion accounted for 9 per cent of suggestions, and surprisingly few informants (3 per cent) thought in terms of innovations in common property resource management, or locally generated technical solutions. Even fewer attended to the question of economic incentives or overall government policy on the environment (though the few suggestions made were generally highly apposite, e.g. the importance of price incentives as a stimulus to more sustainable agriculture and the need for government to decide upon and publish an overall strategy document for the environment in Sierra Leone). Broadly, young Sierra Leoneans are pinning their main hope on the possibility of strong government, increased respect for the law, and technical solutions for sustainable resource management in areas outside reserved forests.

This picture is borne out by their comments on who should be responsible for implementing these suggestions. As many as *half* of all the 584 suggestions involved 'government' or organizations of the state (mainly technical departments of 'line' ministries, or in some cases schools and research institutions). In keeping with the emphasis on technical solutions, much responsibility is seen to lie with experts. There was a strong feeling that strengthening national expertise was an urgent priority in environmental resource management. Clearly, this was linked to the educational ambitions of many of the interviewees, and some interviewees reiterated career ambitions at this point. But there was also an emphasis on the need for international inputs, and a strong awareness that Sierra Leone could not 'go it alone' on environmental issues.

Supporters of 'community conservation' will be reassured to note that quite a good number of regulatory options were assigned, as responsibilities, to local authorities (6 per cent) and groups in civil society, such as farmers' organizations and bush-owning lineages (31 per cent). Strikingly, many informants included themselves at this point, emphasizing that the onus for the future was not on 'traditional' groups, but on 'Sierra Leoneans', 'the people', 'citizens' and, above all, 'us'. This is evidence of a belief, apparently quite widespread among young people, that the nation should and can renew itself 'from within'.

Conclusion

On balance young people in Sierra Leone have a sound grasp of current environmental changes, and clear and cogent ideas about possible solutions. Neo-Malthusian crisis leading inexorably to war is not how young people see the situation in Sierra Leone. They appreciate that the country faces the challenge of managing a threatened resource base. They are accurately informed about where the shoe pinches. They have clear and cogent ideas about solutions. A concerted attack on environmental problems requires technical and (above all) political change. Young women tend to favour technical solutions, young men political solutions. Both genders think not in terms of the violent nihilism of New Barbarism but of a rational modernity. Not only are young Sierra Leoneans remarkably positive about the future, despite the war, but they also see the creation of that positive future as a task for the nation, and a responsibility for young people themselves. Perhaps unhealthy reliance on patrimonialism is beginning to slacken in Sierra Leone? Forest culture in Sierra Leone has a number of precedents for sturdy, but syncretic, self-reliance and these might now come into their own. The problem is that the insurgents have hijacked some of the relevant cultural capital. Donning the guise of bush devils they have tried to frighten the city and the world into granting them metropolitan power and status. New Barbarism compounds the fault by reading this dramaturgical pose as inherent backwardness. My task has been to contradict that reading, and so gain some urgently needed respect and space for the local 'organic intellectuals' who seek to restore healthy links between bush knowledge and forest community, but reject the path of violence.

War–Peace Transitions ▌ Scope for Citizen Action

Bo, Christmas 1994

Early in the morning of 27 December 1994 a group of about a hundred RUF fighters attacked the suburb of New London on the southern edge of Bo town. The group came from the south, first infiltrating the large refugee camp at Gondama, c. 20 km south of Bo, a few days before Christmas, while most of the camp occupants, and the Nigerian soldiers protecting them, were at the stadium in Bo taking part in a Christmas masquerade. The rebels arrived at the camp as civilian refugees in casual clothes, their weapons and uniforms hidden in hold-all bags. They said they were from Pujehun, and having heard the camp was well-stocked with food, had the intention to spend Christmas with their relatives in Gondama. Only later did these RUF fighters reveal themselves in a true light. Once they began to assemble their weapons and don battle fatigues the refugees realized what was going on. Panic ensued, and numbers of refugees were crushed to death or drowned in the Sewa river trying to flee the camp. The rebel combat unit, now fully kitted out in its stolen Sierra Leone army uniforms, slipped away unobserved to the west. Over the holiday period settlements on a back road leading to Bo were attacked by turns. The day after Christmas, and having sacked the town of Tikonko, c. 10 km from Bo, the unit was in position to pay Sierra Leone's most important provincial town and educational centre a holiday recruitment call.

New London is a suburb on the main Kenema–Bo–Freetown highway. The roadside is a busy market, and as usual an early morning crowd had gathered. The rebels emerged from the swamp south of New London, apparently heavily armed with automatic rifles and rocket-propelled grenade launchers (many were carved and painted wooden replicas). A small RSLMF contingent withdrew to brigade headquarters to seek reinforcements. The crowd was exposed to its fate.

The rebels held their fire to appeal to the crowd to join them.[1] A strange thing then happened. A stir began in the crowd. Voices were heard saying 'four years of war for what?', 'we don't want rebels in Bo town' and 'you can only die once'. The stir became a surge, as citizens, heedless of the danger, began to bear down on the momentarily disconcerted rebels. Shots were fired, injuring a couple of people in the crowd. But it was too late to turn back. The crowd's blood was up. The surge quickly became a rout. Startled rebels, meeting civilians unafraid of guns for the first time, panicked and broke ranks as the crowd attacked them with any makeshift weapons to hand.

Surprised by this unexpected civilian counter-attack, the RUF fighters scattered, and were chased into all corners of Bo, a large open town divided by long fingers of swamp land planted to rice. Altogether, pursuing groups caught seven rebels, including one young woman RUF commando in full battle fatigues, who said her name was Alice, and a native of Bo. People remarked on the special trouble she had taken to braid her hair for the attack. Like other rebels caught that day Alice was beaten to death by the crowd.

The town was in a ferment. Mid-morning the army put up a barrage of artillery fire to scare off rebels still lurking in the outskirts. Even late in the afternoon excited groups of young citizens were still bucking and charging through the rice in hope of catching any RUF stragglers. But meanwhile, cooler heads were thinking of the night. A system of vigilante patrols was being rapidly organized, based, in part, on the street-level organization called into play by earlier NPRC town cleansing activities. Traditional organizations such as Poro played their part, as did street and ward-based youth soccer teams. Each sector of the town organized its own night patrols. Suddenly, would-be bathers met a dearth of buckets and basins. The basins were being filled with food for the vigilantes. The buckets were taken for drums, to signal to the neighbouring streets that our people were awake, and to wonder aloud whether the rival team had fallen asleep. Between 4 am and 6 am, when any counter attack might have been most expected, the town rang to the rafters with a bucket symphony.

The night patrols found no rebels, but caught a handful of soldiers attempting to loot. The lucky ones were dragged to brigade headquarters but one or two met a summary fate. The army, alarmed, proposed to take back the town from the vigilantes with a night curfew. The vigilante organizations refused, and the army backed down. For a week or so Bo was a perhaps unique instance of the army having to abide by a curfew imposed by the citizens. On New Year's Eve the army decided it had to act to re-impose its curfew order, and introduce night-time patrols. On

[1]'We have chosen the long and winding road (footpaths and by-passes) to democratic salvation. Sooner or later the citizens of Freetown, Bo and Kenema shall wake up to our call and with brooms and dusters, buckets and pans, sticks and stones, they will rid themselves of the rotten APC system' (RUF/SL 1995: 22).

our street this comprised a nightly visit by an army Land Rover, windows up, corkscrewing into a hand-brake turn at the swamp edge, and issuing a hasty 'all-clear' as the nervous occupants beat it back to barracks. A stand-off ensued, as vigilante organizations negotiated a series of compromises with the army. Thereafter local defence groups secured a recognized position as a regular presence on the security scene in Bo. The RUF shifted its focus to other targets.

Peace from within?

The defence of Bo was a striking instance of citizen action. Vigilantism, Abrahams (1987, 1989) has pointed out, is a phenomenon associated with remote and weak states. It is relevant to ask to what extent civil defence and other forms of citizen action are likely to contribute to restoration of peace in combat zones, and whether outside interventions harm or support this capacity for civil society to institute running repairs. In short, the intention is to conclude this account of 'fighting for the rain forest' with a discussion of scenarios for war–peace transition in Sierra Leone.

If there is a negotiated end to the conflict in Sierra Leone, then a formal process of reconstruction can begin. State and civil society can be repaired 'from above'.

It seems clear, however, that even with clever and honest management, any regime coming to power after a negotiated end to the war would be hard pressed to command the levels of internal resources fully to rebuild a war-damaged economy, and improve on the low pre-war standards of social services that rendered the country vulnerable to war in the first place. It is highly doubtful that the international community is in any mood to step in and meet the shortfall. A senior UN official has already described the donor response to the needs of war-torn Liberia and Sierra Leone as 'pathetic'. Therefore the dangers of sliding back into chronic war are very apparent.

The problem is that the cat is out of the bag. Any opportunist with a few boxes of guns, fighting in forested country, willing to make a virtue of isolation and poor communications, can hold a weak state like Sierra Leone to ransom. The RUF may be drawn into a civil conversation,[2] but other disgruntled opportunists might well step up and fill the breach while ready supplies of detachable youth remain to be recruited. This is a vicious circle. The sociological danger of war feeding on alienable youth will persist while the state is down-and-out, flat on its back.

The question then has to be asked: What if low-level conflict persists indefinitely? Two scenarios can be envisaged.

---

[2] The movement claims (RUF/SL 1995) that this is all it has ever wanted, but offers no clear explanation of why the guerrilla campaign has been targeted on rural civilians.

Scenario 1: the sides (or multiple players) will increasingly develop 'camped' forms of existence, with 'rebels' holding on to their captives and recruits in forest enclaves and other folk – citizens under 'government' rule – living in urban centres and the more secure refugee camps. The economy will revert to the concession company conditions of the late nineteenth century. Resource concessions will be 'let out' to security-cum-mineral operations, such as the South African-based firm Executive Outcomes, with the military capacity to secure an economic return from mining operations in no-man's-land. Executive Outcomes has already taken up a diamond mining concession in Kono District and bought shares in the rutile mine, an operation brought to a halt by rebel attack in January 1995. The rebels will doubtless receive matching offers from similarly organized, but clandestine, mineral outfits, perhaps drawing in ex-combatants from Liberia. It is not yet clear what this return to proto-colonialism might portend, even if it yields a stalemated end to hostilities. It should be recalled, however, that the earlier concession company system led to massive abuses of local human rights and created health and environmental scars from which large parts of the equatorial African forest region still suffer. Formal colonialism was introduced as its *antidote*.

Scenario 2: is one in which civilians give up their understandable nostalgia for 'peace', come to accept war as a normal condition of life, and think creatively about how to build, through civil defence, spiritual sanction, and other inventive uses of a war-oriented, ancestral, informal institutional culture, islands of more regular rural pursuits in the midst of a sea of conflict.

The 'Attack Trade'

Belligerent groups are likely to tolerate civil re-colonization of at least parts of the war-shattered zone, to ensure better supply of basic commodities.[3] Already, women from Bo in central Sierra Leone are trading palm oil from the rebel-ringed palm plantation areas near the coast, having discovered ways to handle the complex check-point culture of the conflict zone.

In the Biafran War such trading ventures were known, collectively, as the 'attack trade'. Trading caravans of up to 30 or more women at a time, roped together, and led by a hunter, would negotiate the bush tracks of the war zone by night, and sleep by day, trading across the enemy lines in old Nigerian coinage (legal tender on both sides of the conflict). In other cases, the 'attack trade' was more open. A field commander might challenge his opposite number to a football match, during which time

---

[3] The RUF makes no bones about collecting cocoa, coffee and palm fruits in areas it controls (irrespective of ownership) and that it 'finds ways to barter them for drugs, clothes, footwear, supplementary food items, school materials *and of course,* radios, cassettes and batteries' (RUF/SL 1995: 13, my emphasis).

the terms of local cease-fires to allow the passage of traders would be agreed. It is plausibly arguable that Biafra depended as much or more on these adjustments between war and commerce as on the highly publicized Oxfam and Caritas 'mercy flights' to Uli airstrip. Charlie (Chapter Four) now pays his school fees by braving the ambush-prone road to Freetown to bring back cigarettes for dealers in Bo. As an ex-child-combatant he reckons he knows war well enough to spot the risks of ambush and survive.

The 'attack trade' may be one of the important processes through which the civil agrarian zones in war-torn Sierra Leone get back on their feet, and extend 'peace from within'. Certainly, such developments have important implications for external, donor-funded, assistance to war-zones in Africa, as will now be discussed.

Relief prolongs conflict?

De Waal (1995) has pointedly challenged the international donor and NGO development communities to compare some of their own worst moments in Africa (the extraordinarily mis-named Operation Restore Hope in Somalia, for example) with some of the concrete, low-level positive developments (like the 'attack trade') to be encountered in the Africa of what he terms 'the Aid Free Zone'.

From Biafra onwards there has been a justified suspicion that high-profile relief operations prolong African wars (Duffield 1994). The argument is not that the high-profile operational agencies are partisan (as was alleged by some supporters of the federal Nigerian cause in the Biafra conflict) but that by concentrating resources (in feeding centres, for example) the relief agencies attract raiding, and successful raiding succours the belligerent parties.

This argument can certainly be applied to Sierra Leone. The pattern of RUF violence, from the outset, has been to concentrate attacks on arms dumps, hospital pharmacies and food stores. At times rebels venture into farming areas to force villagers to harvest, thresh and transport rice back to their camps, but this is time-consuming and dangerous work. Ambushing convoys or raiding feeding centres is less risky. In 1992 the Gola Forest village of Sembehun was raided by the RUF a day or two after radio announcements that the Red Cross was about to deliver supplies of bulgur wheat. More recently, the Freetown government has recognized that convoying food attracts ambushes, whether from rebels or renegade government troops, and has re-opened the ambush-prone road from Freetown to Bo to any willing driver (whatever the risks).

A second area of doubt about high-profile relief activities is that they may undercut commercial developments within and between combat zones that might otherwise support an eventual transition to peace.

Explicitly, the charge is that high-profile relief may weaken an 'attack trade' that would otherwise draw combatants into deals, and provide outlets for the talents of war-zone women and ex-combatants.

Good data are not yet available to test this hypothesis adequately. But it seems possible that the 'attack trade' was least well developed in those parts of Biafra where 'external' relief effort was most prominent (e.g. in towns like Owerri). It is significant that in Sierra Leone the 'attack trade' seems to develop first, or fastest, around commodities (like palm oil, tobacco, cassettes nd batteries) that are local, but not agency, priorities. The International Alert video shows one of the expatriate hostages, a heavy smoker, joking with Foday Sankoh about the special trouble to which he had put the young rebels to keep him supplied with cigarettes. Eye-witness comments from villages close to a main RUF camp in the Kambui South forest reserve suggest that the RUF more regularly obtains such supplies through trading rather than raiding. An alternative to high-profile relief might put 'attack traders' under contract to supply refugee feeding programmes as well as tobacconists.

The ideal scenario envisaged would be to encourage relief agencies to focus on the specialized task of protecting the entitlements of the most vulnerable groups in a public market supplied by the 'attack trade'. Politics in a country like Sierra Leone is the art of patronage, often expressed in its rawest form through the distribution of food. Willy-nilly, relief agencies with large stocks of food become political players, but unconstrained by even the rather elementary procedures of informal political accountability that bind local 'big people' and food-dependent clients in local long-term relationships (cf. Richards 1986). The agencies at times play unwitting food politics without realizing what obligations they are incurring in local eyes.

Smart Relief

The upshot of this kind of analysis is to shift the emphasis away from relief in bulk items and more towards knowledge-intensive assistance. What seems to be required is a more general application of Sen's well-known insight that in famines it is often loss of entitlement rather than absolute food shortage that tends to kill (Sen 1980).

The way to see the problem most clearly is to answer the question 'what relief items can make it through combatant road blocks in a war zone, and how much of the original consignment is left at the end of the day?' I once met a Biafran official whose job was to adjudicate the division of relief supplies coming into Uli airstrip. He described to me the standard carve-up of a supply of six small cars imported for the Caritas relief effort (two for his boss, a senior Biafran political figure, two for the military, and two for the priests supervising a feeding programme). And this, it should be noted, was a consignment that had to pass the scrutiny of only one side in the conflict.

Any bulk supplies must be vulnerable to these kinds of imposts, but there are a number of 'smart', knowledge-intensive, ways to channel help to the civil agrarian islands within war zones without exciting the attention of raiders or road-block controllers.

One way is to shift the focus in food security away from food and towards seed systems, genetic information and farmer invention. In Sierra Leone and Liberia this means fewer bags of white rice (the currency of state patronage) and more 'starter packs' of seed. Work in Sierra Leone has shown that even in low-level insurgency conditions farmers are highly seed-responsive. The routes through which seeds travel in the local community are many and various. The poor have a long tradition of picking over seed-filled elephant dung, hunting unhusked seeds in old sacks, and relying on birds to bring in new seeds from outside, in addition to presenting each other with small handfuls of anything that works. Starter seeds pass through road-blocks without hindrance, at times unintentionally in packing or clothing. African rice (originally only found in West Africa) made it to central America during the time of the slave trade despite the rigours of the Middle Passage.

But farmers need new kinds of seeds (or abandoned favourites) to cope with the contingencies of war. Farmers in Pujehun in 1992 were responding positively to a hardy rice type introduced from northern Sierra Leone as part of a relief initiative, because it was short-duration, weed-tolerant, and resistant to bird damage. Planting this three-month African rice they found something left to harvest after several times being chased out of their farms by fighting.

War-adaptive innovation can be greatly facilitated by knowledgeable back-up from plant specialists (Jusu 1995). Seeds could be bio-engineered to meet reduced labour and management typical of war-zone conditions, for instance. In other cases, the crucial requirement is to facilitate change to less easily raided crop types. A standing field of cassava needs less labour to produce, and can be harvested as the need arises. It cannot so easily be looted, or burnt, as the contents of a rice barn. The historical spread of cassava in Africa is in significant measure a response to the contingencies of war, drought and labour-sapping disease from the nineteenth century onwards. If the longer-term viability of civilian islands within a conflict zone is dependent on raid-resistant cuttings, then undramatic agro-technical research back-up for farmer adaptive innovation has as much to contribute to the solution of complex emergencies as the highly-publicized emergency feeding programmes that currently attract the lions' share of public support.

There are other kinds of 'smart relief' that would also pass the road-block test with flying colours. One such is to use the power of broad-casting to reach deep inside war zones and help facilitate constructive local debate about war–peace transitions, among belligerents as well as civilian activists.

From the outset rebel groups in Liberia and Sierra Leone have shown a street-wise awareness of the importance of international radio. Their unverifiable claims, in phone calls to the BBC Africa service, have stirred up panic. But with good satellite telephone links to London now more widely accessible to the general public in towns such as Bo and Kenema the significance of radio has changed. Claims by Accra-based RUF spokesman, Alimamy B. Sankoh, during the Christmas 1994 campaign, that the rebels had taken Kenema and attacked the road junction settlement at Mile 47 were readily refutable by telephone calls to citizens on the spot.

These improved 'interactive' possibilities render international radio broadcasting more accountable to citizen interests in war zones. Once, international radio was suspect as a hegemonic cultural influence, even where it could be defended from the charge of propaganda. Such suspicions still survive as a legacy from the Cold War. But better local communications mean more channels through which audiences can quickly 'feed back' perceptions to broadcasters. The best international broadcasting is now more 'dialogical' in character, and interesting experiments have been undertaken in ways of catalysing constructive debate about the rebuilding of war-shattered social worlds. One such experiment involves 'soap opera' as a means to extend the information base, and stimulate local discussion of options, for war–peace transitions.

The BBC World Service radio soap opera for Afghanistan, *New Home, New Life*, scripted by Afghan refugees and broadcast in Pashto and Dari, is immensely popular with, and apparently effective in communicating useful messages about war-zone hazards, e.g. land mines, to a large target audience caught up in the continuing insecurity. The longer-term transformative impact of these kinds of initiatives remains to be determined, but modern media research stresses that commercial 'soap opera' is not without its positive impact on the imaginative lives of audiences.

The approach is not exclusive to international broadcasting media, however. Indeed, in many ways, the approach might work best if handled locally, since the 'feed-back' gap is not so great. Sierra Leone certainly has the talent to mount a successful radio 'soap opera', drawing on the lively resources of the West African 'concert party' world of comic drama, to address some of the basic moral and practical dilemmas of war–peace transition in the country. Soap operas used to require sponsors (soap manufacturers). War–peace soap operas need a new generation of sponsors. Relief agencies frequently dramatize their own role for TV audiences 'back home', at times even hogging the limelight. With due regard to the lesson of the dramaturgy of war in Liberia and Sierra Leone they might now also think of investing in local 'strolling players' to refresh the imaginations of war-zone minds temporarily stalled on a surfeit of hazard and horror.

Citizen Action

A hopeful sign concerning the war in Sierra Leone is the new vigour that is beginning to enter debates about citizen action for peace. The Bo civil defence was an important moment of self-realization, in which despair was set aside and citizens said to both rebels and the military 'a plague on both your houses'. Since then debate about citizen action has intensified in a number of quarters. The country divides into those who still have options to escape the war by moving on, and those who have no other place to which to go. Locally, having learnt from the plight of refugees in their midst, a number of individuals and groups have opted to stay put in the face of rebel attack, and thereby discovered useful clues about civil co-existence. In one village north of Bo rebels were trying to set fire to several houses to simulate the damage of a heavy attack. Determined to save his property or die in the process one man discovered that the rebels had struggled to set fire to his house by piling up bedding and using the kerosene from lamps in the house. He attempted to douse the flames, but the rebels came back, to drive him away. His house his only asset, the man challenged the rebels to shoot him if they dared. Puzzled and counting their every bullet, the young RUF insurgents backed down and left the man alone. His discovery was that a certain respect for property creeps into rebel thinking when that property is sincerely defended.

On a rather different level, but in a similar spirit, Sierra Leonean members of the international E-mail Bulletin Board 'Leonenet' have vigorously debated whether the answer to the curse of minerals in Sierra Leone is to seek to re-establish the idea that such resources belong to the chiefdom (*ndɔ* in Mende), where the Paramount Chief is *ndɔ mahɛi* (chief of the land or country). The debate has in effect centred on the notion that healthy government is first and foremost local government, and that many of Africa's problems begin to appear where states have sought to break such local connections between people and resources. The point of interest is not whether or not revived localism would work in the terms proposed, but that the debate is happening at all (among expatriate Sierra Leoneans linked across the global information highway). It seems consistent with the idea that increased globalization allows major re-thinking of the value of localism.

A third area of vigorous interest in re-examining the possibilities of citizen action has come to focus on a possible revitalized role for so-called 'secret societies'. Ellis (1995) reports this debate for Liberia, and it is certainly happening in Sierra Leone as well. A central thought is that where established initiation ceases new forms (like rebel initiation) take their place. It seems to be the case that Poro and other societies have played important roles in the coordination of civil defence. Particular significance might now attach to the potential involvement of the women's initiation associations (Bondo, Sande), an all-but universal aspect of women's social worlds in the Sierra Leone provinces, in local debates about the causes of conflict and healing the social wounds of war. In the past Sande has shown itself to be a flexible and effective forum for debate and training concerned with improved mother-and-child health (cf. Margai 1948; Harding and Mokuwa 1995). Sande may have a specific role in reclaiming female rebel captives for the wider society, and in developing culturally appropriate models for under-standing the circumstances under which young women have become active combatants.

Rethinking patrimonialism

But perhaps the biggest challenge of all for citizen action is to enter into a debate about the nature and future of patrimonialism. As this book has documented, the war in Sierra Leone is best understood as a drama of social exclusion. The rebel leaders are energetic, determined people who feel strongly about being excluded from the networks of patrimonial support under the APC one-party regime. They appeal to a constituency of young Sierra Leoneans who are the victims of state recession in the mining districts. Their political analysis is that violence is justified to recover the nation for the people, on the grounds that patrimonialism favours only the selected few. Patrimonialism is no longer 'sponsorship', it is 'corruption'. Society at large must be made to feel the destructive anger of those for whom patrimonialism no longer works. Meanwhile, the rebels, by whatever means, attempt to construct a model egalitarian society of their own, in the forest. This is no inward-turning survivalism, but an attempt to demonstrate that these rejects of the system have political talents and should never have been ignored in the first place.

The insurgent position enshrines a dilemma. Foday Sankoh does not seek to become president. The state treasury is empty. The international community is loth to top it up. Whoever is president can hardly hope to kick-start the state through massive new patrimonial redistributions. This implies some radical rethinking of the patrimonial political culture that has grown out of centuries of forest insecurity. Sierra Leoneans, as this book has endeavoured to make plain, may not have much material wealth to work with but they do have valuable reserves of cultural capital. Liberia is a warning that sectionalism and tribalism knocks at the door, but the war is not and never has been a regional or ethnic problem and, unlike in Liberia, young Sierra Leoneans can all talk to each other in a single accepted national tongue. The physical isolation of the belligerents is an artefact but also an issue of the war.[4] This difficulty has been to a large extent overcome, by electronics and patient work by conciliators. The idea that talking is a necessity has been

[4] 'Locked up in the forest with no access to the outside world we could not communicate our frustrations and fears' (RUF/SL 1995: 28).

accepted by the parties to the dispute. The question now is what that conversation should be about.

It seems unrealistic to suppose it will simply be about fairer shares of the national cake. Cynics might suppose that the RUF could be bribed to go away. If the war is a crisis of social exclusion then clearly any such move would be ineffective, since the insurgents have a political point to prove. But equally clearly the RUF cannot be readily defeated in the countryside, for, notwithstanding the unacceptable brutality of its methods, the movement has correctly analysed one of the strategic sociological defects of modern Sierra Leone – namely, that the state seeks to command loyalty through patrimonial redistribution at a time when it has lost the wherewithal to meet new and rising demand – and this factor will continue to destabilize the countryside while the state remains weak. Clearly, wise leadership (on both sides) would not go amiss, but it seems that the more basic problem is that society as a whole must begin to re-examine the moral economy of patrimonialism, and decide whether its good points (a parental sense of commitment to the needs of the young) can be separated from the bad (a chronic tendency towards factionalization between those who 'enjoy' and those who feel excluded).

As pointed out, Sierra Leonean culture has long developed ideas about how to limit the abuses of patronage (e.g. through the moral critique encoded within the 'cannibalism' debate, or through the psycho-dynamics of initiation). This cultural creativity needs to be called back into play to explore new options to a moribund patrimonialism. It is not my role to second-guess the outcomes of such local debates, only to point out that it seems likely that, on historical precedent, religious syncretism, and other similarly 'creolizing' approaches to the forging of links between old and new elements in the national political culture will play a part. What does need to be pointed out, however, is the importance of seeking to hold open a space in which such developments can take place. A wise international community might seek to focus some of its help on funding popular participation in seeking the answers to the crisis of patrimonialism. This is perhaps as great a priority as funding elections, for without such a debate the electoral process may only lead to further exacerbation of the unresolved tensions within the patrimonial system.

Two points might be made in conclusion. In opening healthy local debate about a reformed patrimonialism, or what will succeed it, space must be found for young rebel representatives within these developments. It will be important to distinguish between what the movement stands for, and the violence to which it has stooped. Second, it will be essential for the international community to try and guard against the 'ultramontane' elements in the New Barbarism. My critique of New Barbarism is that in essence it splits African ideas from the African social context and uses the ideological material to feed an expatriate intellectual enthusiasm of its own. It is not hard to see that the New Barbarism may be saying more about political concerns in North America (about the politics of multi-culturalism in particular) than it says about West Africa. It is important for Sierra Leoneans not to become too worried by this expatriate intellectual misappropriation.

Mary Douglas's advice is wise. They should press ahead with the task of further elaborating local ideas addressing community dilemmas of social integration in their sector of the 'Atlantic' world, regardless of whether outsiders find the terms in which this debate is carried out 'barbaric' or not. 'Creole' culture has always been open to this kind of misrepresentation, but history is on its side. As Hannerz (1987) implies, 'we are all creoles now'.

A general conclusion: a duty of intellectual care

The central conclusion of this book is that coping with war depends on cultural and institutional resourcefulness in civil society. How can this resourcefulness be supported? Sierra Leoneans have the historical and cultural background to understand how rebels make power through dramaturgical means in zones 'beyond the state'. Green shoots of anti-war grass-roots citizen action are beginning to appear. But in contesting rebel violence citizen action drinks from the same well of institutional culture as the rebels, causing some outsiders to conclude, in error, that all is barbarity. Destructive critique by purveyors of various 'universal' modernisms (whether from the standpoint of neo-liberal market economics or standard theories of human rights) tends to threaten the space in which citizen action might otherwise flourish. Anthropological analysis is useful, I believe, in holding open that space for its rightful tenants, and this is my excuse for the present book. Citizens of weak but modern states in Africa need and deserve room for creative manoeuvre if they are successfully to build islands of security and archipelagos of peace with the limited material resources at their disposal. Given the manifest unwillingness of the rest of the world to involve itself in the problems of countries like Liberia and Sierra Leone, outside commentators owe a duty of care not to weaken, through ill-informed misrepresentation, the cultural mortar with which these fragile structures will be cemented together.

A specific conclusion: postscript for British readers

Britain and Sierra Leone have been in social and economic relationship for more than 450 years. For much of that time our two countries were linked by the slave trade, whose peculiarity was to *confuse* social and economic relationships. It turned people into commodities. The Elizabethan adventurer John Hawkins first acquired slaves on the coast of Sierra Leone as an interloper. He did not even trade for his human cargo; he acquired Sierra Leonean people as slaves *by theft*.

If we follow Kaplan and the proponents of the New Barbarism, 'war' in Sierra Leone is 'crime' fed by overpopulation, a phenomenon for which the West has no responsibility or capacity to solve (other than, perhaps, through offering assistance with birth control). On 1 October 1994, eight months after the publication of Kaplan's influential piece, the British immigration authorities imposed visa controls on Sierra Leoneans seeking to enter the United Kingdom for the first time, to stem at source a potential flow of asylum seekers fleeing the war. Sierra Leoneans in Britain asking for asylum on account of insurgency have since been returned to their home country on the basis that the war is a 'random' violence, not aimed at any specific groups in society. The approach will spread. European Union justice ministers now propose new regulations whereby 'people ... seeking refuge from insurgent groups who are not under state control, will no longer have the right to claim asylum...' (Helm 1995).

But, as this book has argued, rebel violence in Sierra Leone is no instinctive response to population pressure, but a mobilization of youth on behalf of a small group of people angry at their exclusion from an opaque patrimonial political system serving minerals extraction interests. In working through their anger some of the cultural scar-tissue stemming from the days of the slave trade – a trade active in the forests of eastern Sierra Leone until mid-nineteenth century – is once more exposed. The Upper Guinean forests continue to resonate with the seizure of young people and their induction into a world of heightened violence.

Unlike the situation in the Niger delta, resource extraction in the forests of eastern and southern Sierra Leone is not mainly carried out by multi-national mining capital. Nevertheless, patterns of resource extraction in Sierra Leone are matters for international concern since the resources in question have little if any local use. Their market lies overseas.

Business management today operates what is sometimes termed an 'audit culture'. We now need to turn this audit culture towards the issue of resource extraction in countries like Sierra Leone. Put simply, if we believe in a global economy, then the countries that absorb Sierra Leonean minerals or Liberian timber must accept some responsibility for the social damage that results from patterns of resource extraction from which their own economies have benefited. Audit trails would show where, over time, the slaves, ivory, timber, iron ore, diamonds, rutile and bauxite have gone. If responsibility for 'people ... seeking refuge from insurgent groups who are not under state control' were then distributed according to the patterns revealed by such an audit procedure, it is not hard to predict that overseas governments would have a strong impetus to impose new, and less socially disruptive, standards of business ethics on those who continue to engage in the hitherto unrestrained, centuries-old, fight for West African rain forest resources.

I

Recent events

Much has happened in Sierra Leone since this book was finished in January 1996. On 16 January NPRC Chairman Valentine Strasser was deposed by his deputy, Julius Maada Bio. Bio announced his intention to continue with promised elections, but also entered peace negotiations with the RUF. Foday Sankoh was airlifted to Côte d'Ivoire by the International Red Cross to meet Bio. The initial meetings between Bio and Sankoh resulted in an agreement to pursue a negotiated end to the conflict. A temporary cease-fire was agreed. Both sides argued for peace before elections. The RUF leadership wanted time to develop its political programme. Bio was perhaps seeking to enhance the eventual electoral popularity of political affiliates of the NPRC.

But a movement for immediate elections gathered strong popular support. Women peace activists and citizen's organizations, especially in Bo and Kenema, sensed, via trading contacts in rebel districts, that the RUF rank-and-file were deeply war-weary. The young fighters remained very suspicious of the NPRC. The gamble was that they might be more willing to surrender to a civilian regime. Confronted by demonstrations and a determined electoral commissioner (James Jonah) Bio agreed that elections would go ahead on 26 February 1996. The international community helped arrange exit options for leading NPRC members.

Attempts to disrupt polling were made by both dissident military groups and the RUF. Citizens were undeterred. In Bio, eye-witnesses observed soldiers firing in the air to scare off voters. One uniformed group of 'rebels' attacked from the swamp dividing Tengbe Town and Bo Number Two sections of Bo town, but after initial panic citizens were quickly back on the street, vowing openly to 'die in the polling booths'.

The parliamentary elections resulted in a majority for a coalition led by the SLPP. Under the electoral rules a run-off was required between

165

the two leading presidential contenders – Ahmed Tejan-Kabba and John Karefa Smart. This passed off peacefully, with SLPP presidential candidate Tejan-Kabba declared the winner. Karefa Smart noted apparent electoral anomalies but agreed to abide by the result in the interests of national unity. The NPRC stepped down and handed over to the new SLPP-led government on 29 March 1996.

President Tejan-Kabba announced that peace was his first priority and almost immediately began a second round of negotiations with the RUF leadership in Côte d'Ivoire. This resulted in the formation of three joint commissions to work out details of disarmament, encampment and resettlement of ex-fighters. The commissions began work in early May. On 15 May the Ivoirian foreign minister, Amara Essy, held a press conference to report that the RUF had agreed to renounce the armed struggle, though noting that the two parties still held radically different attitudes to the conflict.

Sankoh reacted angrily to suggestions that members of his movement might be offered government posts. The rebel leader insisted the RUF had not fought a war to secure posts. Cease-fire breakdowns were reported. The RUF leadership continued to object to the presence of Executive Outcomes in Sierra Leone. Nevertheless a mood of optimism had begun to take hold in the country. An end to the conflict seemed within sight.

Irrregulars

Although I stand by the material and analysis presented in the body of this book, there are important respects in which I think the account might now be enlarged.[1]

A short visit to Bo in late April 1996 made clear the importance of fully including irregulars in any analysis of the war and the peace process. Irregulars are young people recruited and trained at the war-front by army officers, often as a personal body-guard. Irregulars come from the same pool of patronless war-zone youngsters tapped by the RUF. They should be distinguished from hastily inducted army recruits, some of whom later absconded as 'sobels'.

Some irregulars have become skilled guerrilla fighters. They had a significant impact on the earlier part of the war against the RUF. This impact has not been recognized by the wider society, and irregulars now fear they might in turn become victims of social exclusion.

While the war raged irregulars were equipped and fed from army supplies, but now their future looks very uncertain. Having no army

[1] This is the place to note three items of literature that appeared after this book was finished. Valuable reflections by a Sierra Leonean intellectual with first-hand experience of the conflict are to be found in Squire (1995 and 1996). Riley (1996) is a most useful comparative review of the literature on the crises in Liberia and Sierra Leone.

number they do not fall within the scope of any official demobilization
scheme. Primarily loyal to those who recruited and trained them they
'e potentially a very unstable group. There may be as many irregulars
; there are RUF fighters. (According to 'Rebel Marley' of the RUF Sixth
attalion operating north-west of Bo, April 1996, the RUF has six
/attalions in all, amounting to 3,000 fighters.)

Starved of army resources patrons of irregulars have to find other
ways of providing for their 'boys'. One option has been to pack them off
to areas where there are still signs of RUF activity, ostensibly to defend
outlying villages, but in reality to fend for themselves (from rich local
pickings of cocoa, coffee and diamonds). Irregulars (and their patrons
are as fully enmeshed in the war-zone economy as the RUF.

Lacking any secure place in the peace process irregulars have few
options other than to continue to fight. They might simply decide to
change places in the bush with the real rebels, as and when RUF fighters
are drawn into encampment and resettlement.

Some of the so-called *kamajoisia* may also join the irregulars in this
obscure but violent limbo. *Kamajoisia* are described as 'traditional
hunters'. Sociologically, many come from the same pool as rebels,
captives and irregulars. But they differ from irregulars in two respects.
They deploy hunter skills and technology, and they are loyal to civilian
patrons. Clashes have already been reported between irregulars and
kamajoisia.

Grass-roots civilian groups in Bo in contact with combatants in the
war zone are clear that peace must embrace all classes of belligerent –
irregulars and *kamajoisia* as well as soldiers and rebels. The peace
process must also include, they insist, former inmates released, from
1991 onwards, by RUF raids on jails. These attacks were conceived, it
appears, as a dramatic comment by the RUF leadership on perceived
judicial corruption in Sierra Leone. Deeply scarred by his own
experiences in custody, Foday Sankoh seems to have asked President
Tejan-Kabba to release prisoners and address prison reform as a token of
his good faith in the peace process.[2]

As predicted above, local cultural resources are coming into greater
prominence as citizens seek to build a momentum for peace. In Bo,
Paddle – a 'creolized' masquerade popular among army and police,
linking indigenes and northern migrants – has already attempted to
reach out and incorporate former and would-be belligerents from across
the spectrum of the socially excluded. The organizers of the masque for
1996 were quite explicit about the need for an all-inclusive amnesty,
without which (they argued) the war would flare up again, irrespective
of any peace deal signed with the RUF. The masquerade design for 1996
was topped by a 'white' soldier. Foolishly I wondered if this was a

---

[2] The RUF rebellion was launched 20 years to the day from the coup attempt (23 March 1971)
for which Sankoh was jailed in 1972 (Squire 1995).

reference to the South Africn security firm Executive Outcomes. No, I was told – this was an ex-combatant at peace.

Radicalism and youth

As with recent accounts of 'street children' in Latin America this book tries to make a simple point – that one should see political agency in youth cultures others write off as deviant. This youth culture is presented only in very fragmentary form in the present account. Like a sketch of an iceberg, my text merely hints at the great bulk of material beneath the waterline. Others with better knowledge of politics and street cultures in Sierra Leone will in time illuminate much of that hidden bulk. Participants in the war must be enabled to tell their own story. Various activist fractions (some more sincere than others), have competed to shape this vibrant youth political culture for their own revolutionary (or in some case opportunist) political ends. Although for the greater period of the war many have preferred to remain quiet, these activists also must now have their say. Some are actively engaged in peace-making. Hints at what might emerge are to be glimpsed in Zaya Yeebo's informative account of youth-oriented politics in Ghana in the 1980s. Writing in the year the RUF invasion was launched, Yeebo, already disillusioned with Taylor's 'botched' revolution in Liberia, percipiently seeks to 'jostle some of our non-Ghanaian comrades to pause before jumping on the bandwagon of any "revolutionary" process' (Yeebo 1991: 8). I continue to believe Mary Douglas's 'politics of enclaves' (Douglas 1993) will prove a useful tool in understanding some of the social processes invoked when the RUF 'revolutionary' bandwagon began to roll. But it would be totally wrong to associate Sierra Leonean radicals indiscriminately with this second botched social revolution in West Africa. Millennial dreams are the prerogative of disregarded intellectuals, but there are some grounds for suspecting that in this case hijackers made off with the dream. A healthy political future in Sierra Leone still needs the full and constructive engagement of its radical visionaries.

On Hunters
& Martyrs

Events, July 1996-December 1997

Protracted negotiations between the elected government and the RUF/SL resulted in a peace agreement signed by President Tejan-Kabbah and Cpl Foday Sankoh at the end of 1996. The document recognised the political aspirations of the RUF/SL, provided for the demobilization and reintegration of RUF/SL cadres, and spelled out an active role for the RUF/SL leadership in consolidating peace. Few provisions were implemented. Very different scenarios unfolded on the ground.

The 'permanent' cease-fire agreed in April 1996 was never effective. Distrustful of an army largely recruited under the NPRC the Kabbah government returned large numbers of soldiers to barracks and increasingly shifted attention to the local hunter militias, under the guidance of the Deputy Minister of Defence, Hinga Norman.

Mende-speaking chiefdoms in the war zone were each invited to nominate quotas of young men for initiation and training as *kamajo* fighters. Locally-organized militia units using hunter tactics against the RUF/SL can be traced back as far as 1992, but expansion of *kamajo* units under the Kabbah government was very rapid. Some estimates suggest there may have been as many as 25,000 hunter-style irregulars by mid-1997, surpassing the number of troops in the regular army. Critics alleged that under government patronage the localized hunter civil defence groups were being merged into a regional-ethnic militia.

Backed by elite army units and personnel from the private security company Executive Outcomes, *kamajo* units proved highly effective in carrying the bush war to the RUF/SL, regardless of cease-fire agreements. Located by aerial reconnaissance and radio triangulation, several RUF/SL camps came under intense *kamajo* pressure. The RUF/SL depended on its knowledge and control of bush by-pass routes for communications and supply. *Kamajo* units, comprising rural young men deployed by chiefdom of origin and determined to reclaim local resource-rich territory, used their superior knowledge of the local terrain effectively to surround RUF/SL forest camps and choke off supplies.

Increasingly, RUF/SL units foraging for food or seeking ammunition ran into ambush. *Kamajo* units mounted a major push against key RUF/SL bases during September-October 1996, and attacked RUF/SL concentrations in the Kambui Hills, Soro-Gbema Chiefdom (Pujehun District) and the Gola Forest (culminating in the sacking of Sankoh's headquarters camp, the Zogoda). Few prisoners were taken, though many malnourished civilians were released. Some RUF/SL cadres were killed in fighting or on capture, but many loyalists fled eastward into Liberia where they are camped as refugees.

Facing the prospect of further military reverse, and under strong pressure from West African foreign ministers anxious to end a struggle complicating the higher profile business of resolving the civil war in Liberia, Sankoh made a flying visit, by helicopter, to surviving RUF/SL camps in Kailahun, Kenema and the northern part of Bo Districts in November 1996 to discuss the terms of the draft peace agreement. Perhaps mainly seeking relief from immediate *kamajo* pressure than believing that an acceptable outcome to their struggle was in sight, camp leaders acceded to the draft, and Sankoh returned to Abidjan for a formal signing ceremony on Saturday 30 November.

A small RUF/SL civilian delegation, comprising Fayia Musa, I. H. Deen Jalloh and Agnes Jalloh, then moved to Freetown, ostensibly to act as an advance guard for the fuller incorporation of the RUF/SL in the demobilization and reconstruction planning process. A new ministry had earlier been created to oversee this activity. Progress was painfully slow. The RUF/SL team was largely ignored. *Kamajo* operations against RUF/SL bases still continuing, many of the movement's leading fighters were 'on the run'. Only a handful of mainly young captives under training ever presented themselves for demobilization.

The peace process now thoroughly bogged down Sankoh left Abidjan for Nigeria early in 1997, apparently to try to buy weapons for renewed armed struggle. He was detained by the Nigerian authorities and held under conditions of de facto house arrest in Abuja, seemingly with the agreement of the Kabbah government, from February 1997. Philip Palmer – a veteran of the 1991 cross-border incursion (and an FBC-educated engineer) – stepped up to claim leadership of the movement. Visiting Kailahun, apparently to persuade local RUF/SL groups to accept peace, Palmer and Fayia Musa were seized by Sankoh loyalists.

Meanwhile, discontent within the RSLMF was growing. Some kind of coup attempt against Kabbah in October 1996 was followed by the arrest and detention or sacking of some of the soldiers the regime most distrusted. The coup attempt appeared to reflect a wider concern in the army that the Kabbah government would use demobilization to consolidate a political advantage along regional lines. *Kamajo* militia recruits came from the south and east, the heartland of SLPP support, it being a condition of recruitment that an initiate should speak the Mende language and have a local connection. Many army recruits came from northern districts opposed to the SLPP. The army was to shrink from about 15,000 to c. 6000 men, but definite plans for the demobilization of *kamajo* militia had yet to be announced. The *kamajo* forces would gain any credit from an RUF/SL collapse. *Kamajo* leaders expected to be rewarded with good government jobs and mineral concessions (fights were already taking place between *kamajo* units and regular army groups for control of diamond pits in Tongo Field).

Army rank-and-file knew that in a country still hostile to the NPRC for failing to control 'sobels' their own prospects were poor. Most feared finding themselves back on the street without benefits. The position of the army-linked irregulars – many of whom had played a key role in pushing back the RUF/SL towards Liberia in 1992-3 – was even more tenuous. Those who had opted for demobilization under programmes for child combatants had already found to their chagrin that civilians bracketed all ex-combatants as 'rebels'.

The last straw appears to have been a shipment of some 5000 automatic assault rifles apparently intended for a renewed push by the *kamajo* militia against the RUF/SL in May 1997. Hitherto, *kamajoisia* were occasionally to be seen with AK47s, acquired from RUF/SL fighters killed in combat or renegade military personnel, but perhaps largely for display. Actual *kamajo* operations rely on stalking tactics for which hunters' weapons (knives and shot-guns) are preferred. The prospect of *kamajo* forces routinely equipped with assault rifles offered a radically changed perspective. Now it seemed unavoidable to conclude that the Kabbah government intended to treat the *kamajo* militia as an alternative defence force rather than adjunct to the RSLMF.

On the morning of 25 May 1997 a small group of soldiers led by a Cpl Gborie, bombed the Pademba Road jail in Freetown to release a number of officers detained over alleged involvement in earlier attempts against the Kabbah regime. As the mutiny gained ground President Tejan-Kabbah took off for Conakry in Guinea. A group calling itself the Armed Forces Revolutionary Council (AFRC) led by Major Johnny-Paul Koroma declared that it had taken over the country, and announced that in order to end the war it was inviting the RUF/SL to join a government of national unity. Foday Sankoh, still in detention in Nigeria, gave his approval, before his communications were cut by the Nigerian authorities. The AFRC sent trucks to bring several thousand RUF/SL cadres from the forest into Freetown, whereupon they began to train young recruits from the Freetown underclass for a 'People's Army', arming them with the rifles intended for the *kamajo* militia. Widespread looting and violence against civilians occurred over several days before a semblance of order was restored and the new regime took shape.

Leading RUF/SL fighters Eldred Collins and Sam Bockarie ('Maskita') emerged from the bush to assume positions of influence within the AFRC/RUF alliance. Former NPRC Vice-Chairman Solomon Musa, in exile in Britain, also accepted an invitation to return to join the regime, and was soon active supervising military operations against Nigerian peace-keeping troops. The take-over was deplored internationally, and calls were made for the urgent restoration of democratic government.

Some ministers of the SLPP-led alliance were arrested, but most escaped to Conakry, to form the nucleus of a government in exile. Hinga Norman eluded an assassination attempt and was evacuated to an American warship along with a group of expatriates and foreign-passport holders. In an ironic reversal of fortunes Norman then travelled to eastern and southern Sierra Leone, via Liberia, to organise the *kamajo* militia as a forest-based guerrilla against the new Freetown regime increasingly dominated by cadres of the RUF/SL.

The last stages of the operation to evacuate expatriates nearly ended in disaster, when AFRC soldiers and RUF/SL fighters attacked and overran the Mammy Yoko hotel, the assembly point also used as communications centre by the Nigerian commander of ECOMOG peace-keeping forces. Hopelessly outnumbered, the Nigerians ran out of ammunition after several hours of fighting. The Nigerians had earlier attempted to unnerve the coup makers through naval bombardment of Freetown. The attack on the Mammy Yoko was the AFRC/RUF response. Several Nigerian soldiers were killed. The AFRC later released others captured in the attack as a good-will gesture. With Nigerian troops in control of the international airport at Lungi a stand-off developed.

Several thousand Sierra Leoneans fled from Freetown, by boat and overland, mainly to Guinea and the Gambia, fearing both the chaos of AFRC/RUF rule and further Nigerian bombardment. Sporadic fighting erupted up-country between AFRC/RUF forces and *kamajo* militia elements.

International discussion of the Sierra Leonean case centred on the restoration of democratic government. There was little discussion of the deficiencies of the peace process – the ambiguous role of the *kamajoisia* during the cease-fire, or the detention of Sankoh by the Nigerians, for example.

Attempts to negotiate any resolution to this new crisis foundered on the absolute determination of the RUF/SL elements in the new Freetown regime to secure the release of Sankoh. African states and the United Nations finally decided on a partial trade blockade of the country and mandated ECOMOG to take military action to restore the elected government. This involved bombing by the Nigerian air-force. The irony of asking a Nigerian military dictator to fight to defend democracy in Sierra Leone and the inaccurate, even indiscriminate, bombing in the crowded city of Freetown aside, military pressure bore some political fruit – even at the price of local support – when the AFRC/RUF regime conceded, in October 1997, a return to power by the elected government within a six-month transition period. The agreement, sponsored by West African foreign ministers, made several major concessions to the RUF/SL, including that Foday Sankoh should return to play an active part in full implementation of the signed peace deal. At the time of writing (January 1998) there are few signs that this agreement will be honoured. Junta-leader Johnny-Paul Koroma claims a major sticking point is the continued involvement of Nigerian forces in peace-keeping operations. The AFRC/RUF alliance insists on demobilization only under neutral international inspection. On the other hand, a measure of peace has returned to some rural districts, for which civilians are duly grateful. The situation in the south and east of the country, where *kamajoisia* and AFRC troops confront each other remains very tense and a return to bush war seems a real possibility.

Interpretations

This book was prepared at a time when much still had to be inferred about the RUF/SL, its background, internal organization and motivation. Opportunity to interview a larger cross-section of young people with direct experience of fighting, including some RUF/SL combatants, allows a new sharpening of focus.

I am more than ever convinced that the RUF/SL must be understood against a background of region-wide dilemmas concerning social exclusion of the young. In the remarks below I reinforce the book's central proposition – that the increasing resort to violence stems from past corrupt patrimonial manipulation of educational and employment opportunities. First-hand evidence now confirms my earlier speculation that the RUF/SL became sectarian and peculiarly introverted in response to the unusual circumstances of its forest enclavization. But evidence from the same source – crucially from interviews with young people who have taken up arms *against* the RUF/SL – firmly underscores interpretation of the conflict as an aspect of a more general crisis of youth with regional or continental implications.[1]

Some commentators appeared puzzled by the alliance that emerged between former enemies after the coup of 25 May 1997. They would be less puzzled if they tried to understand the violence as a manifestation of a wider social movement of marginalized youth. Interviews with rank-and-file combatants from all three main factions – the RUF/SL, the NPRC-enlarged army, and the Kamajo militia – show that in one crucial respect it hardly matters to which faction a combatant belongs; all tend to share membership in an excluded and educationally-disadvantaged youth underclass. Young combatants are clear about the specific circumstantial reasons they fight *against* each other. But they are even clearer about what they are fighting *for* – namely, education and jobs.

However, I welcome the chance to be a bit more explicit about an aspect of my argument that has puzzled some critics. I should have been much clearer about what I meant by interpreting the RUF/SL as a movement shaped by its 'excluded intellectuals'.

I was perhaps too ready to credit a greater influence than may have been the case to highly-educated civilian members of the RUF/SL's small 'war council'. This was to manifest a bias towards a conventional notion of the 'intellectual'.[2] I am now inclined to think that the movement's politico-strategic 'motor' lay elsewhere. It seems more likely that the key strategists keeping the movement alive and obdurate against such daunting odds, though at utterly unacceptable civilian costs, were combatant cadres, some at least of mixed Liberian-Sierra Leonean descent, and many with little more than primary education.

It may seem odd, at first sight, to persist in regarding members of such a group as intellectuals in any sense at all. My use of the term – I now need to stress – is broadly compatible with that proposed by Eyerman and Jamison (1991) in their book on social movements. 'Movement intellectuals' (Eyerman and Jamison's coinage) are thinkers

---

1 An exasperated Kenyan educator was heard recently on BBC World Service asking whether her country would have to lapse into war before the government would pay attention to the dangerous state of alienation among young people.

2 My earlier view was perhaps too much influenced by evidence that, for example, abducted college lecturer I. H. Deen Jalloh directed RUF/SL intelligence operations.

(ideologues, apologists, strategists etc, whether highly-trained or autodidacts) who develop their analytical skills on the job, in response to the needs and circumstances of their movement.

That every social movement (however unprepossessing) has its intellectuals, because the social creativity essential to survival requires intellectual shaping, is no great discovery. What is of much greater interest is to examine the kinds of problems such intellectuals address and the resources they draw upon in carrying out their work.

It seems to me important to stress that the intellectual milieu of the RUF/SL is by-and-large a product of basic education. Most abductees possessed some education. The movement excluded the unschooled from guerrilla training; illiterates were kept only as carriers and labourers (Peters & Richards 1998). There is some evidence that leading fighters were for the most part primary school leavers or low-level secondary drop-outs. Opposing the intellectual sophisticates of the Momoh regime as best they could 'movement intellectuals' built with the intellectual resources to hand. These were for the most part attitudes and values derived from primary education.

Primary education concerns itself with basic and objectively verifiable skills. Either you can read, write and count, or you cannot. There are few shady areas where opinions and bias lurk. In so many interviews, informants repeatedly stressed, in naively objective terms, their level of brilliance at primary school, the position they took, the number of double promotions they achieved. This was their golden age. Only later did problems set in. Further up the ladder of educational progress (at secondary and tertiary levels) it is harder to separate right from wrong, brilliance from incompetence. Here, reasons for failure are more complex, and fewer objectively verifiable, and more social factors are invoked. Failure might be explained in terms of lack of support from parents, teacher favouritism, sexual harassment, or corrupt manipulation of examination procedures.

By the time coveted scholarship nominations for overseas study are in prospect educational success and failure are fully enveloped in the fog of political intrigue. The APC regime never resisted the temptation to use higher-education scholarship allocations to make political friends or bring opponents to heel. This was a world of rampant patrimonialism in which it was not unknown for cabinet ministers blatantly to lobby for scholarships for their girlfriends. In such a world educational effort and achievement cannot meaningfully be related. Failure cannot usefully be understood in instrumental terms. It is a world where the very idea of bureaucratic hierarchy that modern education was designed to support is called into question.

One response is to turn away from hierarchy entirely and seek again the transparency of primary educational attainment, forging egalitarian sets of anti-patrimonial social accountabilities as 'objective' in application as a set of tests of basic educational competence. Evidence I review below suggests the RUF/SL's 'movement intellectuals' struggled to create, internally, a movement based on meritocratic and egalitarian ideas about social accountability that 'added up' like primary arithmetic. These principles were paralleled by equally obvious negative 'arithmetic' uses of violence against perceived enemies. In cutting off villagers' hands in response to the growing threat of the *kamajoisia* the movement set out – I suggest below – to confront the murky magic of patrimonial power with the unsubtle obviousness of an elementary subtraction sum.

i. The RUF/SL as a protest against educational collapse

The Kabbah government speaks of the RUF as 'bandits', and even the young people absorbed into irregular and regular units in the government army after the NPRC coup of April 1992 as 'thieves', 'criminals' and 'vagabonds' (Anon. 1997). But when interviewed[3] young combatants of all factions regularly represented themselves as victims of educational collapse (Peters & Richards 1998). Some were 'on the street' before the war due to lack of school fees. Others joined a militia force after war had closed their local schools in order to survive. Frequently it was commented that joining a militia force was a type of education (in weapons and ambush tactics). Combatants volunteered for demobilization having been promised this would be a quick way to re-start their education. Many rejoined irregular units after the coup of 25 May 1997, their hopes dashed.

RUF/SL voices and the voices of young people ranged against them (as RSLMF irregulars and *kamajo* fighters) agree that educational frustration is key to the conflict.

Two testimonies, one from the beginning and the other from the end of the period of fighting, strike at the heart of the RUF/SL perspective on the war. One ex-combatant lectured by Sankoh himself, as the RUF/SL head of ideology at the Vocational School 'training base' in Pendembu in 1991, recalled being taught that the RUF was fighting to right transparent injustices, because 'people were assigned salaries not jobs . . . unqualified people were offered jobs, and qualified people were left unemployed. . .' (Richards et al. 1996). More recent testimony comes

---

[3] The new evidence reviewed in this and following sections is mainly from recent work by Krijn Peters and myself. I am grateful to Krijn Peters for access to his interview material, some of which will be published in a forthcoming joint article (Peters & Richards 1998).

from the feared RUF/SL Kailahun battalion commander 'Maskita' (Samuel Bockarie). Shortly after he had arrived in Freetown after the May 1997 coup Bockarie was invited to speak on radio. In explaining himself, and RUF/SL violence, to a bruised nation he chose to begin by listing the educational frustrations he had experienced in Kailahun and Liberia.

Further evidence emerged in the course of an interview with an apprentice carpenter who had joined the RUF/SL after having been abducted in a raid on a district in north-western Sierra Leone early in 1995 (Peters & Richards 1998). Trained as a guerrilla in the Malal Hills camp, our source portrays the RUF/SL, internally, not as a bandit rabble but a well-organized and disciplined movement with a clearly-articulated pedagogic-political agenda.

According to the young carpenter's account, conveying this agenda was the movement's first priority in relation to abductees. Secure in camp after a forced march of seven days, and a day's rest, the abductees were straight away called to a lecture in which the movement sought to explain itself. This ran as follows. There was no fairness and transparency in the system in Sierra Leone. Despite mineral riches, there was no development of roads, schools and health centres in rural areas. No one in government was listening. Thus the time for talking had passed. Violence was now the only option. Young people had been abducted for guerrilla training to regain their birthright.

Unable to cope with the truly daunting privations of life on the march – the rain, the never-ending toting of heavy loads, the regular shortage of food and ammunition, the constant fear of ambush or beatings – our informant never rose above the ranks, and was glad to have quit. Even so, he was quite clear that the lecture made a lot of sense. He went on to suggest that the movement was very confident its analysis was widely shared by a large number of young Sierra Leoneans with experience of the struggle for education and jobs. This was why it was not contradictory to make cadres through abduction. By way of illustration, he told us about a sizeable group of government soldiers at the Zogoda camp (a place he had visited on operations), held not so much as prisoners-of-war but in the confident expectation that they would in time comprehend and change sides willingly.

What helps explain the war and subsequent developments (such as the merging of a large section of the NPRC-recruited army with the RUF/SL) is exactly this – that the experiences and concerns of the RUF/SL cadres are matched by those of young fighters *opposed* to the RUF/SL. Explicit evidence – and an ominous portent to those who believe that the *kamajoisia* provide a military solution without threatening the patrimonial order – is to be found in the testimony of a young *kamajo* fighter interviewed by Krijn Peters towards the end of 1996 (Peters & Richards 1998). This young man had joined a *kamajo* group only after his school in Kono had been closed by fighting. Until then his dream had been to travel overseas to study microbiology. Typically, he stressed his prowess at school, noting that mathematics, one of his best subjects, was the basis of all science. He hated the RUF/SL for having disrupted his own education – RUF cadres were not fit even to be buried, he opined. But then when asked why the war started he offers a startlingly clearly-focused insight into the mind of his enemy.

Most RUF/SL cadres against whom he fought, he informed us, were students like himself. You could tell this, he said, from the hand-written letters outlining their aims, left scattered in the villages they attacked. From these letters he knew that they fought because they were frustrated. The cause of the frustration was obvious. It lay in the lack of transparency and accountability in provision of educational resources in Sierra Leone. He then went on to develop a critique of Sierra Leoneans who study overseas and put nothing back into the system, condemning the opaque procedures of political patronage through which scholarships were allocated in the first place. The RUF/SL struggle might have been justified, he thought, had the cadres taken their fight straight to the heart of government in the capital where they would have been welcomed by a majority of Sierra Leoneans, rather than unjustifiably turning violence against impoverished rural civilians no better off than themselves.

ii. RUF/SL failure and enclavization

There is much still to learn about the internal organization of the RUF/SL before reaching definitive conclusions about how closely the movement might conform to the ideal egalitarian type of enclave organization theorized by Mary Douglas (a suggestion made in the main body of the book). Forest incarceration may have served to intensify prior enclave predispositions of underclass recruits; alternatively, the RUF/SL may not have been a sect by original choice or intention, but became sectarian through circumstances (including its bungled birth and rejection by the wider community). But there is now definite evidence from informants that the egalitarian tendencies were real, and not just the movement's propaganda.

Informants report that considerable care was taken to control the redistribution and use of items captured in raids (looting for personal use was dealt with by summary execution). Considerable attention was given to health care and education (even though the movement might have no more than a few boxes of aspirins or ripped pages from school readers). Abductees report being able to report sick and draw from the limited medical stores as they had need. Despite obvious hazards, great efforts were made to transfer abducted schoolgirls from the Malal Hills camp to the greater security of the Zogoda during the cease-fire period to resume their education. Even the approach to religion appears to have reflected a carefully-calculated egalitarianism. Each camp had its mosque and church. According to testimony, camp members were free to pray in either (but once a day pray they must or face punishment). In the new social world of the RUF/SL's imagining there was no place for tribalism – care was taken to mix up language groups in camps and Krio (the national lingua franca) was insisted upon as medium of communication. Even that locus of classic hierarchical values – military command – was apparently subject to an egalitarian re-think. One less-than-fully-convinced combatant, objecting to the RUF/SL's abandonment of birth-order ranking, a basic principle of patrimonialism in the wider society, complained that young people his juniors at school were able to order him about due to their greater daring and success in battle. It appears that only a few RUF/SL cadres belonged permanently to an officer class; others – as in 'Shining Path' – were 'commanders for the day' (Richards et al. 1996). Respect within the movement seems to have been based as much on combat success as on rank.

Further, we might wish to note that Sankoh conforms quite well to the profile of an enclave 'leader' suggested by Douglas (1993) – an otiose figure with exhortatory rather than a hands-on executive powers.

Sankoh may have adopted such a style of leadership more by default than intention. By the time of the cease-fire the RUF/SL had six or more major forest camps scattered up and down the country, and a series of defensive outliers. Much time and effort was taken up by the dangerous business of maintaining inter-camp communication. An informant from the Malal Hills group (Peters & Richards 1998) described the process in graphic detail. Everything hinged on field radio sets (like Pol Pot, whose secretive Khmer Rouge forest insurgency is said to be one of Sankoh's sources of inspiration, Sankoh was a trained radio signals technician). Sankoh would contact the group regularly from the Zogoda – typically at the assembly for evening prayers – to encourage, chide, promote. But from time to time sets or batteries failed. If the radio link fell silent for more than a certain number of days a party would be despatched to the Zogoda (several days to the east by hazardous bush by-pass routes) to re-establish communication directly. Our informant conceded, however, that many camp recruits had spent more than a year in the movement without seeing Sankoh in person. Understandably, to them, he was a semi-mythic god-like presence.

His existence long denied, Sankoh came later to be viewed more as some kind of evil genius, manipulating a movement of abducted children against their will. But whether or not Sankoh has assumed some of the characteristics of an enclave leader is an issue of some substance. History shows that the opponents of sectarian rebellions regularly miscalculate the (in reality strictly limited) power and significance of enclave leadership. They focus too much attention on trying to 'take out' the supposed evil genius. Forces besieging the German city of Muenster in the 1530s regularly bombarded the inhabitants with pamphlets offering the millenarian rebels amnesty but only if they would betray their leader (a Dutch weaver, Jan van Bockelzoon, who believed himself to be the Messiah). Leaders of egalitarian enclaves lead by prestige not direct command. Thus attacking the leader solves nothing. It may only strengthen the die-hard resolution of the mass of egalitarian enclavists. This suggests it was an error to remove Sankoh, by detention, from the peace process; egalitarians are fortified by martyrdom.

iii. Sectarian violence

Egalitarian enclaves and hierarchically organized collectivities defend themselves in different ways. The modern state's professional army, with its rigid command structure, and the 'unthinking' responsiveness of trained soldiers, is about as close as it is possible to get to the ideal type of 'bureaucratic' hierarchy. The approach of the enclave to defence is different.

The world within the enclave is 'good' but 'weakly' organized (role specialization is a problem where social harmony is based on sharing and treating people as equals). There is a corresponding emphasis on the 'shell' of the organization, and great concern both that the shell might be breached by hostile forces and that members of the group will defect. The archetypical enclave defensive structure is a moat or wall.

The 'wall' defines the zone of security. Douglas (1993) argues, in effect, that this 'wall' is erected as a 'moral' barrier in the believer's mind. 'Leave if you must' the would-be defector is told, but beyond the 'wall' there lies a great wilderness with many hidden dangers.

If the 'wall' that held together the RUF/SL as a secular sect was erected first through a kind of moral persuasion (exposure to a world of redistributional values) I think we should note that it was kept in place by a set of additional and much more negative forces. The RUF/SL was also, and most significantly, locked in place as an enclave by outside perceptions of the movement's utter *immorality*, and by the enthusiasm of outside agents to act on that perception with a countervailing violence of their own.

The charge of immorality was unfair to the extent that early atrocities were largely the work of alien mercenary elements long since departed the scene of their crime. By 1994-6 most of the movement's members were young Sierra Leonean abductees. But village lynchings and summary executions of rebel suspects by opposing forces (soldiers and *kamajoisia*) never ceased, and served to frighten off defectors right up until the coup of 25 May 1997. This did much of the RUF/SL leadership's work for it by rendering real the movement's mental 'partitioning' of the country into 'safe' forest enclaves and a 'rotten' and 'collapsed' wider society, with two elements separated by a 'dead' zone of devastation and hostility.

It was this 'dead' zone that held the members of the movement together. It was arduous to cross. Survivors turned up at its margins as the perfect picture of the dishevelled 'bush creatures' the wider society so feared (Peters & Richards 1998).

This both secured a kind of protection for the camps but also exemplified the truth of the movement's claims, that the country was a wreck. Informants escaping the RUF/SL reported to us their surprise to discover that beyond the 'dead' zone life continued more or less as normal (Peters & Richards 1998).

This then brings us to the crucial role of *kamajo* groups in shaping the latter part of the conflict. Villagers and RUF/SL cadres we have talked to are equally clear that the patterns of otherwise apparently 'senseless' violence by the RUF/SL – notably the spate of mutilations marring the latter stages of the conflict – were a specific response to the rising 'menace' of the *kamajoisia*.[4]

For example, in June 1996 an RUF combatant captured on active service and held by the army in Bo told me the RUF/SL was no longer 'at war' with the RSLMF – the struggle was now between the movement and the *kamajo* militia. He explained massacre and mutilation of

---

[4] The calculus of violence is as ever a tricky subject. My point is not to rationalize the indefensible but to raise the possibility that we should recognize different 'styles' of violence belonging to the different parties to the conflict. Provisionally, we might recognize conventional RSLMF military violence, certain patterns of atrocity associated with the 'special forces' (deriving from Liberia), RUF/SL 'enclave violence' and vigilante/*kamajoisia* violence (including beheadings). In the culture of hunting in the region special power is seen to reside in the head of an animal and chiefly authority requires that heads be presented to chiefs. There are recent reports of a spate of beheadings by *kamajoisia*. Outside commentators are in danger of lumping all these manifestations of violence together as 'new barbarism' whereas parties to the conflict 'read' the messages in a differentiated manner.

civilians in an isolated village, Gondama, in northern Kamajei chiefdom as 'revenge' for *kamajo* operations against RUF camps. Villagers, he asserted specifically, were guiding the *kamajo* fighters against the RUF, helping them reclaim some of the space serving to protect the RUF/SL.

But why did the 'punishment fit the crime' in this young man's mind? Here it is important to understand that the *kamajo* militia was, by origin at least, a genuine 'grass-roots' reaction to the war, as much a response to the corrupt government army as to the RUF/SL. The young *kamajo* informant cited above pointed out that his unit was called to service on the orders of his local chief. Furthermore, he notes that once *kamajo* groups had been formed they shared the 'right to the land' (freedom of movement) with the army. (Only latterly did the Kabbah government seek to intervene in the recruitment and kitting out of *kamajo* units, thereby risking turning them into an extra-constitutional quasi-governmental 'ethnic' militia.) Thus by origin at least, *kamajo* militia units represented a revival of an older local patrimonial power, untrammelled by state interference. The target of *kamajo* militia intervention was the reclaiming of the 'dead' zone from either of the main parties to the war (RSLMF and RUF/SL) and returning it to the domain of the chiefs. *Kamajo* militia fighters achieved this by re-asserting their 'functionality' in 'dead' zone affairs; they protected farmers re-entering the 'dead' zone, and hunted and killed RUF/SL cadres much as they once hunted wild animals under the authority of the chief, lord of the land. Paramount chiefs, in local tradition, first asserted their title to the forest through prowess in hunting. The young *kamajo* informant stresses that *kamajo* fighters, as revitalized citizens of the 'dead' zone, had the magical power to move at will, and control all spaces, 'appearing in places where you would not expect' (Peters & Richards 1998). *Kamajo* magical powers of movement and bullet protection actually worked, he vehemently asserted, even though he now viewed them as the work of the Devil (having become a born-again Christian while undergoing demobilization in Freetown). The RUF/SL seem, equally, to have been in no doubt that the *kamajo* threat was real. Prepared to battle corrupted state patrimonialism, the movement seems to have become very badly disoriented by this unexpected resurgence of a more authentic local patrimonial power threatening to take away its protective 'wall'.

It is the RUF/SL reaction to this threat that is of present interest. Douglas (1993) has noted that 'enclave' movements regularly reject magic. It might be possible to see mutilation as an extreme form of 'rationalist' response to the patrimonial magic of the *kamajo*. Chiefly power 'flies' to the defence of farmers re-entering the protective 'dead' zone, carrying the battle for authority and accountability to the very gates of the RUF/SL bush camps. If you attack us with 'magic', the RUF/SL seems to say, see, here, we will respond, but with an anti-magical and obvious use of socially-disabling violence. You seek to restore the functionality of the 'dead' zone as land for food production (through the agency of young fighters clad in mystical bullet-proof jackets)? See, here, we will cut off the hands of their mothers seeking to harvest the rice. You want villagers to take part in elections-before-peace (in which, in the chaos, anyone can conjure up the democratic mandate they choose)? See, here, we will cut off the fingers of those who vote. Do some our conscripts plan to run back to their families and hide behind the gowns of the chiefs? See, here, we will cut off their feet.

On this account the political violence of the RUF/SL is a despairing last-ditch deployment of a sectarian elementary-school 'rationalism' against the dark, magical forces of the revived patrimonial authority of the rural chiefs.

Additional References

Anon. 1997. *Restoration to democratic civilian rule in Sierra Leone: a 90-day policy framework for the restoration of the democratically elected Government.* (mimeo).

Eyerman, R. and Jamison J. 1991. *Social movements: a cognitive approach.* Cambridge: Polity Press.

Peters, K. & Richards, P. 1998. 'Why we fight: voices of youth ex-combatants in Sierra Leone.' *Africa*, v. 68(2).

Richards, P., Abdullah, I., Amara, J., Muana, P., Stanley, E., & Vincent, J. 1996/1997. *Reintegration of war-affected youth and ex-combatants: a study of the social and economic opportunity structure in Sierra Leone.* Unpublished draft report.

Abraham, A. 1975. 'Cannibalism and African historiography', In A. Abraham (ed.) *Topics in Sierra Leone history: a counter-colonial interpretation.* Freetown: Leone Publishers.

Abraham, A. 1978. *Mende government and politics under colonial rule: a historical study of political change in Sierra Leone 1890–1937.* London and Freetown: Oxford University Press and Sierra Leone University Press.

Abraham, A. and Sesay, H. 1993. 'Regional politics and social services provision since independence.' In C. Magbaily Fyle, ed. *The state and the provision of social services in Sierra Leone since independence, 1961–1991.* Dakar: CODESRIA.

Abrahams, R. 1987. 'Sungusungu: village vigilante groups in Tanzania', *African Affairs* 86:179–196.

Abrahams, R. 1989. 'Law and order and the state in the Nyamwezi and Sukuma area of Tanzania', *Africa* 59(4): 356–370.

Adams, J. S. and McShane, T. O. 1992. *The myth of wild Africa: conservation without illusion.* New York: W. W. Norton.

Amnesty International, 1992. *The extrajudicial execution of suspected rebels and collaborators.* London: International Secretariat of Amnesty International, Index AFR 51/02/92.

Amnesty International, 1993. *Sierra Leone. Prisoners of War? Children detained in barracks and prison.* London: International Secretariat of Amnesty International, Index AFR 51/06/93.

Ang, Ien 1985. *Watching Dallas.* London: Methuen.

Ang, I. 1994. 'In the realm of uncertainty: the global village and capitalist postmodernity'. In Crowley and Mitchell, eds., *Communication Theory Today.*

Atherton, J. H. 1979. 'Early economies of Sierra Leone and Liberia: archaeological and historical reflections'. In V. R. Dorjahn and B. L. Isaacs, eds., *Essays on the economic anthropology of Liberia and Sierra Leone.* Philadelphia: Institute for Liberian Studies.

Atkinson, P., Hoult, A. & Mills, D. 1992. 'Sierra Leone 1991 – a security crisis'. Unpublished report, Refugee Studies Centre, Oxford.

Barker, M. 1982. *The new racism.* London: Junction Books.

Barrows, W. 1976. *Grassroots politics in an African state: integration and development in Sierra Leone.* New York: Africana Publishing.

Bates, R. H. 1989. *Beyond the miracle of the market: the political economy of agrarian development in Kenya.* Cambridge: Cambridge University Press.

Bayart, J.-F. 1993. *The state in Africa: the politics of the belly.* London: Longman.

Beatty, K. J. 1915. *Human Leopards.* London.

Bellman, B. 1980. 'Masks, societies and secrecy among the Falla Kpelle'. In M. Adams, ed., *Ethnologische Zeitschrift* (Zurich), 1: 61–78.

Bellman, B. 1984. *The language of secrecy: symbols and metaphors in Poro ritual.* New Brunswick: Rutgers University Press.

Bledsoe, C. and Cohen, B. 1993. 'Introduction'. In C. Bledsoe and B. Cohen, eds., *Social dynamics of adolescent fertility in sub-Saharan Africa.* Washington DC: National Academy Press, pp. 5–15.

Block, R. 1992 'EC's timber imports fuel Liberia civil war'. *The Independent on Sunday* (London), 22nd November, 1992.

Bourdieu, P. 1979. *Outline of a theory of practice.* Cambridge: Cambridge University Press.

Bradbury, M. 1995. *Rebels without a cause: an exploratory report for CARE Britain on the conflict in Sierra Leone.* London: unpublished mimeo.

Bradshaw, S. 1996. 'The coming chaos?' *Moving Pictures Bulletin*, Issue 25, February, pp. 18–19.

Braidwood, P. 1994. *Black Poor and White philanthropists: London's Blacks and the foundation of the Sierra Leone settlement 1786–1791.* Liverpool: University of Liverpool Press.

Brehun, L. 1991. *Liberia: the war of horror.* Legon: Adwinsa Publications.

Brownlie, I. 1979. *African boundaries: a legal and diplomatic encyclopaedia.* London: C. Hurst & Co.

Burnham, P. 1980. *Opportunity and constraint in a savanna society: the Gbaya of Meiganga, Cameroon.* London and New York: Academic Press.

Butt-Thomson, F. W. 1929. *West African Secret Societies: their organisations, officials and teaching.* London: Witherby.

Carney, J. 1993. 'From hands to tutors: African expertise in the South Carolina rice economy'. *Agricultural History* 67(3): 1–30.

Carpenter, A. J. 1978 'The history of rice in Africa.' In I. Buddenhagen & G. Persley, eds., *Rice in West Africa.* London: Academic Press.

Cartwright, J. 1970. *Politics in Sierra Leone, 1947–67.* Toronto: University of Toronto Press.

Central Statistics Office 1991. *Report on Labour Force Survey 1988–89.* Freetown: CSO, Government of Sierra Leone.

Chase, R. S., Hill, E. B. and Kennedy, P. 1996. 'Pivotal states and US strategy'. *Foreign Affairs* 75(1): 33–51.

Chaveau, J., Dozon, J. & Richard, J. 1981. 'Histoires de riz, histories d'igname: le cas de la moyenne Côte d'Ivoire', *Africa* 51: 621–658.

Clapham, C. 1976. *Liberia and Sierra Leone: an essay in comparative politics.* Cambridge: Cambridge University Press.

Clausewitz, C. von. 1832. (1968). *On war* (trans. J. J. Graham). Harmondsworth: Penguin Books.

Committee of Investigation. 1994. *Report of the investigation committee set up by the government to inquire into the cicumstances leading to the killing of Rev. Fr. Felim McAllister CSSP and other expatriates at Panguma on 12th March 1994.* Freetown, August 1994. (mimeo).

Conteh, B. K. 1996. *Institutions and rural development: the case of rural banking in Sierra Leone.* Unpublished PhD thesis, University of Leeds.

Cosentino, D. 1982. *Defiant maids and stubborn farmers: tradition and invention in Mende story performance.* Cambridge: Cambridge University Press.

Cosentino, D. 1989. 'Midnight charters: Musa Wo and the Mende myths of chaos.' In W. Arens & I. Karp, eds., *The Creativity of Power.* Washington DC: Smithsonian Institution Press.

Creveld, M. van 1992. *On future war.* London: Brasseys.

Crone, G. R. 1937. *The voyages of Cadamosto: and other documents on Western Africa in the second half of the fifteenth century.* London: Hakluyt Society, vol. LXXX.

Currens, G. E. 1972. 'The Loma avunculate: an exercise in the utility of two models', *Ethnology* 11: 111–121.

Dapper, O. 1668. *The new description of Africa.* Amsterdam.

Dalby, D. 1977. *The language map of Africa.* London: International African Institute.

Davies, A. G. & Richards, P. 1991. *Rain Forest in Mende Life: Resources and Subsistence Strategies in Rural Communities Around the Gola North Forest Reserve (Sierra Leone).* Report to the UK Overseas Development Administration: Department of Anthropology, University College London.

Davidson, B. 1992. *The Black Man's Burden: Africa and the curse of the nation state.* London: James Currey.

D'Azevedo, W. 1962. 'Some historical problems in the delineation of a Central West Atlantic region', *Annals, New York Academy of Sciences* 96(2): 512–38.

Dennis, B. G. 1972. *The Gbandes: a people of the Liberian hinterland.* Chicago: Nelson-Hall.

Douglas, M., 1986. 'The social preconditions of radical scepticism'. In J. Law, ed., *Power, action and belief: a new sociology of knowledge.* London: Routledge and Kegan Paul.

Douglas, M., 1987. *How institutions think.* London: Routledge.

Douglas, M. 1993. *In the wilderness: the doctrine of defilement in the Book of Numbers.* Sheffield: JSOT Press.

Douglas, M. & Wildavsky, A. 1982. *Risk and culture.* Berkeley: University of California Press.

Dorjahn, V, 1959. 'The organization and function of the Ragbenle Society of the Temne', *Africa* 29: 156–170.

Duffield, M. 1994. 'Complex emergencies and the crisis of developmentalism', *IDS Bulletin* 25(4): 37–45.

Duffield, M. 1995. 'The symphony of the damned: racial discourse, complex political emergencies and humanitarian aid', Draft paper – School of Public Policy, University of Birmingham.

Ellis, S. 1995. 'Liberia 1989–1994: a study of ethnic and spiritual violence', *African Affairs* 94, no. 375: 165–198.

Fage, J. D. 1978. *A history of Africa.* London: Hutchinson.

Fairhead, J. and Leach, M. 1996. 'Enriching the landscape: social history and the management of transition ecology in the forest-savanna mosaic (Republic of Guinée)', *Africa* 66(1): 14–36.

Falconer, J. 1990. *The major significance of 'minor' forest products: the local use and value of forests in the West African humid zone. Community Forestry Note,* 6. Rome: FAO.

Ferme, M. C. (1992) *'Hammocks belong to men, stools to women': constructing and contesting gender domains in a Mende village (Sierra Leone, West Africa).* PhD Dissertation, University of Chicago.

Focus on Sierra Leone 1995.

Ford, M. 1992. 'Kola production and settlement mobility among the Dan of Nimba, Liberia', *African Economic History* 20:51–63.

Fulton, R. M. 1972. 'The political structures and functions of Poro in Kpelle society', *American Anthropologist* 74: 1218–1233.

Furley, O. 1995. 'Child soldiers in Africa'. In O. Furley, ed. *Conflict in Africa*. London: Tauris.

Fyfe, C. 1962. *A history of Sierra Leone*. London: Oxford University Press.

Fyfe, C. 1964. *Sierra Leone Inheritance*. London: Oxford University Press.

Fyle, C. and Jones, E. 1980. *Krio-English Dictionary*. Oxford: Oxford University Press.

Fyle, C. Magbaily, ed. 1993. *The state and the provision of social services in Sierra Leone since independence, 1961–1991*. Dakar: CODESRIA.

Gaddafi, M. n.d. *The Green Book*. Benghazi.

Gaisseau, P.-D. 1954. *The sacred forest: the fetishist and magic rites of the Toma* (trans. A. Ross). London: Weidenfeld and Nicolson.

Garrett, L. 1996. 'The return of infectious disease', *Foreign Affairs* 75(1): 66–79.

Giddens, A. 1989. *The consequences of modernity*. London: Polity Press.

Gilroy, P. 1993. *The Black Atlantic: modernity and the double consciousness*. London & New York: Verso.

Gittins, A. J. 1987. *Mende religion: aspects of belief and thought in Sierra Leone*. Studia Instituti Anthropos 41. Nettetal (Germany): Steyler Verlag.

Glanville, R. R. 1938. 'Rice production on swamps', *Sierra Leone Agricultural Notes*, No. 7.

Goodwin-Gill, G, & Cohn, I. 1994. *Child soldiers: the role of children in armed conflicts*. Oxford: Clarendon Press.

Greenberg, J. H. 1963. *The languages of Africa*. Bloomington: University of Indiana Press.

Greenhouse, S. 1995. 'The greening of US diplomacy: focus on ecology.' *The New York Times International*, Monday, October 9th, 1995.

Guyer, J. and Eno Blinga, S. M. 1995. 'Wealth in people as wealth in knowledge: accumulation and composition in Equatorial Africa', *Journal of African History* 36: 91–120.

Guyer, J & Richards, P. 1996. 'The invention of biodiversity: social perspectives on the management of biological variety in Africa', *Africa* 66(1), (Special Issue *The Social Shaping of Biodiversity: perspectives on the management of biological variety in Africa*).

Hair, P. 1964. 'An early seventeenth-century vocabulary of Vai', *African Studies* 23(3/4): 129–39.

Hair, P. 1967. 'Ethnolinguistic continuity on the Guinea coast', *Journal of African History* 8(2): 247–68.

Hair, P. 1968. 'An ethnolinguistic inventory of the Lower Guinea Coast before 1700: Part 1', *African Language Review* 7:47–73.

Hair, P. 1987. 'Colonial Freetown and the study of African languages', *Africa* 57: 560–65.

Hancock, I. 1983. 'Manding lexical behavior in Sierra Leone Krio.'. In I. R. Dihoff, ed., *Current approaches to African linguistics*. (Vol. 1). Dordrecht: Foris Publications.

Hannerz, U. 1987. 'The world in creolization', *Africa* 57: 546–559.

Hannerz, U. 1992. *Cultural complexity: studies in the social organization of meaning*. New York: Columbia University Press.

Hardin, K. L. 1992. *The aesthetics of action: continuity and change in a West African town.* Washington: Smithsonian Institution Press.

Harding, F. and Mokuwa, E. 1995. *AIDS awareness and the Sande Society in Sierra Leone.* Unpublished report to ESCOR, Overseas Development Administration, London.

Helm, S., 1995. *The Independent*, Wednesday, 22nd November 1995

Henkemans, A. B. 1995. *Forest products are a free gift of nature: gender issues in the exploitation and trade of non-timber forest products in the Korup Project Area, SW Province, Cameroon.* Dissertation, TAO, Wageningen Agricultural University.

Hill, M. H. 1984. Unpublished. 'Where to begin? The place of the hunter founder in Mende histories', *Anthropos* 79: 653–6.

Hodges, R. K. 1992. 'A view of psychological problems resulting from the Liberian civil conflict and recommendations for counselling and other corrective activities'. Appendix V, in *A Report of the Round Table Conference on Strategies and Direction for the Reconstruction and Development of Liberia.* The New African Research & Development Agency, Monrovia.

Hoejbjerg, C. K. 1995. *Staging the invisible: essays on Loma ritual and cultural knowledge.* PhD Thesis, Institute of Anthropology, University of Copenhagen.

Holsoe, S. 1966. 'The Condo confederation in western Liberia.' *Liberian Historical Review*, 3(1): 1–28.

Holsoe, S. 1979. 'Economic activities in the Liberian area: the pre-European period to 1900'. In V. R. Dorjahn and B. L. Isaacs, eds., *Essays on the economic anthropology of Liberia and Sierra Leone.* Philadelphia: Institute for Liberian Studies.

Huntington, S. P. 1993. 'The clash of civilizations?' *Foreign Affairs*, 72 (Summer).

Innes, G. 1969. *A Mende–English dictionary.* Cambridge: Cambridge University Press.

Jackson, M. 1989a. *Paths towards a clearing: radical empiricism and ethnographic enquiry.* Bloomington: Indiana University Press.

Jackson, M., 1989b. 'The man who could turn into an elephant'. In *Paths towards a clearing: radical empiricism and ethnographic enquiry.* Bloomington: Indiana University Press.

Jedrej, C. 1976. 'Medicine, fetish and secret society in a West African culture'. *Africa* 46: 247–257.

Johnny, M., Karimu, J. and Richards, P. 1981. 'Upland and swamp rice farming systems in Sierra Leone: the social context of technological change', *Africa* 51(2): 596–620.

Jones, A. 1981. 'Who were the Vai?', *Journal of African History*, 22(2): 159–178.

Jones, A. 1983. *From slaves to palm kernels: a history of the Galinhas country (West Africa) 1730–1890.* Wiesbaden: Steiner Verlag.

Jones, A. 1990. 'Decompiling Dapper: a preliminary search for evidence?...' *History in Africa*, 17: 171–209.

Jordan, T. G. and Kaups, M. 1989. *The American backwoods frontier: an ethnic and ecological interpretation.* Baltimore: Johns Hopkins University Press.

Jusu, M. S. 1995. *The genus Oryza: sources and uses of genetic variability by Susu and Limba farmers in Sierra Leone.* (Unpublished research proposal, Working Group for Technology and Agrarian Development and Department of Plant Breeding, Wageningen Agricultural University).

Kalous, M. 1974. *Cannibals and Tongo Players of Sierra Leone.* Auckland: privately printed.

Kaplan, R. D. 1993. *Balkan Ghosts: a journey through history*. London: Macmillan.

Kaplan, R. D. 1994. 'The coming anarchy: how scarcity, crime, overpopulation, and disease are rapidly destroying the social fabric of our planet.' *Atlantic Monthly*, February pp. 44–76.

Keen, D. 1994. *The benefits of famine: a political economy of famine and relief in south-western Sudan, 1983–1989*. Princeton: Princeton University Press.

Keen, D, 1995. ' "Sell-game": the economics of conflict in Sierra Leone', paper given at *West Africa at War: Anarchy or Peace in Liberia and Sierra Leone?* A one-day Conference held at the Department of Anthropology, University College London, London WC1E 6BT, 21st October 1995.

Kellner, D. 1995. *Media culture: cultural studies, identity and politics between the modern and the post-modern*. London: Routledge.

Kilson, M. 1966. *Political change in a West African state: a study of the modernization process in Sierra Leone*. Cambridge, Mass.: Harvard University Press.

Kpundeh, S. J. 1995. *Politics and corruption in Africa: a case study of Sierra Leone*. Larnham, MD: University Press of America.

Kriger, N. 1992. *Zimbabwe's guerrilla war: peasant voices*. Cambridge: Cambridge University Press.

La Fontaine, J. 1985. *Initiation: ritual drama and secret knowledge across the world*. Harmondsworth: Penguin Books.

Laan, H. L. van der 1965. *The Sierra Leone diamonds: an economic study covering the years 1952–1961*. London and Freetown: Oxford University Press & Sierra Leone University Press.

Launay, R. 1982. *Traders without trade: responses to change in two Dyula communities*. Cambridge: Cambridge University Press.

Lave, J. 1986. 'The values of quantification'. In J. Law, ed., *Power, action and belief: a new sociology of knowledge*. London: Routledge.

Leach, M. & Fairhead, M. 1994. *The forest islands of Kissidougou: social dynamics of environmental change in West Africa's forest-savanna mosaic*. Report to ESCOR, Overseas Development Administration (mimeo, 96 pp.).

Leopold, R, 1991. *Prescriptive alliance and ritual collaboration in Loma society*. Unpublished PhD Dissertation, Indiana University.

Linares, O. 1981. 'From tidal swamp to inland valley: on the social organization of wet rice cultivation among the Diola of Senegal', *Africa* 51(2): 557–595.

Linares, O. (1992). *Power, Prayer and Production: the Jola of Casamance, Senegal*. Cambridge: Cambridge University Press.

Lipsedge, M. and Littlewood, R. 1996. 'Psychopathology and its public models: a provisional typology and a dramaturgy of domestic sieges', submitted to *British Journal of Medical Psychology.*

Little, K. 1949. 'The role of the Secret Society in cultural specialization', *American Anthropologist* 51: 199–212.

Little, K. 1965–6. 'The political function of the Poro'. Part I *Africa* 35(4): 349–365, Part II *Africa* 36(1), 62–71.

Littlefield, D. C. 1980. *Rice and slaves*. Baton Rouge: Louisiana University Press.

LRD 1980. *Bush fallow in Sierra Leone: an agricultural survey.* (Technical Report No. 6) Freetown: Land Resources Division, Ministry of Agriculture.

Luke, D. F. and Riley, S. 1989. 'The politics of economic decline in Sierra Leone', *Journal of Modern African Studies*. Norwood NJ: Ablex.

Luttwak, E. N. 1995. 'Great-powerless days'. *Times Literary Supplement*, June 16th, p. 9.

MacCormack, C. P. 1979. 'Sande: the public face of a secret society'. In B. Jules-Rosette, ed., *The new religions of Africa*. Norwood NJ: Ablex.

MacCormack, C. P. 1983. :Human leopards and crocodiles: political meanings of categorical ambiguities'. In P. Brown & D. Tuzin, eds., *The Ethnography of Cannibalism*. Washington: Society for Psychological Anthropology.

Margai, M. 1948. 'Welfare work in a Secret Society', *African Affairs* 47: 227–231.

Marks, T. 1992. 'Making revolution with Shining Path'. In D. S. Palmer, ed., *Shining Path of Peru*. London: C. Hurst.

Martin, C. 1990. *The rainforests of West Africa: ecology, threats, conservation*. Basel: Birkhaeuser Verlag (trans. Linda Tsardakas).

McCall, M. 1974. *Kailondo's Luawa and British Rule*. D.Phil Thesis, University of York.

Migeod, F. W. H. 1926. *A view of Sierra Leone*. London: Kegan Paul, Trench, Trubner.

Moran, Mary. 1994. 'Warriors or soldiers: masculinity and ritual transvestism in the Liberian civil war'. In Constance R. Sutton, ed., *Feminism, nationalism and militarism*, Arlington VA: American Anthropological Association/Association for Feminist Anthropology.

Muehlhaeusler, P. 1986. *Pidgin and creole linguistics*. Oxford: Blackwell.

Murphy, W. P. 1980. 'Secret knowledge as property and power in Kpelle society: elders versus youth', *Africa* 50: 193–207.

Murphy, W. P. and Bledsoe, C. H. 1987. 'Kinship and territory in the history of a Kpelle chiefdom (Liberia)'. In I. Kopytoff, ed., *The African Frontier: the reproduction of traditional African societies*. Bloomington: Indiana University Press, pp. 123–47.

Musa, S. and Musa, J. Lansana. 1993. *The invasion of Sierra Leone: a chronicle of events of a nation under siege*. Washington DC: Sierra Leone Institute for Policy Studies.

Nordstrom, C. 1992. 'The backyard front'. In C. Nordstrom and J. Martin, eds., *The paths to domination, resistance and terror*. Berkeley: University of California Press.

Nyerges, E. 1989. 'Coppice swidden fallows in tropical deciduous forest: biological, technological and socio-cultural determinants of secondary forest successions', *Human Ecology* 17, 379–400.

Nyerges, A. E. 1996. 'Ethnography in the reconstruction of African land use histories: a Sierra Leone example'. *Africa* 66(1): 122–144.

Opala, J. A. no date [1986?] *The Gullah: rice, slavery, and the Sierra Leone-American connection*. Freetown: United States Information Service.

Opala, J. A. 1993. *Ecstatic renovation!: street art celebrating Sierra Leone's 1992 revolution*. Freetown: Sierra Leone Adult Education Association. (see also *African Affairs* vol. 93, 1994)

Palmer, D. S. ed. 1992. *Shining Path of Peru*. London: C. Hurst.

Parren, M. P. E. and de Graaf, N. R. 1995. *The quest for natural forest management in Ghana, Côte d'Ivoire and Liberia*. Tropenbos Series 13. Wageningen, NL: Tropenbos Foundation.

PEA, 1989. *Bras, greens and ballheads: interviews with Freetown 'street boys'*. Freetown: People's Educational Association of Sierra Leone.

Peterson, J. 1969. *Province of Freedom: a history of Sierra Leone, 1787–1870*. London: Faber & Faber.

Phillips, R. B. 1978. 'Masking in Mende Sande Society initiation rituals', *Africa* 48: 265–77.

Portères, R. 1976. 'African cereals: Eleusine, Fonio, Black Fonio, Teff, Brachiaria, Paspalum, Pennisetum, and African Rice'. In J. Harlan, et al. eds., *The origins of African plant domestication*, The Hague: Mouton, pp. 409–452.

Prins, H. H. T. & Reitsma, J. M. 1989. 'Mammalian biomass in an African equatorial rain forest.' *Journal of Animal Ecology*, 58:851–861.

Rayner, S. 1982. 'The perception of time and space in egalitarian sects: a millennarian cosmology.' In M. Douglas, ed., *Essays in the Sociology of Perception*, London: Routledge & Kegan Paul.

Reno, W. 1993. 'Foreign firms and the financing of Charles Taylor's NPFL', *Liberian Studies Journal* 18(2): 175–188.

Reno, W. 1995. *Corruption and state politics in Sierra Leone*. Cambridge: Cambridge University Press.

Richards, J. V. O. 1974. 'The Sande: a socio-cultural organization in the Mende community in Sierra Leone', *Baessler-Archiv* 22: 265–81.

Richards, P. 1974. 'Kant's geography and mental maps', *Transactions of the Institute of British Geographers*, 61: 1–11.

Richards, P. 1985. *Indigenous agricultural revolution: ecology and food production in West Africa*. London: Hutchinson.

Richards, P. 1986. *Coping with hunger: hazard and experiment in a West African farming system*. London: Allen & Unwin.

Richards, P. 1987. 'Africa in the music of Samuel Coleridge Taylor', *Africa* 57(1): 566–571.

Richards, P. 1990. 'Indigenous approaches to rural development: the agrarian populist tradition in West Africa'. In M. Altieri and S. Hecht, eds., *Agroecology and small farm development*. Boca Raton, USA: CRC Press.

Richards, P. 1992a. 'Saving the rain forest? Contested futures in conservation'. In S. Wallman, ed. *Contemporary futures: perspectives from anthropology*. London: Routledge.

Richards, P. 1992b. 'Rural development and local knowledge: the case of rice in central Sierra Leone', *Entwicklungsethnologie*, 1: 33–42.

Richards, P. 1992c. 'Landscapes of dissent: Ikale and Ilaje country, 1870–1950'. In J. F. A. Ajayi and J. D. Y. Peel, eds. *Peoples and empires in Africa: essays in memory of Michael Crowder*. Harlow: Longman.

Richards, P. 1993. 'Natural symbols and natural history: chimpanzees, elephants and experiments in Mende thought'. In K. Milton, ed., *Environmentalism: the view from anthropology*, ASA Monograph 32, London: Routledge (in press).

Richards, P. 1994. 'Videos and violence on the periphery: Rambo and war in the forests of the Sierra Leone-Liberia border.' *IDS Bulletin*, special issue, *Knowledge is Power? The use and abuse of information in development*, ed. Susanna Davies, 25(2): 88–93.

Richards, P. 1995a 'Rebellion in Liberia and Sierra Leone: a crisis of youth?' In O. W. Furley, ed., *Conflict in Africa*. London: Tauris.

Richards P. 1995b. 'The versatility of the poor: wetland rice farming systems in Sierra Leone', *Geoforum*, 35(2), 197–203.

Richards, P. 1995c. 'Local understandings of primates and evolution: some Mende beliefs concerning chimpanzees'. In R. Corbey and B. Theunissen, eds., *Ape, Man, Apeman: changing views since 1600*. Leiden: Department of Prehistory, Leiden University.

Richards, P. 1996a. 'Agrarian Creolization: the ethnobiology, history, culture and politics of West African rice'. In R. Ellen and K. Fukui, eds., *Redefining nature: ecology, culture and domestication*. Oxford: Berg.

Richards, P. 1996b. 'Culture and community values in the selection and maintenance of African rice'. In S. Brush and D. Stabinsky, eds., *Intellectual property and indigenous knowledge*. Covelo CA: Island Press.

Richards, P. 1996c. 'Chimpanzees, diamonds & war: the discourses of global environmental change and local violence on the Liberia-Sierra Leone border', H. Moore, ed., *The changing nature of anthropological knowledge*. London: Routledge.

Richards, P. 1996d 'Indigenous peoples: concept, critique, cases'. *Proceedings of the Royal Society of Edinburgh*, Thematic Issue on the Lowland Rain Forest of the Guinea-Congo Domain 104B: 349–365.

Riley, S. 1996. *Liberia and Sierra Leone: anarchy or peace in West Africa*. Conflict Studies 287. Research Institute for the Study of Conflict and Terrorism.

Rodney, W. 1970. *A history of the Upper Guinea Coast, 1545 to 1800*. Oxford: Oxford University Press.

RUF/SL. 1995. *Footpaths to democracy: toward a New Sierra Leone*. No stated place of publication ('The Zogoda'?): The Revolutionary United Front of Sierra Leone.

Ruiz, Hiram A. 1992. *Uprooted Liberians: casualties of a brutal war*. US Committee For Refugees, 1025 Vermont Ave., NW Suite 920, Washington DC.

Sanday, P. R. 1986. *Divine Hunger: cannibalism as a cultural system*. Cambridge: Cambridge University Press.

Savill, P. S. and Fox, J. E. D. 1967. 'Trees of Sierra Leone'. Mimeo.

Schick, T. W. 1977. *Behold the Promised Land: a history of Afro-American Settler Society in 19th Century Liberia*. Baltimore: Johns Hopkins University Press.

Schwartz, J. M. 1996. *Pieces of a mosaic: an essay on the making of Makedonija*. Hoejbjerg DK: Intervention Press.

Sen, A. 1981. *Poverty and famines: an essay on entitlement and deprivation*. Oxford: Clarendon Press.

Sengova, J. 1987. 'The national languages of Sierra Leone: a decade of policy experimentation'. *Africa* 57: 519–530.

Seymour, G. L. 1860. 'The journal of the journey of George L. Seymour to the interior of Liberia: 1858'. *New York Colonization Journal* 105, 108, 109, 111, 112.

Sierra Leone, Government of, 1924. *Annual Report of the Lands and Forests Department for the year 1923*. Freetown: Government Printer.

Sims, J. 1859–1860. 'Scenes in the Interior of Liberia: being a tour through the Countries of the Dey, Goulah, Pessah, Barlain, Kpellay, Sualong, and King Boatswain's Tribes in 1858'. *New York Colonization Journal* 9(12) (December 1859), 10(6) (June 1860), 10(8) (August 1860).

Squire, C. B. 1995. *Ill-fated nation*. Freetown.

Squire, C. B. 1996. *Agony in Sierra Leone*. Freetown.

Stanley, W. B. 1919. 'Carnivorous apes in Sierra Leone', *Sierra Leone Studies* (old series), March, 1919.

Stewart, C. and Shaw, R. eds. 1994. *Syncretism/antisyncretism: the politics of religious syncretism*. London: Routledge.

Tarazona-Sevillano, G. 1992. 'The organization of Shining Path'. In D. S. Palmer, ed., 1992. *Shining Path of Peru*. London: C. Hurst.

Tarr, S. Byron 1993. 'The ECOMOG initiative in Liberia: a Liberian perspective', *Issue: a Journal of Opinion*, vol. 21 (1–2): 74–83.

Thomas, W. Northcote, 1920. 'Who were the Manes?', *Journal of the African Society*, 19: 176–188, 20: 33–42.

Thornton, J. 1992. *Africa and Africans in the making of the Atlantic world, 1400–1680.* Cambridge: Cambridge University Press.

Tiffen, M., Mortimore, M. and Gichuki, F., 1994. *More people, less erosion: environmental recovery in Kenya.* Chichester: Wiley.

Todd, L. 1984. *Modern Englishes: Pidgins and Creoles.* Oxford and London: Blackwell in association with Andre Deutsch.

Toffler, A. and Toffler, H. 1994. *War and Anti-war: survival at the dawn of the 21st Century.* London: Little, Brown & Co. (UK).

Unwin, A. H. 1909. *Report on the forests and forestry problems in Sierra Leone.* London: Waterlow, for the Government of Sierra Leone.

Vansina, J. 1990. *Paths in the rainforests: toward a history of political tradition in equatorial Africa.* London: James Currey.

Waal, A. de 1995. 'Human rights and famine: some heretical thoughts.' West Africa Seminar, Dept. of Anthropology, University College London.

Waldock, E. A., Capstick, E. S. and Browning, A. S. 1951. *Soil conservation and land use in Sierra Leone.* Freetown: Government Printer.

Wallerstein, I. 1980. *The modern world-system: mercantilism and the consolidation of the European world-economy, 1600–1750.* New York: Academic Press.

Waters, J. 1995. *Globalization.* London: Routledge.

Wilson, K. B. 1992. 'Cults of violence and counter-violence in Mozambique', *Journal of Southern African Studies,* 18(3): 527–582.

Winterbottom, T. 1803. *An account of the native Africans in the neighbourhood of Sierra Leone.* London: C. Whittingham.

Wit, de, T. and Gianotten, V. 1992. 'The center's multiple failures'. In D. S. Palmer, ed., 1992. *Shining Path of Peru.* London: C. Hurst.

Wonkeryor, E. L. 1985. *Liberia military dictatorship: a fiasco 'revolution'.* Chicago: Strugglers' Community Press.

Wylie, K. 1967. *The politics of transformation: indirect rule in Mendeland and Abuja.* PhD Thesis, East Lansing: Michigan State University.

Wylie, K. 1969. 'Innovation and change in Mende chieftaincy, 1880–1896', *Journal of African History,* 2: 295–308.

Wyse, A. J. C., 1977. 'The Sierra Leone/Liberian boundary: a case of frontier imperialism', *Odu* n.s. 15, 5–18.

Yeebo, Z. 1991. *Ghana: the struggle for popular power.* London and Port of Spain: New Beacon Books.

Young, T. 1990. 'The MNR/RENAMO: external and internal dynamics'. *African Affairs,* 89, no. 357, pp 491–509.

Zack-Williams, A. B. 1990. 'Diamond mining and under-development in Sierra Leone – 1930–1980', *Africa Development/Afrique et Développement* 15(2): 95–117.

Zack-Williams, A. B. 1992. 'Diamond mining in Sierra Leone, 1930–80'. In G. Thomas-Emeagwali, ed., *Science and Technology in African History.* London: The Edwin Mellen Press.

Zack-Williams, A. B. 1995. *Tributors, supporters and merchant capital: mining and under-development in Sierra Leone.* Aldershot: Avebury Press.

Zack-Williams, A. B. and Riley, S. 1993. 'Sierra Leone: the coup and its consequences', *Review of African Political Economy* 56: 91–98.